Islam, Christianity, and the West

FAITH MEETS FAITH

An Orbis Series in Interreligious Dialogue
Paul F. Knitter, General Editor
Editorial Advisors
John Berthrong
Julia Ching
Diana Eck
Karl-Josef Kuschel
Lamin Sanneh
George E. Tinker
Felix Wilfred

In the contemporary world, the many religions and spiritualities stand in need of greater communication and cooperation. More than ever before, they must speak to, learn from, and work with each other in order to maintain their vital identities and to contribute to fashioning a better world.

The FAITH MEETS FAITH Series seeks to promote interreligious dialogue by providing an open forum for exchange among followers of different religious paths. While the Series wants to encourage creative and bold responses to questions arising from contemporary appreciations of religious plurality, it also recognizes the multiplicity of basic perspectives concerning the methods and content of interreligious dialogue.

Although rooted in a Christian theological perspective, the Series does not limit itself to endorsing any single school of thought or approach. By making available to both the scholarly community and the general public works that represent a variety of religious and methodological viewpoints, FAITH MEETS FAITH seeks to foster an encounter among followers of the religions of the world on matters of common concern.

FAITH MEETS FAITH SERIES

Islam, Christianity, and the West

A Troubled History

Rollin Armour, Sr.

ORBIS BOOKS

Maryknoll, New York 10545

Library of Congress Cataloging-in-Publication Data

Armour, Rollin S. (Rollin Stely), 1929-
    Islam, Christianity, and the West : a troubled history / Rollin
Armour, Sr.
        p. cm. — (Faith meets faith series)
    Includes bibliographical references and index.
    ISBN 1-57075-407-1 (Paper)
    1. Islam—Relations—Christianity.   2. Christianity and other
religions—Islam.   3. Islamic countries—Relations—Europe.   4.
Europe—Relations—Islamic countries.   5. Islam—History.   I. Title.
II. Faith meets faith
    BP172.A736 2002
    261.2'7'09—dc21
                                                    2001008228

To
MARY ANNE

Ζωή μου σᾶς ἀγαπῶ
—George Gordon, Lord Byron

caritas aeterna est

Contents

List of Maps

Prologue

After September 11, 2001

The two attacks on the World Trade Center, first the bombing in 1993 and then its destruction in 2001, with the concomitant attack on the Pentagon and the aborted fourth highjacking, stand as bookends for the chapters that follow. I began the project about the time of the first incident and am completing it just after the second. In between came the bombings of the American embassies in Nairobi and Dar es Salaam and the bombing of the USS *Cole*. Other bombings took place in Riyadh and the Khobar army barracks in Saudi Arabia. These incidents and others like them are the work of terrorists whose violent activities enjoy no sanction from traditional Islam and have been denounced by numerous Muslim leaders. But because they were carried out by Muslims, followers of Islam who believed their deeds were blessed by God, these occurrences must be placed within the broad scope of the interaction between the Western world and the Islamic world.

Alarming is a modest word to use for these affairs, for they raise the fear of another long struggle between the two great regions. Whether that will come to be is unknown at the present, but it seems clear that, at a minimum, difficult days lie ahead for the people of these two areas. One can hope, however, and I believe with some reason, that on the other side of the coming events—many of them doubtless to be violent—may lie a time when the people of the West and the people of the Islamic world will develop a better understanding of each other. We can all pray to that end. This book is intended as a modest contribution to that goal.

Preface

In the thirty-eight years I taught courses in world religions, the religion that consistently raised the greatest problems among students was Islam: not Hinduism, not Buddhism, not Shinto, or Sikhism. It was as though there were something in the students' genes that provoked this response. Islam and Judaism are closer to Christianity than other religions, and Islam would seem the closer of the two because of the high esteem in which it holds Jesus. This consistent response from students has been a matter I have often pondered.

The idea of doing a book on the subject of Christian–Muslim relations came to me during a study leave at Münster, Germany. While perusing materials on Islam in the library of the Catholic Faculty at the University of Münster one afternoon, I saw a long shelf of books and pamphlets on Islam that Catholic scholars had written for lay people, and I wondered why it was important for German Catholics to know about Islam more than some other religion. The answer quickly came—the presence of large numbers of Turkish workers, the *Gastarbeiter,* who had come to Germany. Germans now had Muslim neighbors, people they saw at the market and in the shops, whose children their own children met at school. Then a second thing came to mind. Martin Luther, the great German reformer, wrote a number of tracts on Islam in the sixteenth century because of the fear that the approaching Turkish armies of Suleiman II would overrun Germany. The Turks did not arrive then, but they had come now, though not as conquering warriors. Luther wrote to inform German Christians about Islam, and now, four and a half centuries later, Catholic writers were doing the same. I decided that there might be a story in there somewhere, one that could relate to my old question of how our society views Islam. In a day when contacts with Muslims are increasing rapidly, such a study would seem to be timely. Thus I began collecting materials on the history of the encounter of the two religions, and this book is the result of that research.

Among the many people who assisted me in this work were three of my students, Jason Pepe, Curt Moore, and Joey Bishop, who gathered bibliography and reviewed sources. I owe them my special thanks because they were in this project early. Dr. Walter B. Shurden, Calloway Professor of Christianity, then chairman of the department at Mercer University, and Dean Douglas Steeples of Mercer's College of Liberal Arts provided research funds at important times.

Four people have read drafts of all or most of the manuscript. Professor John Kaltner of Rhodes College has shared generously of his wide knowledge of Islam. He has recommended readings, caught errors, and made numerous suggestions in both content and style that have strengthened the book, and his encouragement has been a boost when my spirits flagged. Professor Jamie

Cockfield of Mercer made many helpful suggestions of style and of fact, as did Professor O. Suthern Sims. My son Steve has helped greatly with both English expression and content. My wife, Mary Anne, has made suggestions on several chapters as well. Walter Price provided information on evangelical views of the nation of Israel, and Hunter Godsey offered a valuable insight on current theory of language that relates to one of the subjects in the study. To all of these I offer my heartfelt thanks. Needless to say, the errors that remain are of my making.

This work would have been impossible without the good efforts of the librarians of Mercer's Jack Tarver Library. They have procured books and articles from far and wide, producing them almost magically, and I am greatly indebted to them for their help.

Farther away in time and space, but near in spirit, have been two important mentors, Professor George Huntston Williams, my graduate instructor in the art of church history, and Professor Wilfred Cantwell Smith, my teacher in the study of world religions. I regret that neither is here in the flesh to receive my thanks. Only recently has it come to my attention that Dr. Williams had planned to write a history of the involvements of the Christian movement with both Judaism and Islam, news that encouraged me in this work.

I have used the word "research" in regard to writing this book, but the real research has been done by others, scholars who have read the original sources in the original languages. The books of Norman Daniel, Bernard Lewis, Daniel Sahas, John Esposito, R. W. Southern, Benjamin Kedar, James Kritzeck, Clinton Bennett, Hugh Goddard, and many others lie behind almost every page that follows. Their names appear in the documentation. I hope I have been faithful to them and have reported on them accurately.

An early form of this material was given as the inaugural R. Glenn Eaves Lecture at Mississippi College in October 1993, and the positive response of that audience was an encouragement to proceed with the project. I thank Dr. Eaves for that invitation.

I want to say a special word of tribute to my good friend and graduate school classmate, the late Dr. Robert Walton. Mary Anne and I came to Münster through his invitation. Not only did he arrange an appointment for me as Guest Professor in the Protestant Faculty that gave us entree to a place to live and provided access to the rich libraries of the university, but he offered many suggestions and strong encouragement for taking up this subject. Were he still alive, he would have been an advisory reader, and his comments would have helped greatly. While my principal dedication of this book is to my wife, a secondary dedication is to Bob and his good wife, Charlotte, in memory of the many wonderful visits Mary Anne and I had in their home.

I want to thank Professors John Kuykendall, Charles Kimball, and Hani Khoury for their support of my efforts to put the manuscript out for publication. Professor Kuykendall helped me early, and Professor Kimball supported my proposal to Orbis Books. Professor Khoury has encouraged me all along and as an Arab Israeli has been an especially important source for the study of present-day Israel.

The editors and staff of Orbis Books, especially my editor, Dr. William Burrows, have done wonderful work in readying the manuscript for publication. Because Orbis has published for years in the area of interreligious studies, I had thought that this book might fit into their publishing program, and I am honored that they have accepted it. More than that, they are due thanks from the religious world at large for the courageous stands they have taken in publishing books in theology and religious history that might have been frowned upon not many years ago.

Finally to my family I owe a special thanks—to my children, Ellen and Rod and Steve, who have kept up with my work and lent their own encouragement. And especially I thank my wife, Mary Anne, who has had to contend with a husband not only absent-minded as usual, but often preoccupied with the work of writing. She has encouraged this project from the beginning, has made numerous suggestions about the book, and it is to her that I dedicate it, with my love.

MACON, GEORGIA
OCTOBER 5, 2001

Introduction

With two world religions, sustained by the same convictions, driven by the same ambitions, living side by side in the same region, it was inevitable that, sooner or later, they would clash.

—Bernard Lewis[1]

The idea behind this book is simple: to recount the history of the responses of the Christian West to Islam. This interaction between Christendom, East and West, and Islam has gone on for the better part of fourteen centuries as the two civilizations have lived side by side, their land borders coterminous. Contact between them has been continuous and has increased in recent decades. Rarely was the contact peaceful, and almost never was it based on mutual understanding. In the early centuries Eastern Christians encountered Islam far more than Christians in the West, but as the centuries passed the West's contacts increased, first in the Islamic invasion of Spain, then in the Middle East through the Crusades, and finally over almost the entire Islamic world through European colonialism.

Islam, like Judaism and Christianity, traces its faith back to the patriarch Abraham and belongs thus to the family of Abrahamic religions. All three are monotheistic; all three make reference in varying ways to the prophets of Israel and Judah; and the three have a long history of interaction. As descendants of a common ancestor, they may be called siblings, and as with most siblings, rivalries have developed over the centuries, rivalries that have been expressed in books and writings, but also in overt action, including war and persecution. The burden of this book may be said to be the tracing of the sibling rivalry between Christians and Muslims, the Western world and the Islamic world. Jews will enter the story at several points as well, but more as counterpoint than as a direct theme.

From the beginning Christian thinkers had difficulty dealing with this new religion. In Islam Christians met people who worshiped the same God as Jews and Christians and affirmed the truth of the original revelations to ancient Israel. Muslims honored Jesus as a prophet who had no sin, was born of a virgin, ascended into heaven, and is expected again at the Last Day. Islam called upon its people to follow lives of morality and piety, and it looked to the final day of judgment. All of this echoed Christianity. But Islam also denied the legitimacy of both Old and New Testaments as they exist, holding that their texts

---

[1] Bernard Lewis, *The Middle East: A Brief History of the Last 2000 Years* (New York: Scribner, 1995), 32.

1

O T + N T

had been corrupted; and it denied the divinity of Jesus and the doctrine of the Trinity, as well as many other items of Christian orthodoxy. What were Christians to make of a religion that at one and the same time affirmed and denied basic Christian tenets? That question has baffled Christians ever since they first encountered Islam.

Islam is more than a religion—it became a total civilization. In its first century the Islamic movement captured great pieces of Christendom, later the entire Byzantine empire, and then threatened the very heartland of Europe. During the early Middle Ages, when western Europe was little more than a backwater area, overrun and disrupted by barbarian invaders, Islamic civilization led the world in science and culture and boasted cities with streets, libraries, and amenities the equal of any city on earth. No problem would vex medieval leaders and thinkers more than Islam, as a religious movement to be interpreted and understood, as a cultural rival, and as a political and military adversary to defend against.

Christians failed in their attempts to understand and interpret Islam—unless one considers writing to confirm one's misinformation and prejudice as success. Mostly theologians, these writers possessed no categories for reading Islam save those they found in scripture and Christian orthodoxy, but Islam did not fit them. Further, Christians, particularly those in the West, assumed the worst about Islam. Expecting the worst, they saw the worst. One would hope for more, for evidence that Christians, West or East, could have described Islam for what it was in itself, but that rarely happened. Perhaps one should not rush to judgment too quickly here, however, since modern-day Christians have not done a great deal better. Indeed, one of the things to be learned in this study is that much of the prejudice and misinformation of the past continues today.

Two major themes will intertwine in this study, the intellectual-theological and the military-political. The intellectual and theological will examine what the West thought of Islam and how Christian theologians evaluated it. The military-political will trace the movements of power and force, the pushes and pulls between these two great civilizations.

The Christian apologetic against Islam would develop along several lines. It began by seeing Islam as another of the heresies that plagued the church. Later, Christians recognized that they were opposed not just by a heresy, but by a whole civilization. They preferred to call their opponents by their ethnic names, Saracen, Turk, or Tatar, avoiding the word *Islam*. Placing the movement within the broad sweep of divine history, some considered Islam to be the precursor of the Antichrist and thus a harbinger of the Last Day. One of the most popular approaches was to denigrate Muhammad, and Christian writers did this with abandon through countless defamatory stories about him. Muhammad was a lecher and a blasphemer, a man of violence who used religious claims for his own self-interest, altogether the opposite of a prophet of God. And theologians disputed Muslim doctrine and teachings: the Muslim views of God, of Jesus, of the Bible, of faith and salvation, of paradise, and so on. Muslim practices were a parody of Christian ways, they said, and Muslims were more interested in sex and material things than in the life of the spirit.

In most of this, Christians were reading Islam through their own eyes with little ability or interest in learning about Islam as Muslims knew Islam. Prejudgment was the rule, not the exception; denigration was the norm, not understanding. In these ways they accounted for a religion that presented false views of Jesus. It had to be not only wrong, but evil, possibly inspired by Satan, and certainly held by people of dubious sincerity and faithfulness. There were exceptions to these views, but in the main there could be no middle way. In sum, one must not, in most of this history at least, expect to find the more tolerant and open-minded attitude shared by many contemporary theologians and students of religion.

The military-political encounter began when Islamic forces conquered great sections of Christian lands in the seventh century. Four centuries later Christians responded with Crusades to the Holy Land and the Reconquest of Spain and Portugal. In the fifteenth century the Ottoman Turks engulfed the Eastern Christian empire and thereafter threatened Western Europe. Finally in the nineteenth and twentieth centuries the colonial powers of Western Europe commandeered almost all of the Islamic lands, a control they relinquished after World War II, save for their continuing support of the new state of Israel, carved as it was out of Arab and Muslim land.

The encounter of these two civilizations has affected both. It was through the Arabs that Western Europe first reclaimed the Greek classics of philosophy and science, materials lost to the West during the barbarian invasions. Through the Arabs came numerous fruits and vegetables, oranges and rice, plus cotton, sugar cane, and coffee, not to mention Arabic numerals, the notational system that Arabs adapted from the mathematics of India, without which modern science would be impossible. Both astronomy and medicine in the West drew on the knowledge of Arab tutors, and many stars still bear Arabic names. Today the direction is reversed as the West contributes to both the Islamic and the non-Islamic worlds the powerful tools of modern science and technology.

Contact between Muslims and Westerners has increased markedly in recent decades. The power struggles in the Near East involving Israel, Iran, Iraq, and other Mideastern countries are regular fare in our press. Turks, Arabs, and other Muslims have immigrated into European countries and America in sizable numbers, so that people and a religion once distant from us are now near. And some Westerners have converted to Islam. We meet Muslims at work, in our shopping centers, or in our neighborhoods. The encounter continues apace, and because the amount of interchange has increased and the power stakes are now very high, exacerbated by the problem of terrorism, the need for knowledge and understanding is perhaps greater than ever. The study of this history would seem to be appropriate.

To understand this history, however, one must first know a few fundamentals about the Islamic faith, its founder, the Prophet Muhammad, and its underlying tenets. The study begins, therefore, with a brief account of Muhammad, the principles of Islam, and the story of Islam's early spread into the world of the Mediterranean and the Middle East.

1

Muhammad and the Establishment of Islam

When Muhammad the apostle of God reached the age of forty God sent him in compassion to mankind, "as an evangelist to all men."
— Muhammad ibn Ishaq[1]

Muhammad was a complex man. . . . But there was a power in him which, with the help of circumstances, was to make him one of the rare men who have turned the world upside down.
— Maxime Rodinson[2]

The story of Islam begins with the Prophet Muhammad, or, in his full name, Muhammad ibn 'Abdallah. Muslims name him "the Prophet (or Apostle) of God," "the Rightly Guided One," "the Seal of the Prophets," and consider him not only the greatest of God's prophets, but the great exemplar of human life. They insist, however, that he was only human and in no sense divine, though without sin just as Islam says all prophets have been. As both prophet and apostle, Muhammad is held to stand in the line of prophets God has sent to the nations of the world, including the prophets of ancient Israel and Jesus.

A native of Mecca and a sometime merchant and caravaner, a trade typical of Mecca of that day, Muhammad was the son of 'Abdallah ibn 'Abd al-Muttalib, who died shortly before Muhammad's birth, and grandson of 'Abd-al-Muttalib ibn Hashim, founder of the Hashimite clan that belonged to the Quraysh tribe of Mecca. Muhammad's mother, Amina bint Wahb, reared him until her death when he was seven years old. Then his uncle, Abu Talib, took the boy into his home.

Muhammad was born about the year A.D. 570. The name Muhammad means

---

[1] Muhammad ibn Ishaq, *The Life of Muhammad: A Translation of Ishāq's "Sīrat Rasūl Allāh,"* trans. A. Guillaume (Karachi, Oxford, New York, and Delhi: Oxford University Press, 1997), 104.
[2] Maxime Rodinson, *Muhammad*, trans. Anne Carter (New York: Pantheon, 1971, 1980), 313.

"the praised one," or "he who is glorified." Huston Smith reports that "his name has been borne by more male children than any other in the world."[3]

Of Muhammad's early years, the Prophet's early biographer, Muhammad ibn Ishaq (d. ca. 767) says:

> The Apostle of God grew up, God protecting him and keeping him from the vileness of heathenism because he wished to honour him with apostleship, until he grew up to be the finest of his people in manliness, the best in character, most noble in lineage, the best neighbour, the most kind, truthful, reliable, the furthest removed from filthiness and corrupt morals, through loftiness and nobility, so that he was known among his people as "The Trustworthy" because of the good qualities which God had implanted in him.[4]

A good illustration of this honorific title occurs in an account of the refurbishing of the Ka'aba, the sacred, cube-shaped building of Mecca (the word *ka'aba* means "cube") sometime before Muhammad began his reform. When the builders were ready to reset the sacred Black Stone for which the building was noted, the workers held back, debating which tribe would have the honor of handling the holy object. The stone, probably a meteorite, is held to date from the earliest of days, perhaps even from Adam himself, and as an object of veneration and reverence it had reposed in an outside corner of the Ka'aba for centuries. To reinstall it would be a great privilege. Unable to name one of their own group, the workers agreed to bestow the distinction upon the next person to come into the Sanctuary. That person was Muhammad, and they gave the honor to him, whereupon he instructed them to place the stone on a cloak, have a representative from each of the four tribes take a corner, and raise the stone toward its place. When they did so, Muhammad took the stone from the cloak and lifted it into its position.

THE REVELATIONS AND EARLY YEARS IN MECCA

About the year 610 on the Western calendar, while devoting himself to prayer in the month of Ramadan, Muhammad says he found himself visited by the angel Gabriel. He heard his visitor command him to recite the words he would speak. Overwhelmed by the majesty of this mysterious visitant, Muhammad could do nothing at first, but after repeated admonishments by the angel, he discovered he could recite the divine message word for word. Muslims call this "the Night of Destiny" or "Night of Power."

Muhammad reported this experience to his wife, Khadija bint Khuwaylid,

---

[3] Huston Smith, *The World's Religions* (San Francisco: HarperSanFrancisco, 1991), 223-24.
[4] Ibn Ishaq, *Life of Muhammad,* 81.

who immediately believed that her husband had been visited by a messenger from God, even though Muhammad was not sure, fearing he had been deceived by the spirits of the desert. Khadija consulted her cousin, Waraqa ibn Naufal, a *hanif,* that is, an Arab monotheist committed to neither Judaism nor Christianity. Waraqa, who was knowledgeable in the scriptures of the two religions, listened to Khadija's account of Muhammad's story, whereupon he announced that Muhammad had received a great revelation like that sent to Moses ages before. Waraqa, like Khadija, assured Muhammad that the revelations were to be believed.

As the visitations continued, they brought terror to Muhammad. He would perspire heavily, swoon, and even fall to the ground, and then he would seek Khadija for comfort and understanding, sometimes going to her on hands and knees. Later Christian critics would claim that these fits were epileptic seizures, but the descriptions match those of other seers and prophets, including King Saul in the Old Testament, who lay naked on the ground all night in a coma, and the apostle Paul, whose dramatic vision of Jesus left him blind.

In later revelations Muhammad sometimes heard the words of an angel, sometimes he saw only a vision, and at other times the revelation was "like the reverberations of a bell." Putting nonverbal revelations into words was an arduous and painful task for him. He spoke of how difficult these revelations were: "Never once did I receive a revelation without thinking that my soul had been torn away from me."[5] These messages were later collected as the Qur'an (the name means "recitation"), the Muslim holy book. The Arabic word *sura* ("row") names the individual revelations that form the chapters of the Qur'an.

More visitations followed until Muhammad did believe. Some two years after the first revelation, the *sura* entitled "The Forenoon" (all of the *suras* are named) brought to Muhammad the following beautiful and convincing message:

> Thy Lord has neither forsaken thee nor hates thee
> and the Last shall be better for thee than the First.
> Thy Lord shall give thee, and thou shalt be satisfied.
>
> Did He not find thee an orphan, and shelter thee?
> Did He not find thee erring, and guide thee?
> Did He not find thee needy, and suffice thee?
>
> As for the orphan, do not oppress him,
> and as for the beggar, scold him not;
> and as for thy Lord's blessing, declare it. (Qur'an 93:4–11[6])

---

[5] Karen Armstrong, *Muhammad: A Biography of the Prophet* (San Francisco: HarperSanFrancisco, 1992), 89.

[6] Unless otherwise noted, quotations from the Qur'an are from Arthur J. Arberry, *The Koran Interpreted* (New York: Macmillan, 1955). Verse numbers for the *suras* tend to vary from translation to translation.

When Muhammad's cousin, Ali, heard these things, he believed, as did Zayd, his former slave whom he had freed; Abu Bakr, the first of his successors; and Muhammad's three daughters. Another key figure in the Prophet's career, his uncle, Abu Talib, a man well placed among Mecca's leaders, did not convert, explaining that he could not leave the tradition of his people, although he later provided Muhammad crucial support against his enemies. Without Abu Talib's aid in the days of trouble later on, Muhammad would probably not have survived, since in the tribal culture of Arabia no individual was safe without the protection of a strong individual within the tribe. A lone individual could be killed with impunity.

These mysterious messages remained within Muhammad's inner group for some three years, when the newly commissioned prophet began preaching to the people of Mecca at large, calling upon them to pull down their false idols and turn to the one true God, *al-Lāh* (literally, "the God," usually spelled "Allah" in English), and to share their wealth with the poor.

Meccans had often spoken of a deity named al-Lāh who created heaven and earth, but this creator deity seems to have receded into the distance in favor of fertility deities, the *banat al-Lāh*, the "daughters of al-Lāh," though some see evidence of a growing interest in al-Lāh prior to Muhammad. There were many other deities in Mecca—polytheism was the reigning religion, and some 360 idols were said to grace the interior of the holy Ka'aba.

Mecca had been an important religious center for Arabs for centuries, in part because of its association with Abraham and his son, Ishmael. According to the Qur'an as well as Arab tradition, Abraham and Ishmael built the original Ka'aba. Further, a well named Zamzam, also in Mecca, was connected with Ishmael and Hagar, Ishmael's mother. As the story has it (parallel in part to the narrative in Genesis 16:1-14), when Abraham and Sarah were unable to have children, Abraham, following the custom of their day, had a child by Hagar, Sarah's servant, who served as a surrogate for Sarah. Ishmael was the child. Later, after God gave Sarah her own child, Isaac, she became jealous of Abraham's older son and ordered Abraham to send Hagar and Ishmael away. Banished to the desert, the servant woman and her child nearly died of thirst, until God answered Hagar's prayers and caused a well to spring up, according to Arab tradition the holy well Zamzam. The story is important to both Hebrew scriptures and the Qur'an, and thus to Judaism, Christianity, and Islam: all three traditions hold that the Arabs descended from Ishmael, as the people of Israel descended from Isaac, though the Bible places these events in southern Palestine. Long before Muhammad's time these two sites, the Ka'aba and the well Zamzam had become sacred places that brought large numbers of pilgrims to Mecca and with them money that filled the coffers of Mecca's businessmen. Muhammad called upon Meccans to honor the pilgrimage and make it more a holy occasion rather than one for profit, but this demand threatened the purses of the merchants. While the reforms he proposed in worship would unsettle cherished traditions in Mecca, these changes would affect the Meccans' income.

Arabia in the early seventh century

Bostra
Jerusalem
SYRIA
PALESTINE
Eilat
Magna
Dumat al-Jandal
N
EGYPT
RED SEA
Khaybar
MEDINA (Yathrib)
Badr
Quba
Well of Maunah
Qudayd
Well of Usfan
MECCA
Taif
ABYSSINIA

Miles
0   100   200   300

Approximate line
of Byzantine frontier

Byzantine Empire

Muhammad's preachments attacked yet another Arab tradition, tribalism, the social system that had organized Arab life for centuries. Possessing no overall ruler or system of government, Arabs had lived within their separate tribes, competing and clashing as they chose with no comprehensive system for righting wrongs save for blood vengeance. This new religion required a personal commitment to the one God who transcended clan and tribe, and the acceptance of a single system of law, God's law, as revealed through Muhammad, that would bind individuals and tribes into a single society. This reform would be thorough, affecting the total society, not just religious belief and practice. It is no surprise that Muhammad's announcements were not welcomed.

In spite of criticisms, the Prophet was undaunted, and he warned that any who refused to turn and serve the one God and follow his commands would suffer in God's fearsome day of judgment:

When the sun shall be darkened,
when the stars shall be thrown down,
when the mountains shall be set moving,
when the pregnant camels shall be neglected,
when the savage beasts shall be mustered,
when the seas shall be set boiling,
when the souls shall be coupled [with their bodies in the resurrection],
when the buried infant shall be asked for what sin she was slain [a reference
to infanticide],
when the scrolls shall be unrolled,
when heaven shall be stripped off,
when Hell shall be set blazing,
when Paradise shall be brought nigh,
then shall a soul know what it has produced. (Qur'an 81:1-14)

For the most part Muhammad's message was ill received, and he soon found himself rejected, taunted, and chastised. Even worse, persecution struck his followers. They were criticized, even beaten, and one was killed, a slave woman remembered as the first martyr of Islam. The leaders of Muhammad's tribe, the Quraysh, had become enraged. As the opposition to his preaching grew, Muhammad's situation became precarious. Resistance became so strong at one point that he sent a number of his followers into Abyssinia, an erstwhile enemy of the Quraysh, to live in exile among Christians for their protection.

MUHAMMAD'S MOVE TO MEDINA

Then a new opportunity presented itself. Representatives from Yathrib, the native city of Muhammad's mother, an oasis town some 280 miles to the north, contacted Muhammad and urged him to come to their city and initiate a reform of government and life. Impressed with the courage and leadership of the fiery

Muhammad, they thought he might bring the order and organization that their town needed. Apparently Muhammad's call to worship the one God did not bother them, perhaps because of their long association with the town's rather sizable Jewish population. On July 16, 622, on the Western calendar, Muhammad emigrated from Mecca to Yathrib, where he joined some seventy of his Meccan followers. Muslims call this trip the "Emigration," *hijra* in Arabic, and say that it was the turning point of Muhammad's work as prophet and reformer. Indeed, they consider Muhammad's journey to Yathrib the central happening in world history and accordingly date their calendar to that event, naming earlier history "before the *hijra*" (B.H.) and later events "in the year of the *hijra*" (A.H.), parallel to the Christian dating that begins with the birth of Jesus.

In Yathrib, Muhammad worked slowly to establish his leadership and bring about reforms. Even though some opposed him, in time he met with great success, so much so that the city's name was changed to the "City of the Prophet," *Madinat al-Nabi*, or in short Anglicized form, Medina.

Here Muhammad organized the entire society in conformity with his recurring revelations. The change was radical. Economics, marriage and divorce, social welfare, and the power of the sword, as well as religion, came under Muhammad's control and the rule of Islam. Muhammad allowed a camel to choose a site where he built his small house, which he made into a house of prayer, the first mosque. He established Friday noon as the principal time of prayer, marking his movement off from Judaism and Christianity with their Saturday and Sunday holy days. Friday was market day for Arabs, a convenient day for an assembly. The month of Ramadan, already an Arab holy month, became a time of fasting from dawn until dusk. In the words of Ishaq: "Legal punishments were fixed, the forbidden and the permitted prescribed, and Islam took up its abode. . . ."[7] In Mecca, Muhammad was a preacher, reformer, and prophet. In Medina he was all of these plus lawgiver and ruler. Thereby was born a total human system—social, legal, military, economic, and religious— whose elements would later provide the materials to form a world-class civilization. This inclusive quality of Islam with its emphasis on community became a continuing mark of the movement, one clearly in evidence even now.

Meanwhile, Muhammad's conflict with the people of Mecca continued, now in the form of military engagements. The tribal society of Arabia was accustomed to raiding parties that occasionally attacked merchant caravans and to jousting contests among tribes, but the conflict between Medina and Mecca was more intense. Three battles ensued. The first, something of a raid on a merchant caravan, was decisively won by the Medinans. They lost the second, a full-fledged clash between the two towns, in which Muhammad himself took a wound. Had the Meccans pursued their victory, they could probably have overrun Medina and ended the Prophet's regime, but they did not.

The third conflict is called the Battle of the Ditch. Muhammad ordered a

---

[7] Ibn Ishaq, *Life of Muhammad*, 235.

Islam
total human system includes social, legal, military, economic +
where as Christian + Judean legal + military are separated out.
and given over to nationality religious

trench dug outside Medina. It was a simple strategy, and it worked. When the Meccans arrived, they could find no way for their horses to leap the chasm, and they were driven away by the arrows of Muhammad's forces. The victory was decisive, and it left Muhammad in clear control of his new city. One thing remained, to enlarge his rule to include Mecca. Meanwhile, a new problem emerged, namely, his relation to the Jewish tribes who lived there.

RELATIONS WITH JEWS

In his early days in Medina, Muhammad worked well with the Jews of the city. He drew up a charter "granting them equal rights of citizenship, full religious liberty and military protection on condition that they take part in the defense of the city,"[8] an action of considerable significance in a time not noted for religious freedom. The Jews of Medina apparently felt that his appeal to the one God and his call for lives of morality comported well with their faith. At first Muhammad had his followers face Jerusalem when they prayed, as Jews did, and for a time he made the Jewish Yom Kippur a holy day for Muslims.

When the Jews realized that his new revelation differed from theirs and was intended to replace it, the relationship with Jews worsened, causing Muhammad to shift the direction of prayer to Mecca and its holy building the Ka'aba. This step was significant because it brought Islam into a close relationship with Abraham, the *hanif* (as Arabs believed) whom Muhammad often cited for his refusal to worship idols and his submission to the one God. The rejection of Jerusalem as the direction of prayer was an affront to the Jews that convinced them that they could not work with Muhammad.

Problems then intensified. A Jewish man played an indecent prank on an Arab woman and was killed by an Arab, who was in turn killed by a Jew. As punishment Muhammad forced the Jewish man's tribe into exile, requiring the members to leave their possessions behind. Another Jewish man who wrote satiric poems opposing Muhammad—no small thing in a culture that lived by the spoken word—was killed at Muhammad's request.

Muhammad's problem with the Jews of Medina came to a head after the Battle of the Ditch. Muhammad discovered evidence that the remaining major Jewish tribe had sided with the Meccans in violation of the covenant they had made to assist Muhammad in the defense of Medina. He ordered them surrounded, and when they appealed for relief he agreed to let Sa'd ibn Mu'adh, the chieftain of a group friendly to the Jews, pronounce judgment on them. Sa'd, who was dying of wounds he had suffered in the battle, announced that all 700 Jewish men should be beheaded, their property divided among the Medinans, and the women and children sold into slavery. Muhammad responded, "Truly Sa'd

---

[8] Robert Payne, *The History of Islam* (New York: Dorset, 1990), 30. Muslims often cite this charter as an early instance of Islam's tolerance of other religions.

has declared the judgment of God from beyond the Seventh Heaven,"[9] and he implemented Sa'd's decision.

Muhammad viewed Jewish recalcitrance as a violation of the covenant he had made with them and a threat to the success of his reform and thus saw it as tantamount to treason. Mercy, therefore, was out of the question, and the severity of the punishment did not seem out of line to him. Justified as the executions may have been from Muhammad's point of view, the incident remains an unfortunate blot on his career, representing what appears to many to have been unnecessary violence.

A POLITICAL LEADER

Because Muhammad led Medina's forces in battle and ordered punishments and executions as a governor and political leader would do, Christian critics would later accuse him of being a man of war who sought to advance himself through violence, thereby either directly or indirectly comparing him unfavorably with the peaceful Jesus. The debate is probably beyond a resolution, because the appeals are to entirely different purposes of leadership. Like Moses of old, often cited in the Qur'an for his faithful obedience to God, Muhammad was a prophet, a lawgiver, and a military leader. Jesus' role differed: in his work as teacher, healer, and preacher, he more nearly resembled the writing prophets of the Old Testament. Muhammad was reforming an entire society; Jesus was announcing the kingdom of God. Muhammad offered a new political rulership, a new governing authority. Jesus offered no alternative to Roman rule; he and his followers lived within the *Pax Romana* with its powerful system of law and sought to carry out Jesus' principles of love within that setting. The careers of the two leaders are not parallel. As to Muhammad, if one asks whether he was a political reformer, or a prophet, or a military leader, the answer is that he was all of these at once. The contrast with Jesus is sharp.

While Muhammad's political and military activity might seem to be greatly different from Christianity, that is correct only in comparison with the beginnings of the Christian movement, but not if compared to the Christianity of Muhammad's day. The Christendom of the Middle Ages was exactly like the society Muhammad had in mind, namely, a society in which religion, law, politics, economics, and all of social life merged into one interlocking system. In that sense Islam would become a mirror image of Christendom, and much of the difficulty between the two societies would come from that fact. Christendom's pattern of an inclusive society that blended religion and law into a unity would not change until the eighteenth-century Enlightenment introduced its principles of human rights and individual freedom. At that point medieval Christendom died, and the modern secular state began to emerge. Since we live

---

[9] Ibid., 47

in the latter setting with freedom of religion, it is difficult for us to imagine any other kind of society. Our kind is new, however, and it is radically different from the Christian society of the Middle Ages and the Islamic society that Muhammad founded. Islamic societies tend to perpetuate the older pattern, a fact that places them in sharp contrast to contemporary Western societies with their principles of human rights and separation of church and state. Islamic doctrine has principles of human rights also, but Islam understands these to derive from God and his revelation, namely, the Qur'an, not to be inherent in humans by a law of nature.[10] Hence, an Islamic society is to be ruled by God's law as found in the Qur'an and the *shari'a*, the system of Islamic law that Muslims have developed over the centuries.

THE QUR'AN

The divine visitations to Muhammad continued throughout his career, and powerful messages they were, carrying a poetic force that mesmerized his hearers. Citing the quality of these recitations as proof of their divine inspiration, Muhammad challenged his hearers: "Bring a sura like it . . . and you will not" (Qur'an 2:23). And no one did. After Muhammad's death Muslims collected these special sayings and brought them together as the Muslim holy book, the Qur'an or the "Recitation."[11] Muslims call these collected preachments the "Standing Miracle," in honor of the beauty and power they possess and their quality as divine revelation.

Recognizing the sense of divinity the book can create in believers, Karen Armstrong, a former Catholic, likens the Qur'an to the Catholic Eucharist in that it can provide "a Real Presence of the divine word in our midst."[12] It is held to be perfect, inerrant, absolute, an earthly copy of what has been since eternity in Heaven. Since the Qur'an properly exists only in Arabic and strictly speaking cannot be in any other language,[13] Muslims have sometimes taught their converts Arabic rather than translate their holy book. Thus, Arthur J. Arberry, whose English-language rendering is the principal edition cited in this study,

---

[10] In 1980 to mark the beginning of the fifteenth century of the Islamic era, the Islamic Council for Europe meeting in London enacted a *Universal Islamic Declaration of Human Rights*. It may be found in *Islam: A Challenge for Christianity* edited by Hans Küng and Jürgen Moltmann (London: SCM Press; Maryknoll, N.Y.: Orbis Books, 1994), 140-50. The *Declaration* is nonbinding. The sponsoring organization is a private umbrella organization for European Muslims. A relatively traditional statement, it is based on the Qur'an and *shari'a*, though it does speak to some contemporary issues.

[11] "[A]n Arabic word which combines the meanings of 'reading' and 'recitation'" (Bernard Lewis, *The Middle East: A Brief History of the Last 2000 Years* [New York: Scribner, 1995], 52).

[12] Armstrong, *Muhammad*, 50.

[13] One of the four main schools of law within Islam allows translations, namely, the Hanafite, the dominant school in India; the others do not (Gustave E. von Grunebaum, *Medieval Islam: A Study in Cultural Orientation,* 2nd ed. [Chicago: University of Chicago Press, 1953], 152-53).

entitled his "translation" *The Koran Interpreted*. Mohammed Marmaduke Pickthall, the translator of the greatly admired English version entitled *The Meaning of the Glorious Koran*, himself a Muslim, says of his text: "[This] is not the Glorious Koran, that inimitable symphony, the very sounds of which move men to tears and ecstasy. It is only an attempt to present the meaning of the Koran—and peradventure something of the charm—in English."[14]

The exalted status of the Qur'an becomes clear if one asks for the Islamic parallel to Jesus. The answer is not Muhammad but the Qur'an. Muhammad is a prophet and, rather like Paul or Mark of the New Testament, a human being, inspired but not divine, a person who announces a holy revelation. The Qur'an, however, is the divine revelation itself, the eternal Word of God in human language, just as Jesus in Christian teaching is the eternal Word of God in human form. In popular piety, however, Muhammad is a highly spiritualized figure, the ideal human being, whose behavior, demeanor, and unwavering faith are the model for Muslims. Frithjof Schuon, a convert to Islam and a noted Islamics scholar, says very bluntly that "Islam is the Prophet," suggesting how Muhammad is held to embody Muslim ideals.[15]

The compelling quality of the Qur'an's poetry, particularly when chanted in the traditional manner, is still attested to by Arabic-speaking hearers. Even Arab Christians have said that no other Arabic-language literature can equal it. Islamic tradition has made much of this fact, particularly in light of the Qur'an's description of Muhammad as "the unlettered Prophet," or as another translation renders the text, "the Prophet who can neither read nor write" (Qur'an 7:157).[16] Arabs, a people of the desert, had little visual art, so they put their artistic energies into poetry, in which they excelled, though never more so than in the Holy Qur'an from Muhammad.

RECLAIMING MECCA

The Medinans' victory over the Meccans in the Battle of the Ditch was so decisive that it put the formerly aggressive Meccans on the defensive, allowing Muhammad to travel to his native city if only briefly. The year was 628 on the Western calendar. When he arrived at Mecca accompanied by a substantial force of men under arms, the Meccans chose to negotiate rather than fight. A

---

[14] Mohammed Marmaduke Pickthall, *The Meaning of the Glorious Koran* (New York: New American Library, 1953), vii.

[15] Clinton Bennett, *In Search of Muhammad* (London and New York: Cassell, 1998), 227.

[16] Abdallah Yusuf Ali (*The Holy Qur'ān: Text, Translation and Commentary* [Brentwood, Md.: Amana Corp., 1983]) in the first case, and Pickthall (*Meaning of the Glorious Koran*) in the second. The meaning of the text is disputed by translators. While the word *ummi*, literally "unlettered," is traditionally applied to Muhammad, some think it should be applied to his audience. Thus Arberry, "the Prophet of the common folk" (*Koran Interpreted*). Or in yet another turn, Maxime Rodinson, "the gentile prophet" (*Muhammad*, 252 n. 1).

written treaty resulted that committed the two parties to ten years of peace and guaranteed Muhammad a pilgrimage visit the following year. The agreement signaled that the conflict was nearing its end: it effectively recognized Muhammad's leadership and the cancellation of the Meccans' alliances with others.

A year later, March 629—it was the month of pilgrimage—Muhammad returned to Mecca accompanied by some 2,600 other pilgrims. The group entered the city in peace with their swords sheathed. When he arrived at the Ka'aba, he dismounted, kissed the sacred Black Stone in its corner, and made seven circumambulations around the holy building, part of the ritual of the "lesser pilgrimage." His faithful friend and supporter, Bilal, a black Abyssinian, climbed to the top of the Ka'aba and announced the call to prayer, following his practice in Medina. The astonished citizens of Mecca could only watch in amazement as the Medinans knelt, bowing toward the Ka'aba in prayer.

Muhammad's final conquest of Mecca came less than a year later. When an incident involving Meccans and Muslims reflected poorly on the Meccans, Muhammad saw an advantage for him in the situation, and he took the opportunity to complete arrangements for his victorious entry. He arrived at the city on January 11, 630. By prior agreement, the Meccan warriors had withdrawn, and, save for one small skirmish by his troops in a corner of the city, the Prophet's entrance was peaceful. He announced a general amnesty for the Meccans, although he did order the execution of some ten persons who had spread anti-Muslim propaganda or were charged with murder. Any who asked forgiveness seem to have been spared. Of the event Karen Armstrong says:

> He had come to Mecca not to persecute the Quraysh but to abolish the religion which had failed them. . . . [M]ounted on [his camel] Qaswa, he rode round the Ka'aba seven times, touching the Black Stone each time and crying "al-Llahu Akbar!" [God is great.] The shout was taken up by his 10,000 soldiers and soon the whole city resounded with the words that symbolized the final victory of Islam. Next Muhammad turned his attention to the 360 idols around the shrine: crowded on to their roofs and balconies, the Quraysh watched him smash each idol while he recited the verse:

> the truth has come, and falsehood has vanished away;
> surely falsehood
> is certain to vanish. [Qur'an 17:82][17]

He then commanded that the pictures of pagan deities that adorned the walls of the Ka'aba be obliterated, though it is said that he allowed the representations of Jesus, Mary, and Abraham to remain for a time. After receiving assurances of fealty from the Meccan citizens, Muhammad quietly returned to Medina. Muslim tradition names the Prophet's conquest of Mecca "the opening."

---

[17] Armstrong, *Muhammad*, 243.

Muhammad returned to Mecca only once, in March 632, again as a pilgrim, the only complete pilgrimage he made from Medina. He died a natural death the following June while resting in the arms of the most beloved of his wives, Aisha. His body was placed in a simple grave under her little house, and a mosque was raised over the tomb. The last words heard from his mouth were, "No, the friend, the highest in paradise."[18]

IN PRAISE OF MUHAMMAD

While Islam denies divinity to Muhammad, the Qur'an identifies him as "the Messenger of God, and the Seal of the Prophets" (33:40). In recognition of his holiness and place of honor, devout Muslims, upon pronouncing his name, customarily follow with the words "may God's blessing and peace be upon him," a Muslim practice for the names of Jesus and Mary as well.

Although Muhammad denied that he had the power of miracles—and none are reported in the Qur'an—the traditions of Islam contain many such. It is said that, while still a child, Muhammad was visited by two angels who cut open his chest, removed his heart, and washed it clean. He once put his hand in a jar of water and the water sufficed for the ablutions of three hundred men. With only a few scraps of food he fed a multitude of some eighty men.[19]

Perhaps the best known of these supernatural stories is that of his night journey to the presence of God. The Qur'an reports:

Glory be to Him, who carried His servant by night
from the Holy Mosque to the Further Mosque
the precincts of which We have blessed,
that We might show him some of Our signs.
He is the All-hearing, the All-seeing. (17:1)

This brief Qur'anic account was enlarged to say that the angel Gabriel roused the sleeping Prophet and led him to the winged steed, Buraq. The heavenly mount carried him to the site of the ancient Jewish temple in Jerusalem, where he prayed alongside Abraham, Moses, Jesus, and other prophets. The area is called al-Aqsa (*aqsa* means "further"), and the Dome of the Rock covers the stone from which it is said that Muhammad ascended to heaven. When a

---

[18] Tor Andrae, *Mohammed: The Man and His Faith*, trans. Theophil Menzel, rev. ed. (New York: Harper & Brothers, 1955), 172.

[19] A contemporary statement of Muhammad's miracles by a Muslim scholar is quite sober. "When he came, he showed forth many Clear Signs, for his whole life from beginning to end was one vast miracle. He fought and won against odds. Without learning from men he taught the highest wisdom. He melted hearts that were hard, and he strengthened hearts that were tender and required support. In all his sayings and doings men of discernment could see the working of God's hand" (Ali, *The Holy Qur'ān*, 1540 n. 5439).

ladder was brought, Muhammad and Gabriel climbed upward through the seven heavens. On the way the Prophet was granted a vision of the sufferings of hell, and when he arrived at the top he came into the presence of God, who confirmed Muhammad's divine commission. The Lord commanded him that his people should pray fifty times a day, a number reduced to five through Moses' intercession during Muhammad's descent to earth. Tradition identifies the two parts of the story by a two-part name, "the Night of the Journey and the Ascension." The reader may recognize a parallel journey through Purgatory and paradise in Dante's *Divine Comedy*, a work some have said drew inspiration from the account of Muhammad's wondrous experience.

Words of adulation of the Prophet are almost unbounded. The Egyptian writer al-Damiri (d. 1405), described him thus:

> God sent [Muhammad] after a long break (in the succession of Messengers) to be a mercy to mankind, and he delivered His message. He strove with true diligence in the cause of God, gave proper advice to the people, and served his Lord till death came to him. He was the most favored of all creatures, the noblest of the Messengers, the Prophet of Mercy, the leader of convinced believers, who on the Day will bear the Standard of Praise, be the general intercessor, occupy the glorious station, have the pool which many will frequent, and gather under his banner Adam and all who came after him.
>
> He is the best of the Prophets and his community is the best of communities. . . . He performed astonishing miracles, possessed great natural abilities, had a sound and powerful intelligence, a most distinguished genealogy, and perfect beauty. His generosity was boundless, his bravery unchallengeable, his forbearance excessive, his knowledge profitable, his actions ever honorable, his fear of God complete, his piety sublime. He was the most eloquent of men, perfect in every respect, and the furthest of all mankind from things base and vicious. Of him the poet has said:

> "None like Muhammad has the Merciful ever created,
> Nor such, to my thinking, will He ever again create."[20]

At the same time, no other renowned religious leader, whether Gautama the Buddha, or Confucius, or Lao-tzu, or any comparable figure, has drawn the controversy and ire that Muhammad has, particularly from Christians. The basis of course is Muhammad's rejection of traditional Judaism and Christianity, and his claim to improve upon them. The history of that animosity will be a considerable part of this study.

---

[20] Quoted by F. E. Peters, *Judaism, Christianity, and Islam: The Classical Texts and Their Interpretation*, vol. 1, *From Covenant to Community* (Princeton: Princeton University Press, 1990), 247.

ISLAM, THE RELIGIOUS SYSTEM

Muhammad called the religious system he established "Islam." The principal meaning of the word is "surrender" or "submission," Muslims being "submitters" to God—the word "Muslim" is cognate to the word "Islam." While "surrender" is primary, a second meaning relates to the Arabic word *salam*, "peace," parallel to the Hebrew *shalom*. So "Islam" is the way of surrender to God, the way to create peace.

While non-Muslims may speak of Islam as originating with Muhammad, mainstream Islam says otherwise, claiming that even though Muhammad's message was new to his fellow Arabs, the revelations to Muhammad were a renewal of God's earlier revelations to Adam, Abraham, Moses, Jesus, and many other prophets, revelations that Muhammad said had been corrupted. Indeed, God had sent "warners" to every people on earth. The Arabs, descendants of Abraham's oldest son, Ishmael, as they were, had long since forsaken God's way and turned to idolatry, just as the Jews had in the famous story of Aaron's golden calf. As for Christians, Muhammad said that they had erred in portraying Jesus as divine.

The sin of idolatry was a fundamental sin, an unforgivable sin, and Muhammad consistently inveighed against "associating" anything with God, whether an image or a person or anything else.

> Those on whom you call apart from God, are
> servants the likes of you;
> call them and let them answer you, if you speak truly.
> What, have they feet
> wherewith they walk,
> or have they hands wherewith they lay hold,
> or have they eyes
> wherewith they see,
> or have they ears wherewith they give ear? (Qur'an 7:193-94)

Even so, Muhammad honored Jews and Christians as "People of the Book," that is, the Bible, whether in Jewish or Christian form, and saw them as people striving to worship the One God, even if they did so partly in error.

The late Wilfred Cantwell Smith, a prominent scholar of Islam, has underscored the importance of monotheism for Islam:

> From [Muhammad's] day to this, Islam has been uncompromising in its doctrine of monotheism, and its insistence on transcendence: God the Creator and Judge is Lord of all the universe, is high above all his creatures and beyond them, and beyond all their imaginings—and certainly beyond all their representations. Other deities, it asserts, are but the fig-

ments of men's wayward imagination, are unadulterated fiction; they just do not exist. Man must not bow down to worship them, or look to them for help, or think about them. God is God alone; on this point Islam is emphatic, positive, and clear.[21] *No Trinity*

One can easily imagine how this forceful message would bring opposition from the tradition-bound people of Mecca with their many images in the Ka'aba.

This faith was to inform all of society. Laws for marriage were set down (a maximum of four wives, if the husband loved and provided for them equally), laws for commerce (no usury or interest on loans, though profits gained thereby would be shared with the lender), a tithe for the poor (two-and-one-half percent of that value that has been held for one year), daily prayer (established as noted above to be five times a day), and at least one pilgrimage to the holy places of Mecca if health and resources would permit. The bulk of these teachings are enshrined in the Qur'an, but many oral traditions about Muhammad, both teachings and narratives, were collected as the *hadith*, often translated as "Traditions," or more literally the "Narratives" or "Accounts," which provide a secondary source for Muslim law and doctrine. Muslim jurists, applying and interpreting these laws as times and conditions required, developed the *shari'a*, the Islamic system of law that in its classical form covered all aspects of society, though in many areas a system of secular law developed alongside it.

Muhammad banned any and every form of idolatry in favor of the unadorned worship of the One God. Muhammad demanded high levels of social justice and morality, ideals that were to be rigidly enforced. Violence was to be *really?* avoided, save in cases of self-defense and correction of injustice. Here was a social and religious tradition immediately recognizable to Jews and Christians, seemingly formed from their own cloth but changed within the context and practices of Arab life and the mystic visions granted to Muhammad. Indeed many contemporary scholars hold that Muhammad did not think of replacing Judaism and Christianity with Islam but instead sought to establish Islam alongside Judaism and Christianity. On this point Karen Armstrong says: "Muhammad never had any idea that he was founding a new world religion. This was to be a religion for the Arabs, who seem to have been left out of the divine plan."[22] Jews had their religion and holy book as did the Christians, but his people did not. In time, however, the universal claims of Islam became clear, and classical Islam acted on that principle. Mainstream Muslims would say that the universal claims were there from the beginning. Indeed, a *hadith* quotes Muhammad as having said: "The prophets were formerly sent to their people alone, whereas I have been sent to all mankind."[23]

---

[21] Wilfred Cantwell Smith, *The Faith of Other Men* (New York: Harper & Row, 1962, 1972), 61.

[22] Armstrong, *Muhammad*, 86.

[23] Quoted by Bennett, *In Search of Muhammad*, 142.

When Muhammad began his reform, Arabs were a tribal society ruled by traditions of tribal competition and blood vengeance, but by the time he died they had a common system of law based on Islam. He turned a divided people into a coherent unity and replaced their tradition of idolatry and polytheism with a clear monotheism. Thereby he forged a brotherhood based not on race but on a common faith, no small achievement among the desert tribes of that day.

On the surface the parallels of the new religion with Judaism and Christianity were numerous: worship of the one God, the importance of Abraham, Moses, and Jesus, a society informed by a single religious view that sanctioned its religious and civil laws—all of this was familiar in type to Jews and Christians from the history of ancient Israel and from life in the Middle Ages. But Muhammad's religion was not Judaism or Christianity. Whether intended for Arabs alone or not, Islam was a rejection of both earlier religions in favor of a system that corrected what Muhammad saw as their errors. Therein lay the problem for both Jews and Christians, who were certain to resist this new religious way. However, when Islam moved out of Arabia and took control of Christian lands, Muslims did not attempt to abolish Judaism and Christianity. Instead, both Jews and Christians were allowed to continue their ways even if under special restrictions.

THE MUSLIM VIEW OF JESUS

For Christians, the biggest problem with Muhammad was his denial of the deity of Jesus. Much of the rest of Christian teaching about Jesus is there: he was born of the Virgin Mary, he lived a sinless life, he ascended to heaven, and is expected at the Last Day. As to Jesus' crucifixion, Muhammad said that God would not have allowed one of his prophets to suffer such a calamitous end. On this point, contemporary Western scholars, inclined to look for historical antecedents, observe that Muhammad had likely encountered Christian Gnosticism, a branch of early Christianity noted for its claim that denied to Jesus a physical body and therefore held that Jesus could not have suffered crucifixion—another was crucified in his place, either Simon of Cyrene, who carried Jesus' cross, or a spirit who took the form of Jesus.

THE RIGHTS OF WOMEN

Muhammad seems to have had a free and accepting relationship with women, and the laws of the Qur'an granted them certain important rights. He spoke openly with women and heard and answered their questions about Islam and the Qur'an. Muhammad's greatest contribution to women was the elimination of the practice of infanticide, which was used mainly against baby girls, less desired than males. The sixteenth *sura* speaks of this grim practice with considerable irony.

When news is brought
To one of them, of (the birth
Of) a female (child), his face
Darkens, and he is filled
With inward grief!

With shame does he hide
Himself from his people,
Because of the bad news
He has had!
Shall he retain it
On (sufferance and) contempt,
Or bury it in the dust?
Ah! what an evil (choice)
They decide on? (Qur'an 16:58-59, Ali)

That Muhammad envisioned equality of the sexes in some sense at least is seen in several things. This passage suggests equality:

Women shall have rights
Similar to the rights
Against them, according
To what is equitable

It is immediately followed by something a little different:

But men have a degree
(of advantage) over them. (2:228, Ali)

More telling is *sura* 33:35, whose very structure places men and women on the same level:

Men and women who have surrendered
believing men and believing women,
obedient men and obedient women,
truthful men and truthful women,
enduring men and enduring women,
humble men and humble women,
men and women who live in charity,
men who fast and women who fast,
men and women who guard their private parts,
men and women who remember God oft—
for them God has prepared forgiveness and a mighty wage. (Arberry)

Before this *sura* came, the revelations were given to men, but afterwards women were sometimes especially noted. The practice of polygyny preceded

polygamy before

Muhammad, but he limited the number of wives to four. The woman could contract for a monogamous marriage. Divorce was permitted, largely as a man's right, but Muhammad called it "abhorrent to God." Women had some rights in divorce too, including the right to initiate divorce. The right of women to inherit property was ensured (though only one-half the amount of her brothers, who would have to pay dowry for their sisters), as well as her control over her dowry, even in divorce, an important safeguard for economic help. To a degree Muhammad was accepting earlier practice, but even so it is notable that the West granted women no property rights at the time. Muslim women took part in battles, mainly caring for the wounded, though the oft-told story of Muhammad's widow Aisha sitting on her camel at a battle in support of the caliph Ali suggests a more active role. When, on the orders of Uthman, the third caliph, the official copy of the Qur'an was compiled, the holy book was placed in the care of a woman for safekeeping, not a man. Aisha and others contributed accounts to the *hadith*, the great collection of oral tradition about the Prophet. In these instances and more, women participated directly in the Islamic movement.

At the same time there were restrictions. The Prophet ordered his wives behind a curtain in their home (the Arabic word for curtain can also be rendered "veil"), in order to seclude them from contact with his many visitors (Qur'an 33:59), but since his home was virtually a public place where he conducted the community business, family privacy would seem in order. His only other mention of the veil for women was for purposes of modesty: "Let them cast their veils over their bosoms, and not reveal their adornment save to their husbands" (24:31). The seclusion instituted with the curtain in his home was eventually required of all women, as was the veil, especially after Islam's spread into Syria and Persia, where Christian and Zoroastrian women were already covered head to foot. In general, the early Islamic movement was male-oriented and placed women in a subordinate position.

The Abbasid dynasty that moved the caliphate to Baghdad tightened the restrictions even more. The veil was required of all women by then, and they no longer could participate in group deliberations. The husband's right of divorce became absolute (though in some Muslim societies portions of women's rights in divorce were continued), and women were segregated from men in the mosque, when they were allowed in at all. Even though a woman's property rights remained, the male's right to control the woman had become the norm in Islam. Even so, women have had significant roles in Islam, particularly in the Sufi movement, the tradition of Islamic mysticism, which was begun in the eighth century by a woman, Rabi'a al-Adawiyya.

While the practice of restrictions on women has clearly been the norm in Islam, Leila Ahmed, who has written one of the more authoritative books on women in Islam, sees an ambiguity, even a tension within the tradition, in respect to the place of women. The quotations of equality cited above bespeak an egalitarianism that apologists for Islam often cite. Ahmed believes the rhetoric of equality, the "ethical vision" of Islam as she terms it,[24] may account for the way many Muslim women defend their acceptance of the veil and other restrictions, saying that they feel no subordination or oppression. Ahmed believes that the broad principles are so strong that these register in the minds of many Muslims, both men and women, more than the practices that modern Westerners find limiting. And, of course, those principles can be the basis for appeals for changes in practice.

THE FIVE PILLARS OF ISLAM

Muslims summarize the major points of their belief and practice in the Five Pillars of Islam: they are the Two Sentences, prayer, almsgiving, fasting, and the pilgrimage to Mecca. Each has been alluded to but a larger discussion is in order.

1. The Two Sentences

The confession of Islam is simple and direct: "I bear witness that there is no god but God, and Muhammad is his Apostle."[25] The first words recited over a new-born infant and the last said at the grave, they are heard on innumerable occasions in between, particularly as the *muezzin,* or cantor, sings them five times a day from his post in a minaret atop the mosque in his call to prayer. Reciting them three times with a believing heart before two witnesses makes one a Muslim. Muslims call this creed "The Two Sentences," or "The Two Words," or sometimes simply "The Word." In Arabic the confession reads: "*Lā-'i-lā-ha-'il-lal-lāh; Mu-am-ma-dur-ra-sū-lul-lāh.*" The Arabic has a pleasing, rolling sound, poetic and engaging, and the Arabic script can be highly decorative, but most of all, the words announce the heart of the Muslim faith: worship of the one God as revealed to the Prophet Muhammad.

2. Prayer

A Muslim is to pray five times a day: at dawn, midday, mid-afternoon, sunset, and the fall of darkness. The prayers are traditional and follow a defined routine beginning with standing, then kneeling, then touching one's forehead to the ground, a physical enactment of the surrender to God for which Islam calls. The most common of the numerous prayers is the first *sura* of the Qur'an, the latter portion of which reads:

---

[24] Leila Ahmed, *Women and Gender in Islam: Historical Roots of a Modern Debate* (New Haven and London: Yale University Press, 1992), 65-66.

[25] "Apostle," *rasul.* The Arabic uses two words for Muhammad's office: *nabi,* "prophet," and *rasul,* "apostle."

> Thee only we serve; to Thee alone we pray for succour.
> Guide us in the straight path,
> the path of those whom Thou hast blessed,
> not of those against whom Thou art wrathful,
> nor of those who are astray. (Qur'an 1:5-7)

Prayers may be offered at any place, though the Friday noon prayers are customarily said at a mosque. The scene in a mosque is impressive: row upon row of men in straight and exact lines (the women separate, usually behind a screen), kneeling and bowing in unison following the *imam,* an officer who serves much like a rabbi. The posture of kneeling and bowing in prayer symbolizes and acts out the ideal of submission and surrender to God as perhaps nothing else can. Following the prayers, the *imam* ordinarily gives a sermon for the occasion.

3. Alms

The Third Pillar, almsgiving, is a tax collected for charity. Usually given to the mosque for distribution, the practice has sometimes been used as justification for economic socialism. The classical rule, already mentioned, calls for an annual contribution of two-and-one-half percent of that value that has been held for one year, but implementation varies.

4. Fasting

Fasting is commanded for the month of Ramadan, the ninth month of the Muslim year. A holy month by pre-Islamic tradition, and the month in which Muhammad received his first revelation, by his command Ramadan became a time for fasting. During daylight hours nothing is to pass one's lips, even the smoke of a cigarette, but the restriction ends at sunset. In spite of the somber implication of the word "fasting," Ramadan is a season of celebration when families and friends gather in the evening to enjoy what has been prohibited during the day-long fast, a practice Islam's Christian critics would often criticize. The month concludes with a three-day feast, a major festival in Islamic life. The Muslim calendar follows the lunar year, which is some eleven days shorter than the solar year of the Western calendar, and as a result the monthly rotation gradually brings Ramadan, like other Muslim celebrations, through the entire range of the year's seasons.

5. Pilgrimage

The *hajj* or pilgrimage, to Mecca in the twelfth month of the Muslim year is to be completed by every Muslim male at least once unless illness or poverty prevents it. Women are encouraged to make the journey if accompanied by a man. Upon entering Mecca pilgrims dress in simple white robes symbolic of their desired purity before God and their equality before each other. The pilgrimage lasts several days and includes walking around the Ka'aba seven times, and then making two traditional journeys. One journey, called the "lesser pilgrimage," is a short and hasty trip to the well Zamzam, a reenactment of Hagar's frantic search for water after Abraham had sent her and her son Ishmael away. The "greater pilgrimage" is a two-day trek into the desert in remembrance of Abraham's attempt to offer his son as a sacrifice to God, parallel in part to Genesis 22. The *hajj* concludes with a three-day period of celebration and festivity and a final visit to the Ka'aba.

Those who have made the pilgrimage testify that it is a profoundly moving experience, not only because its actions recall ancient sacred events but also because they create a sense of community with other Muslims from around the world. Pilgrims, dressed alike, with no covering but tents, suffer equally from the daily heat and the night's cold, and even eat the same feast, the well-to-do sharing their food with the poor. Pilgrimage, like group prayer in the mosque on Friday and the fasting of Ramadan, reinforces the communal nature of Islam, a profoundly important characteristic of the Muslim tradition.

CONCLUSION

When Muhammad died in 632, Arab tribes once divided by tribal and family loyalties, often at odds with each other, possessed a larger loyalty, namely, to Islam and the deity Islam proclaimed. Not only had a sense of unity developed among Arabs, but also an energy and enthusiasm that would carry them and their new faith outside Arabia into the Mediterranean and Asian worlds, and even into Europe.

Now there were three religious traditions claiming their ancestry in the ancient patriarch, Abraham—Judaism, Christianity, and Islam. Judaism was the oldest and smallest. Dispersed among the nations of the Near East, Jews had no land of their own, no nation state, and no army to defend them. They lived in a Diaspora. Yet God (of Abraham) has promised them land + Moses took them there

The Christian church had long since joined hands with the Roman empire to become a political power as well as a religious movement, though the barbarian invasions in Western Europe had left that power intact only in the East. The Christian diatribe against Judaism was in full swing, having been given a great boost by the sermons and writings of John Chrysostom (the "Golden-tongued") in fifth-century Constantinople.

Now a new rival to both Judaism and Christianity had appeared. Because Christianity had become a political power as well as a religion, it would be the political antagonist of Islam, and their conflict would sometimes turn into war. Whether simple controversy, or war, or persecution, as in the case of the Christian persecutions of the Jews, the three traditions from Abraham, siblings in a sense, would have a complex and often bloody history with each other. That would begin with the expansion of the Islamic movement in its first century.

2

The Spread of Islam

If someone in the first third of the seventh Christian century had had the audacity to prophesy that within a decade or so some unheralded, unforeseen power from the hitherto barbarous and little-known land of Arabia was to make its appearance, hurl itself against the only two world powers of the age, fall heir to the one (Sassanid) and strip the other (the Byzantine) of its fairest provinces, he would undoubtedly have been declared a lunatic. Yet that was exactly what happened.

—Phillip K. Hitti[1]

Because Muhammad neither named a successor nor established a plan for choosing one, upon his death Islam's first crisis was the question of leadership. Muhammad's followers answered by turning to the Prophet's "Companions," the innermost circle of his associates. They chose as their new leader Abu Bakr, one of the earliest and most respected of Muhammad's converts, named him "caliph" (Arabic *khalīfa*, "successor" or "deputy"), and granted him political and military authority over Muslims, though not religious authority—that belonged to Muhammad alone and would be enshrined in the Qur'an and the *hadith*.

Abu Bakr and his comrades had a second decision—What should they do now that the Prophet was no longer with them? Their answer was to take Islam to the regions around them, particularly to their fellow Arabs.[2] Did not the Qur'an say (in Arberry's rendering), "We have sent thee not, except to mankind entire, good tidings to bear, and warning . . . ?" (34:27). The revelation to Muhammad needed to be carried abroad, and the Muslim leaders were moved to a sense of divine mission.

---

[1] Philip K. Hitti, *The Arabs: A Short History,* 5th rev. printing (Chicago: Henry Regnery Co., 1949), 56.

[2] The term "Arab" has an interesting history. Originally it named the inhabitants of the Arabian peninsula, Semites like the Jews. As the Islamic movement spread, the term came into broader usage for those who spoke Arabic as their mother tongue. That is pretty much its current meaning. In that sense it names those peoples who live in North Africa, the Arabian peninsula, the Levant (i.e., Syria-Palestine), and Iraq. Iranians, for instance, strong Muslims as they are, are not Arabs. They descend from the ancient Persians, as their language, Farsi, suggests.

Muhammad had sent an earlier expedition north to the border of Byzantium that was led by Zayd, Muhammad's former slave and adopted son, and one south to the head of the Gulf of 'Aqaba that Muhammad led himself. The first brought defeat; the second resulted in treaties with the local rulers. After Abu Bakr consolidated the support of the tribes within Arabia, his successor, Caliph Umar, led the Muslim warriors northward out of the peninsula. Convinced of the truth given by the Prophet of God, and with few skills other than horsemanship and combat, they rode forth to conquer.

Beyond the goal of uniting Arabs inside and outside Arabia, the motives of the Arab warriors were probably mixed. Many sought gold and glory, for the spoils were to be divided among both commanders and warriors. Devout believers entertained the hope of eternal reward, for it was said that any who died in this holy campaign would immediately attain paradise with its wondrous pleasures of plush oases, well supplied with dates and luscious food, not to mention the dark-eyed *houris, women* who would serve their men's every want and need. Therefore, the Arab warriors heeded the call to *jihad*—the word means "struggle," or more largely, "to struggle in the Way of God"—the undertaking of war to carry Islam into new areas.

Arab warriors moved with surprising speed into the area of the Byzantine empire. Within three years they had taken Damascus. Then Jerusalem fell, then Egypt, and then Syria. Reports indicate that Jews sometimes aided the Arabs in capturing Byzantine cities. In A.D. 632, on the very eve of the Arab invasion, the emperor Heraclius had ordered the baptism of all Jews within the Byzantine empire. Jewish sympathies would hardly have been with the Byzantines.[3]

When the Arabs emerged from their peninsula, two empires dominated the Middle East, the Byzantine and the Persian. The former, the continuation of the Roman empire, now the Christian empire, was presided over by Constantinople, one of the greatest cities of the day, with great libraries, beautiful churches, and a well-run civic system. In the early seventh century this empire included Syria-Palestine, present-day Turkey, and the Balkans, as well as most of North Africa and Italy. Byzantium's strong army and navy made it a major military power. Persia, its rival and enemy, based in present-day Iran, stretched from the Middle East to India and continued the culture and prestige of the earlier Persian regimes. The two empires, one born in Europe, the other in Asia, had fought on and off for centuries in a rivalry that stretched back to the days of Alexander the Great and before. Now they faced a common enemy.

Within twenty years the bulk of these two empires had fallen to Arab armies, as Byzantine and Persian garrison cities offered little resistance, exhausted as they were from the wars the two great states had long waged against each other. Arab warriors, accustomed to desert fighting, maneuvered well in the battles.

---

[3] The emperor Justinian had earlier placed several severe restrictions on Jews and in effect removed from them full legal rights. Jews in turn responded with fighting, including several military actions, but they were defeated and severely punished.

The Persian capital, Ctesiphon, fell in 645, but the Christian capital of Constantinople remained free owing to a valiant defense.

The surrender of the towns and cities in areas controlled by Byzantium was aided not only by the few Jewish residents but by the resentment many Christians had against their rulers because of both religious oppression and high taxation. For three centuries Christian theologians had argued and debated doctrines about Jesus and his divine and human natures. When decisions were reached, the imperial authorities enforced the views of the winning side, usually the orthodox, but not all conformed and many nonorthodox remained, usually among the subject ethnic groups, Syrian Christians in Lebanon and Syria, and Coptic Christians in Egypt. These groups, along with Jews and Samaritans, had suffered from the demands of the Christian emperors, and so resistance to the Byzantine rulers was already considerable when the Muslims arrived.

Once vanquished by the Islamic forces, Arabs, whether Christian or other, came under the strictest rule—they were required to become Muslims upon pain of death. Non-Arabs, whether Christian or Jew, the so-called "people of the Book," could surrender their arms and continue their own religious practices on the condition that they pay the required poll tax, refrain from criticizing Muhammad and the Qur'an, and keep to any other restrictions that might be required. Islam has called such people "protected minorities." In Persia, Zoroastrians were generally assigned protected status but with more restrictions than those for Christians and Jews because the Arabs wanted to prevent a revival of Persian nationalism. Some Christians, wearied by the detailed and seemingly interminable theological debates, probably found the simple Muslim confession, "There is no god but God," a breath of fresh air and yielded to their new masters on that basis, though few chose to convert.

The position of nonorthodox Christians and Jews within the former Byzantine empire improved with the Arab conquest—the new restrictions were much less severe than those that had been imposed by orthodox Christian emperors. But the ruling Byzantine elite lost their privileged status—they were reduced to the same level as their nonorthodox fellow Christians. The condition of Jews improved, however. For the first time in five hundred years Jews could live more or less at will in Jerusalem, from which they had been evicted by the emperor Hadrian when he put down the Bar-Kokhba rebellion in the 130s. Hadrian's decree permitted Jews to return to Jerusalem only for the Day of Atonement, though that restriction had been somewhat relaxed by Christian rulers over the centuries. Jews were now also free from the emperor Heraclius's edict of 632, which ordered them to be baptized.

Christians and Jews within Persia exchanged Persian-Zoroastrian rule for Arab-Muslim rule, and both groups accommodated to the change very well. (The Christians in Persia were mostly Nestorian Christians, a branch named for a fifth-century division that, in a manner of speaking, emphasized the humanity of Jesus.) The Nestorian patriarch Yeshuyab III wrote to another cleric about the Arab conquest: "They have not attacked the Christian religion, but rather they have commended our faith, honoured our priests . . . and conferred benefits on churches and monasteries."[4] When the caliphate moved to Baghdad a century later, only the Nestorian patriarchate was allowed to move there. In fact, the Nestorian Christians were the most favored Christian group under Islamic rule anywhere. The Nestorians are noted for a successful and important mission to China that they launched not long after the Islamic conquest of Persia.

The Islamic practice of permitting Christians and Jews ("the people of the Book") and others to continue in their own religion, if under restrictions, has been a striking feature of the Islamic faith. Islamic law viewed idol worshipers differently and allowed them only two choices, conversion or death. This law, however, was rarely implemented, as evidenced by the way the Mogul rulers of India some centuries later allowed Hindu polytheism and image worship to continue.

The Islamic pattern of relative toleration contrasts rather sharply with Christian Europe, which moved more and more to persecution and expulsion as the Middle Ages passed. Exceptions to the Islamic system that allowed Jews and Christians to live undisturbed occurred from time to time, but usually as a result of mob violence or the aberrant behavior of a local ruler. Over the centuries it was generally better to be a Christian or a Jew in an Islamic society than a Jew or Muslim in a Christian society. It is also true that as time passed more and more of the populations of North Africa and the Middle East converted to Islam, until, after several centuries—the date is uncertain—the great majority were Muslims, although pockets of Christians and Jews remained here and there (Coptic Christians in Egypt and Syrian Christians in Syria-Palestine, for example). In many areas the church disappeared altogether. Judaism generally persisted better than Christianity—Jews had learned how to survive through their three-hundred-year struggle with Christian rulers.

THE QUESTION OF WAR

On the surface it seems that Islam was spread by military conquest. The historian Bernard Lewis enters a mild disagreement, observing that while the spread of Islam was made possible by war, conversion to Islamic faith was not forced upon the conquered. The Qur'an is explicit on this point: "No compulsion is there in religion" (2:258). Lewis explains: "The primary war aim of the conquerors was not to impose the Islamic faith by force. . . . The conquered peoples were given various inducements, such as lower rates of taxation, to adopt Islam, but they were not compelled to do so."[5]

---

[4] Quoted by Samuel Hugh Moffett, *A History of Christianity in Asia*, vol. 1, *Beginnings to 1500* (San Francisco: HarperSanFrancisco, 1992), 339.

[5] Bernard Lewis, *The Middle East: A Brief History of the Last 2000 Years* (New York: Scribner, 1995), 27.

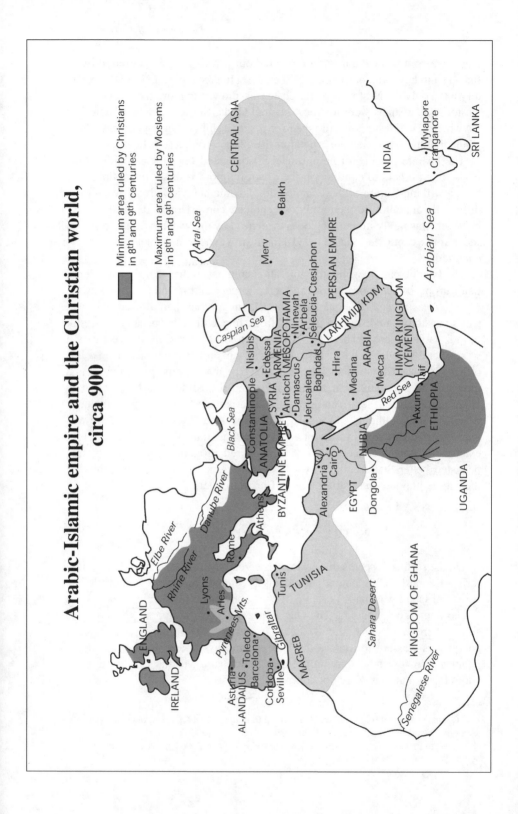

Arabic-Islamic empire and the Christian world, circa 900

Minimum area ruled by Christians in 8th and 9th centuries

Maximum area ruled by Moslems in 8th and 9th centuries

In one passage the Qur'an seems to order war, though reluctantly—"Prescribed for you is fighting, though it be hateful to you" (2:212[6])—and even war against unbelievers:

> Fight those who believe not in God and the Last Day
> and do not forbid what God and His Messenger
> have forbidden—such men as practise not the
> religion of truth, being of those who have been given
> the Book—until they pay tribute out of hand
> and have been humbled. (9:29)

> And fight the unbelievers totally even as they fight you totally;
> and know that God is with the godfearing. (9:36)

These latter Qur'anic texts call for "*jihad* of the sword." No element of Islam has caused as much disagreement and debate between Christians and Muslims as this command.

The Arabic word *jihad*, "struggle," is used in two senses in Islam: spiritual struggle and military struggle. The spiritual "struggle in the way of God" (9:24) against unbelief and injustice has always been held as primary, a battle waged within one's own soul and behavior as well as in society. Islam calls this the "greater *jihad*" and identifies it as a duty incumbent upon every Muslim. The importance of this effort is paramount. "Struggle for God as is His due, for He has chosen you" (Qur'an 22:78). The second form of *jihad*, often termed the "lesser *jihad*" and in the media rather incorrectly called "holy war," is the physical struggle of combat in defense of Islam. While all Muslims must undertake the greater *jihad*, not all are required to participate in the lesser *jihad*, actual warfare, though all are obligated to support such a war when it is under way.

Islamic teaching requires that such a military campaign may be undertaken only in certain instances. One is the defense of Islamic people and territory if attacked, exactly parallel to the Western and Christian doctrine of just war, a war fought in self-defense. A second purpose is a war fought to right a wrong. The Christian just war theory allows this view also. The Gulf War of 1991, which was fought to repel Iraq from its invasion of Kuwait, was such a war. The expansion of Islam in the seventh century would also be an example of righting a wrong, the idea being that it was wrong for the Middle East and North Africa not to be exposed directly to Islam and ruled by Islamic law.

At that point formal Islamic doctrine and language divide the world into two parts, the *dar al-Islam*, that is the "House [or Home] of Islam," or as some translators render it, "the peaced abode," and the *dar al-harb*, that is, the "House of War," or "the unpeaced abode." The first is the Islamic area proper, where, ideally speaking, all have surrendered or submitted to God as Muslims

---

[6] 2:212 in Arberry's translation quoted here; 2:216 in Ali's translation.

or, if not, have at least submitted to Islamic rule and thus to the rule of God's law in society. By virtue of this conformity to God and God's law, such societies are considered, in principle at least, to be at peace, both with God and with themselves. Other societies, not submitting to God, are held to be in disorder from internal conflict as well as from conflict with the Deity because they have not accepted divine law. Muhammad taught that Muslims are to fight such societies and that war against them is justified. At that point the situation becomes more controversial. According to Bernard Lewis, "In principle, this war was to continue until all mankind either embraced Islam or submitted to the authority of the Muslim state."[7] Any who are attacked under such conditions will charge that the Muslim forces have undertaken a war of aggression, and later Christians in Europe launched their Crusades on just that claim, namely, that the Holy Land was unjustly taken from them by Arab Muslims.

While Muslims did not require the people they conquered to convert to Islam, they presumed their subjects would eventually do so, and they believed, furthermore, that Islam would eventually cover the entire world. Of course, Christians have presumed their faith to be potentially universal as well, and therein lay, and lie, the seeds for conflict between the two traditions. Both claimed, and still claim, to possess universal and absolute truth, and both were and are under some compulsion to spread that truth.

That Muslims used military force to spread Islamic power, if not the Muslim faith, is well known; less familiar is the fact that Christian rulers did the same. Illustrations are the Christian Roman empire with laws that favored Christianity; conversions compelled by Charlemagne, medieval laws ordering capital punishment for heretics, and baptism, death, or exile for non-Christians; and even nineteenth- and twentieth-century colonialism, in which Christian missionaries rode to their mission fields on the shoulders of Western military and economic power. Christians are probably less aware of their history on this point than they are of Islamic history, but in many respects the pattern was the same.

THE CALIPHATE

The first two caliphs, Abu Bakr and Umar, completed the organization of Arabia under the rule of Islam and began the spread of Islam beyond. Umar was the first to assume what became the traditional title for caliphs, "Commander of the Faithful," and he established the Islamic calendar by naming the year of the *hijra* as the first year of the Muslim era. Uthman, the third caliph, supervised the editing of the Holy Qur'an.

A struggle for power broke out upon Uthman's death, however, and the party of Ali, Muhammad's cousin and son-in-law won out; he was named the fourth caliph and the last of those called by Islamic tradition "the Rightly Guided

---

[7] Bernard Lewis, *Islam and the West* (New York and Oxford: Oxford University Press, 1993), 9.

Caliphs." The view of Ali and his supporters was that the caliph should be a descendant of Muhammad. Although Ali was not a blood descendant, he was related to Muhammad by his marriage to Muhammad's daughter, Fatima, and their two children were Muhammad's grandsons.

Disputes over the selection process, internecine quarrels among Muhammad's followers, and a disagreement over the importance of familial succession finally led to war among the factions, and upon Ali's assassination in 661 the Islamic movement divided into two separate traditions, one named *sunni*, literally "tradition," the other *shi'a*, "party," the "party" of Ali. The assassination of Ali and the subsequent death of his son in battle turned them into martyrs among their followers, and Shi'ite Islam has ever since placed great value on vicarious suffering. Sunni Islam is by far the larger of the two and the branch medieval Christians encountered in the main. Recent events, however have included a great deal of Western involvement with Shi'ite Islam, since both Iran and Iraq are large centers of Shi'ite population.

Two great dynasties would come from the Sunni side. The Umayyad dynasty ruled from Damascus from 661 to 750, the Abbasid in Baghdad from 750 to 1258. Sunni Muslims accept these caliphs, but Shi'ite Muslims, who were never able to gain the caliphate again, consider them "usurpers." Alongside the Abbasid dynasty were two others, a surviving branch of the Umayyad dynasty in Spain from 777 to 1236, and the Fatamid dynasty in Cairo from 909 to 1171.

When the caliph Muawiya, who established the Umayyad line, moved the Islamic capital to Damascus in 661, he effectively turned Muslim eyes toward Byzantium and the Greek-language world, a move that resulted in the transformation of Islam and later in the revival of Greek and classical ideas in Latin Europe. Further, Muslim armies, now better organized, their ranks enlarged with volunteers from the new subject peoples, Arab and non-Arab, Muslim and Christian, turned eastward and moved across present-day Iran, Afghanistan, and Pakistan to the very banks of the Indus River, carrying Islam with them. The area is still Muslim today. Islamic warriors rode westward as well, across the sands of North Africa, where once again, native groups, both religious and ethnic, found new freedom through their Muslim conquerors. In the East the Byzantines held the line at the Taurus Mountains, and the capital city of Constantinople remained secure, while northern Africa became the launching pad for attacks on Europe.

The Islamic invasion of Spain came in 711, when Berber troops led by a general named Tariq were invited into the Iberian peninsula to aid a Christian ruler in his power struggle (the name Gibraltar is derived from the Arabic words *Jabal Tariq*, "mount of Tariq"). Muslim armies advanced north across the Iberian peninsula and into central France, where in 732 (some say 733[8]) at a site

---

[8] Benjamin Z. Kedar, *Crusade and Mission: European Approaches toward the Muslims* (Princeton: Princeton University Press, 1984), 25: "the all-too-often misdated Battle of Tours-Poitiers of 733"; John Beeler, *Warfare in Feudal Europe, 730–1200* (Ithaca and London: Cornell University Press, 1971), 12: "The action at Tours in 733."

between Tours and Poitiers they met the troops of Charles Martel, Charlemagne's grandfather. Islamic and Christian forces engaged once, but when Charles's scouts returned the following morning, they found that their opponents had withdrawn. While the battle is sometimes described as a major turning point in Western history, the Arab and Berber retreat to southern France and the Pyrenees may have been not so much a military defeat as a strategic withdrawal due to their having exceeded the limits of their resources and supply lines.[9] In the East, the last of these early attacks on Constantinople came in 717, but it failed, and so by the middle of the eighth century the frontiers of the Islamic empire were relatively stable in both the west and the east. Had the two prongs of the pincer movement aimed at the eastern and western flanks of Europe been able to meet, Arabs would have been in a position to establish an empire rather like that of ancient Rome.

Even so, their accomplishments were almost as impressive. One hundred years after leaving Arabia, most of Spain and Portugal, all of North Africa, Palestine, and Syria, plus the territory eastward to the Himalayas and to the borders of China were in Islamic hands. Muslim warriors, reflecting on their success, concluded that their victories were providential. Only God could have brought these wondrous things to pass. If proof were needed of the truth of Islam and the message of the Prophet, there it was for all to see—an extraordinary series of conquests, particularly for warriors ill equipped for such massive and spectacular victories. When Christians looked back on these events, they also appealed to providence, but in reverse—they saw these disturbing events as punishments upon Christians for their sins. which sins 'in particular?

ISLAMIC CIVILIZATION

What happened in succeeding centuries may have been even more impressive, namely, the formation of a world civilization out of Arab culture and Muslim faith and the materials of the various peoples now under their sway. The development came in three steps. First, Arabs conquered and established their political rule, as already described. The second stage came with the spread of the Arabic language, which became the standard language for public life, diplomacy, and scholarship, and in time became either the first or second language for the common people. Within two centuries a new cultural entity had developed that used the Arabic language but began to draw on the resources of the Middle East and the classical world of Greece and Rome. Third was the gradual conversion over several centuries to the Islamic faith of the majority of the

---

[9] Norman Daniel speaks of the battle "which Gibbon over-stressed as decisive, in order to tease the theologians of Oxford about their escape from interpreting the Quran. . . . After that date there was no serious northward prosecution of *jihad* or holy war. . . . The northern climate never attracted the Arabs seriously" (*The Arabs and Mediaeval Europe* [London: Longman, 1975], 7).

population, save for the pockets of those Jews and Christians who remained as protected minorities.

In 762 the new Abbasid caliphate established its capital in Iraq on the west side of the Tigris River at the site of an ancient Babylonian town and named it Baghdad, thereby bringing the Muslim movement into direct contact with the cultures of Persia and India. At its peak Baghdad had marvelous buildings, clean streets, and great libraries, and we are told, with perhaps some modest exaggeration, that the city stood "alone as the rival of Byzantium."[10] For five centuries the Abbasid Caliphate ruled the Asian half of Islam from Baghdad, and in that period Islam experienced its golden age.

Meanwhile, 'Abd al-Rahman, a member of the Umayyad family, escaped the overthrow of the Umayyad dynasty in 750 and fled to Spain in 755 to continue his family's rule there. He developed his capital, Cordoba, into a city that soon rivaled Baghdad in splendor. With a half million inhabitants at its height, seven hundred mosques, and three hundred public baths, Cordoba's showpiece was the great mosque, which matched the mosques of Mecca and Jerusalem. Later converted to a Christian church, the building is still called "La Mezquita," the Mosque.

The late Philip Hitti says that the Spanish city "enjoyed miles of paved streets illuminated by lights from the bordering houses 'whereas seven hundred years after this time there was not so much as one public lamp in London,' and in 'Paris centuries subsequently, whoever stepped over his threshold on a rainy day stepped up to his ankles in mud.'"[11]

The great period of Muslim civilization came in the ninth and tenth centuries as Arabs in Baghdad adopted the learning and sciences of Greece and India as well as the culture of Persia. In the words of Professor Hitti, a noted historian of the Arabs and himself an Arab:

> By the conquest of the Fertile Crescent and the lands of Persia and Egypt the Arabians came into possession of the earliest seats of civilization in the whole world. In art and architecture, in philosophy, in medicine, in science and literature, in government the original Arabians had nothing to teach and everything to learn. And what voracious appetites they proved to have! With sharp curiosity and latent potentialities never aroused before, the Moslem Arabians in collaboration with and by the help of their subject peoples began now to assimilate, adapt and reproduce their intellectual and esthetic heritage. In Ctesiphon, Damascus, Jerusalem and Alexandria they viewed, admired and copied the work of the architect, the artisan, the jeweler and the manufacturer. To all these centers of ancient culture they came, they saw—and were conquered.[12]

---

[10] Hitti, *The Arabs,* 110.

[11] Ibid., 169. "The splendor of Cordova [*sic*] dazzled the eyes and stirred the imagination of the Latin world" (Gustave Grunebaum, *Medieval Islam: A Study in Cultural Orientation,* 2nd ed. [Chicago: University of Chicago Press, 1953], 57).

[12] Hitti, *The Arabs,* 71-72.

From India the Arabs took the system of numerals we call Arabic (Arabs call it Indian), adding to it the decimal system. In the ninth century Arab translators led by Hunayn ibn Ishaq (also called Joannitius), a Nestorian Christian, turned into Arabic the writings of Plato, Aristotle, and Galen; astronomical works from India; and a host of other important Greek-language texts that had been unavailable to scholars of the West since the barbarian invasions. Baghdad flourished as a world-class center of learning, while, as Hitti says, "Charlemagne and his lords were reportedly dabbling in the art of writing their names."[13] Here Semitic culture that stretched back to the ancient Babylonians and Assyrians "found its final culmination," incorporating the riches of the Hellenistic tradition with the older ideals of the Semites. With these developments, Arabic, once the language of poetry and religion, became a language of philosophy and science, not to mention its role as the diplomatic language in use from the Atlantic to central Asia. In this expansive empire the Muslims achieved what both Christian emperors and Persian rulers had earlier dreamed.

Politically, however, the Islamic domains were divided and were destined to divide further. In addition to the Umayyad caliphate in Spain, a Fatamid dynasty was founded in Cairo in 909, falling finally in 1171 to the great Saladin, who founded the Ayyubid dynasty, which lasted some 150 years and figured prominently in the defense against the Crusades. The ideal of the early caliphs of a united Islam headed by one supreme caliph did not survive.

In contrast to the splendor and learning of Islam, Europe at the height of the Umayyad dynasty was poor and backward. Divided among small, petty kingdoms, riven by the long-standing quarrel between Rome and the Eastern Church, and struggling almost continually with invaders from the north and east, Western Christendom was no match for the powerful culture of Islam. Judaism had long since been surpassed by Christianity, but now the Christian world stood second after Islam, the new member of the family of Abraham.

THE MEDITERRANEAN

The move of Islamic forces into the Mediterranean itself began in 823 with an invasion of Crete, and then Sicily in 827, thereby establishing a base for landings in Italy. Rome itself was pillaged in 846. An Islamic colony in northern Italy caused disturbances in Provence and the Ligurian Alps, but these incursions onto the Continent were short-lived. Sicily remained in Arab hands until the late eleventh century, when Normans created their own state in Sicily and southern Italy and the Italian maritime cities began to grow in prominence and influence.

---

[13] Ibid., 120.

11ᵗʰ C   13ᵗʰ C

INVASIONS: TURKS AND MONGOLS

At the peak of the Abbasid dynasty in the ninth century, the caliph in Baghdad possessed more power than any other ruler on earth, but a century later he was hardly in charge of his own city. Internal struggles and divisions were destroying the Baghdad caliphate. Heavy taxation, the division of Islamic religious leaders into factions, and the inability of the ruling families to control their passions and family life had weakened the Islamic empire. When the Seljuk Turks arrived in the eleventh century, Baghdad could not withstand them, and the capital and the eastern part of the Islamic settlement came more and more under the control of people who were not Arabs. But when the Turks converted to Islam, the conquerors became the conquered. The threat of these same Seljuk Turks against Byzantium was the event that triggered the Crusades.

In the thirteenth century Mongols streamed down from the plateaus of central Asia and in 1258 decimated Baghdad, putting the caliph and three hundred of his officials to death plus a sizable portion of the citizens. The city was left in ruins; the great Abbasid dynasty was at an end; and the Islamic caliphate was no more. Philip Hitti notes: "For the first time in its history the Moslem world was left without a caliph whose name could be cited in the Friday prayers."[14] The Mongols, led by Helagu, a grandson of Genghis Khan, pressed on into Syria, which they subjugated, conquering both Aleppo and Damascus. Later the seventh Khan converted to Islam, and again the pattern of conqueror and conquered reversed. With those victories the power of the Islamic forces was well spent, but it would rise again through the Ottoman Turks in the fourteenth century.

CONCLUSION

With the establishment of Islam there were three religious traditions claiming their ancestry in the ancient patriarch Abraham—Judaism, Christianity, and Islam. The first of these, Judaism, was the oldest and the smallest. Dispersed among the nations of the Near East, Jews had no nation-state and no army to defend them. They lived in a Diaspora. By the seventh century the church had joined hands with the Roman empire and had plenty of power to defend itself with. Also by then the diatribe against Judaism was in full swing, having been given a great boost by the sermons and writings of John Chrysostom (the "Golden-tongued") in fifth-century Constantinople. Now a new rival to both Judaism and Christianity had appeared. Because Christianity had become a political power as well as a religion, and because Islam was from the beginning

---

[14] Ibid., 218.

the same, competition would develop between Christianity and Islam more than between Christianity and Judaism, though the Christians would in time develop actual persecutions of the Jews. The Christian–Muslim conflict would often turn into war, though usually wars over land rather than wars to convert. The rivalry with Islam would prove to engage and confound the Christians almost more than the one Christians had with Jews. Christians would find that they could only contend against Islam; they could not defeat it.

3

The First Christian Responses to Islam

It is interesting to note that at first the Byzantine Empire viewed Islam as a kind of Arianism [an early Christian heresy] and placed it on a level with other Christian sects. Byzantine apologetic and polemic literature argues against Islam in the same manner as it did against . . . the adherents of other heretical teachings. Thus John Damascene . . . did not regard Islam as a new religion, but considered it only an instance of secession from the true Christian faith similar in nature to other earlier heresies.

—A. A. Vasiliev[1]

The first Christian writers to report on Islam were Byzantine Christians who identified the Islamic soldiers as Arabs and called them hostile, powerful, and fearsome enemies but seemed to know nothing about their Islamic religion. In the 630s, Maximus the Confessor—theologian, monastic, and defender of the orthodox faith—wrote Peter the Illustrious exhorting him to be vigilant in his prayers, reminding him of the recent invasion by Arabs, whom he describes but does not name:

> To see a barbarous nation of the desert overrunning another land as if it were their own! To see our civilization laid waste by wild and untamed beasts who have merely the shape of a human form![2]

Thinking of the Jews whom the emperor Heraclius had recently ordered to be baptized, Maximus calls these assailants "a Jewish people who . . . delight in human blood . . . whom God hates, though they think they are worshiping God." His letter charges that they are "announcing the advent of the Antichrist" and

---

[1] A. A. Vasiliev, *History of the Byzantine Empire, 343–1453* (Madison: University of Wisconsin Press, 1952), 207.

[2] John C. Lamoreaux, "Early Eastern Christian Responses to Islam," in *Medieval Christian Perceptions of Islam: A Book of Essays*, ed. John Victor Tolan, Garland Medieval Case Books 10, Garland Reference Library of the Humanities 1768 (New York and London: Garland, 1996), 14.

are, in John Lamoreaux's words, "storing up wrath against themselves on the day of judgment."[3] Maximus believed that the sufferings imposed on the Christians were a divine punishment for their sins, but he also believed that widespread repentance and reform would turn back the tide of these invading Arab warriors. Although Maximus's description of the Arabs as "a Jewish people," who "think they are worshiping God," seems to reflect religious elements, his language probably indicates little more than their being Semites, descendants of Abraham.

Sophronius, patriarch of Jerusalem, a compatriot of Maximus and an eyewitness of the Arab victories, also complained of the violence of the "Saracens." He called them Arabs and charged that their leader was the devil: "Why is the flow of blood continual? Why are bodies prey for the birds of the sky? Why are churches destroyed and the cross insulted?"[4] He called the Arabs the "Abomination of Desolation" that was predicted by Daniel and reaffirmed by Jesus,[5] a sacrilege of the holy things of God that would portend the end of the age. Sophronius's sense of alarm is clear, but his report seems exaggerated. Archaeological evidence suggests little if any destruction of churches. In fact, there are reliable accounts of church construction during this period.

Among these dire and woeful descriptions we do not hear the word "Islam," nor, save for Maximus's report that the Arabs say they believe in God, anything about a war to spread religion. Indeed, during the Middle Ages neither side used religious terminology to identify the other, except for "infidel," a term that both groups adopted later and of which Bernard Lewis says: "It was in the exchange of this insult that they achieved their fullest and most perfect mutual understanding."[6]

The patriarch Sophronius, emphasizing the violence that he saw, called the Arabs "godless Saracens,"[7] the name Christians understood to derive from Sarah, Abraham's wife. In the eyes of these Christian writers, Arabs were another in the series of invading peoples, barbarians, who had attacked the empire for centuries, this time from the south rather than the north, advancing against the eastern empire, not western Europe. Byzantines believed, like the Greeks before them, that they and their culture were superior to all others, in

---

[3] Ibid.

[4] Ibid., 15.

[5] Daniel 9:27; Matthew 24:15. Most scholars understand the text in Daniel to refer to the sacrilege of the Jerusalem temple by Antiochus IV in 167 B.C. One is tempted to think that Sophronius is thinking of the al-Aqsa Mosque, which was built on the site of the ancient Jewish temple, but Sophronius died before that was built. Perhaps he saw it coming.

[6] Bernard Lewis, *Islam and the West* (New York and Oxford: Oxford University Press, 1993), 8.

[7] Lamoreaux, "Early Eastern Christian Responses," 15. "Saracen" is an ancient term, predating the Christian era, but its origin is uncertain (Lewis, *Islam and the West,* 133). R. W. Southern has observed: "[The Europeans] were happier discussing the spelling of 'Sarah,' whether it should have one or two *r*'s than in discussing the nature of the Saracens" (*Western Views of Islam in the Middle Ages* [Cambridge, Mass., and London: Harvard University Press, 1962], 18).

this case not only superior but divinely established and blessed. Other people were held to live on a vastly lower plane.

EARLY CRITICISM OF THE ISLAMIC RELIGION

A few decades later, descriptions became more exact. John of Damascus, a saint of both Eastern and the Western churches and one of the most prominent theologians of the Orthodox tradition, met Islam at first hand and reported on its beliefs. He is often described as the author of the Christian attitude toward Islam.

A strong tradition, uncertain but believable, claims that the Damascene's grandfather participated in negotiating the surrender of Damascus to the Arabs in 635, and that John, like his father and grandfather before him, served for years in the Arab civil administration of the city. As such a background might suggest, John's writings reveal a good knowledge of Arabic. He left Damascus and his civic post about 716 and enrolled as a monk in the Monastery of St. Sabas near Jerusalem, where he was ordained to the priesthood. There he wrote the great theological tracts and hymns upon which his fame as a Christian theologian rests. Revered as a saint soon after his death, he was declared a doctor of the church by Pope Leo XIII in 1890. Three later Byzantine writers spanning the eighth to the tenth centuries also discussed Islam: Bishop Theodore of Carra (usually called by his Arabic name, abū-Qurrah), Nicetas of Byzantium, and the emperor Constantine VII Porphyrogenitus.

John's principal statement on Islam appears in his major work, *The Fount of Wisdom*, in a section entitled *On Heresies*, which catalogues aberrations from orthodox Christianity. John wrote to instruct his Christian readers in the evils of Islam so they could avoid the heresy. The first part of his statement follows. Though lengthy, it merits reading to see how Christian descriptions of Islam began. Having discussed some one hundred religious errors, he writes:

> There is also the still-prevailing deceptive superstition of the Ishmaelites, the fore-runner of the Antichrist. It takes its origin from Ishmael, who was born to Abraham from Hagar, and that is why they also call them Hagarenes and Ishmaelites. They also call them Saracenes, allegedly for having been sent away by Sarah empty; for Hagar said to the angel, "*Sarah has sent me away empty* [*kene* in Greek]." These, then, were idolaters and they venerated the morning star and Aphrodite, whom notably they called *Habar* in their own language, which means "great"; therefore until the times of Heraclius [Byzantine emperor, 610-641] they were, undoubtedly, idolaters. From that time on a false prophet appeared among them, surnamed Mameth, who, having casually been exposed to the Old and the New Testament and supposedly encountered an Arian monk, formed a heresy of his own. And after, by pretense, he managed to make the people think of him as a God-fearing fellow, he spread rumors that a scripture was

brought down to him from heaven. Thus, having drafted some pronounce-ments in his book, worthy (only) of laughter, he handed it down to them in order that they may comply with it.[8]

John had several things right: the story of Sarah, Hagar, and Ishmael; Ishmael as an ancestor of the Arabs; the name Muhammad, if under a different spelling; a scripture allegedly sent down from heaven; contacts of Muhammad with Jew-ish and Christian sources; and the claim that the Arabs, presumably of Mecca, once worshiped Aphrodite (Venus). The story of Muhammad's meeting a Syr-ian monk (named Bahira) was often told in Islam, but John's claim that the man was an Arian Christian is a departure. Arianism, a heresy concerning the doc-trine of Christ, made sense to John because it held that Jesus was human, less than fully divine, a view John thought he saw in Islam.

According to the biographer ibn Ishaq, Bahira was a Christian monk in Syria. When the monk saw Muhammad approaching, accompanied by his com-panion, Abu Talib, he witnessed a cloud over Muhammad's head that made the leaves droop on the tree where Muhammad stood. Bahira had learned from a holy book that a prophet could appear, and when he saw Muhammad, he rec-ognized that Muhammad bore the signs of prophethood that the book had pre-dicted, including "the seal of prophethood between his shoulders."[9]

The story of Muhammad and Bahira prompted John and his successors to consider Muhammad's calling and teachings to be from human sources, not from God. Muslim tradition sees the matter otherwise. According to an account in the *hadith* (the collection of oral traditions about Muhammad), when Bahira first saw Muhammad, he recognized him as a prophet-to-be, and thus Islamic tradition sees the report as a vindication of Muhammad's prophethood and an answer to the Christian charge that Muhammad was not a genuine prophet because he was "unannounced."

John says that Muhammad formed his teachings from elements he took from Judaism and two unorthodox branches of Christianity, the Arian and the Nesto-rian. Orthodox Christians had charged the former with denying the divinity of Jesus, the latter with overemphasizing Jesus' humanity—views that accord to some degree with Islam—and thus in John's view were the probable sources of Islamic teaching on Jesus.

The Damascene's reference to the word *habar* reveals that he, like other Christian interpreters, was mystified by the oft-repeated Muslim chant *Allahu akbar*, commonly translated, "God is great." John's compatriot, Constantine Porphyrogenitus, offered this explanation of the Muslim formula:

> They pray also to the star of Aphrodite [Venus] which they call *Koubar*, and in their supplication cry out *'Alla oua Koubar*, that is, God and Aphrodite.

[8] "The Chapter 100/101 of the *De Haeresibus*," trans. Daniel J. Sahas, in *John of Damascus on Islam: The "Heresy of the Ishmaelites"* (Leiden: E. J. Brill, 1972), 133.

[9] Muhammad ibn Ishaq, *The Life of Muhammad: A Translation of Ishāq's "Sīrat Rasūl Allāh,"* trans. A. Guillaume (Karachi, Oxford, New York, and Delhi: Oxford University Press, 1997), 116.

For they call God *'Alla;* and *oua* they use for the conjunction *and* and they call the star *Koubar.* And so they say *"'Alla oua Koubar."*[10]

Constantine believed that the sacred Ka'aba represented Venus, and thus he described Islam as both polytheistic and idolatrous even though both practices were adamantly rejected in Islamic teaching. John erred here also, thinking that the Black Stone in the corner of the Ka'aba had once represented the head of Venus.

Muhammad's allowance of as many as four wives plus additional concubines comes in for special criticism by John, and particularly the case of Muhammad's marriage to Zaynab, the divorced wife of the Prophet's adopted son, Zayd. The story is that Zaynab bint Jahsh (the Prophet had two wives named Zaynab, this one the daughter of Abdallah ibn Jahsh) was married by arrangement to Zayd, the former slave of Muhammad given to him by his first wife, Khadija. Muhammad went to Zayd's tent to see his former slave and was greeted by Zayd's wife, Zaynab, who, not expecting visitors, was lightly clad. The Prophet turned away quickly but, moved by the charms of the beautiful woman, is reported to have said, "Praise be to God who changes men's hearts."[11] It seems that Zaynab had never wanted to be married to Zayd in the first place, and her descriptions of the encounter with Muhammad so troubled her husband that he went to the Prophet and offered to divorce Zaynab. No action was taken immediately, but the marriage worsened, and Zayd finally divorced her. In time Muhammad decided to marry her, but he faced criticism. Zayd was Muhammad's adopted son, and Zaynab was therefore legally his daughter-in-law, and many thought marriage to a daughter-in-law was highly improper. Then a solution emerged: Muhammad received a revelation that the marriage would not be incestuous. The reasoning underlying this message was that since Zayd was a foster son, not a son by birth, the relationship had been humanly arranged and would be no obstacle to Muhammad's planned marriage. The Prophet's favorite wife, Aisha, is said to have been present when the revelation came to Muhammad. Her response was: "Truly thy Lord makes haste to do thy bidding."[12]

The Damascene and his successors shared Aisha's critical view. Moreover, John charged Muhammad with lechery, criticizing the Prophet's exceeding the Qur'an's limit of four wives per man (Zaynab was his fifth wife), as well as claiming that Muhammad had committed incest in marrying Zaynab. Muhammad's marriage to Zaynab was consistently troublesome to Christians, and it was, according to Norman Daniel, perhaps the best-known story about Muhammad in the West.[13] Muslims, more pragmatic here, have accepted this seeming

---

[10] John Meyendorff, "Byzantine Views of Islam," in *Dumbarton Oaks Papers,* no. 18 (Washington, D.C.: Dumbarton Oaks Center for Byzantine Studies, 1964), 118. I have romanized (in italics) Meyendorff's Greek characters.

[11] Karen Armstrong, *Muhammad: A Biography of the Prophet* (San Francisco: HarperSanFrancisco, 1992), 196.

[12] Ibid.

[13] Norman Daniel, *Islam and the West: The Making of an Image* (Edinburgh: University Press, 1960), 346 n. 51.

departure by their leader, understanding that God gave "his Messenger a few extra privileges," to use the words of Karen Armstrong,[14] and have used the incident as a precedent for exempting adoptive relationships from the laws of consanguinity.

These criticisms and objections by Christians indicate more than a difference over stories and specific doctrines, they demonstrate conflicts between two religious systems, each claiming divine sanction for its beliefs and practices, holding itself to be the final and perfect revelation and therefore judging the other to be fraudulent. What Muslims held to be revelations and mandates from God, Christians would see as humanly inspired preachments, some of them—the one just referred to in particular—designed largely to serve Muhammad, the preacher. Because of this wide difference in evaluation, arguments between the two traditions were inevitable. John Meyendorff calls this disagreement a "permanent misunderstanding between the two cultures and the two religious mentalities."[15] This deep level of misunderstanding consistently caused Christians to see Islam in its worst light, often a false light, producing what Norman Daniel terms "a deformed image of Islam."[16]

In assessing the Damascene's judgment of Islam, one must remember that the Byzantines were fighting Arabs at the time to defend what was left of the Christian empire, and perhaps regain what they had lost. John's hymns pray for "the victory of the Emperor over his enemies [Islam]" and hope that the emperor "will trample under his feet the barbarian nations [Arabs among them, of course]"[17] (additions by present author). Proud of their heritage of Greek culture and the Christian religion as the Byzantines were, they thought of their empire as the kingdom of God on earth, with their emperor as *theotokos*, the "God-bearer" (a term used also for the Virgin Mary). Anyone outside these righteous and privileged domains was held to be barbarian. The division of the world into these two areas paralleled the classic Islamic distinction between the *dar al-Islam*, "the peaced abode," and *dar al-harb*, "the abode of war."

Perhaps John's harshest criticism of Islam—though less harsh than the charges some would bring—came in his calling the Islamic movement "the forerunner of the Antichrist," the evil power predicted for the Last Days by the New Testament book of Revelation. John had used the term earlier for the emperor Leo III, an opponent of images in the churches (John defended the use of icons), but in that usage he meant a person who denies that Jesus is the incarnate Son of God. In criticizing Islam, John speaks more directly of the book of Revelation's idea of the Antichrist as a forerunner of the Last Day, as the monk Maximus had done earlier, but he does little more than mention the thought.

If John of Damascus had an imperfect knowledge of Islam, his contempo-

[14] Armstrong, *Muhammad,* 197.
[15] Meyendorff, "Byzantine Views of Islam," 122.
[16] Daniel, *Islam and the West,* 8.
[17] Meyendorff, "Byzantine Views of Islam," 117-18.

rary, the philosopher Nicetas of Byzantium, was worse. Nicetas expressed two grave falsehoods about passages in the Qur'an. The first is *sura* 112, a text often quoted for its clear monotheism. A. J. Arberry renders the words of Gabriel to Muhammad thus:

> Say: "He is God, One,
> God, the Everlasting Refuge,
> who has not begotten, and has not been begotten,
> and equal to Him is not any one!"

Here "everlasting" translates the Arabic word "solid," "massive," or "permanent," something on the order of a hammered-out piece of metal. Nicetas, who had several Greek versions before him, took the word in its literal or physical meaning and reported that Muslims think of God as "all-spherical," that is, solid or material and not spiritual. The Damascene did better, rendering the Arabic "God the Creator of all."[18]

The second error of Nicetas came in his treatment of one of the best known *suras* in the Qur'an (96), which tells of Gabriel's first appearance to Muhammad when he commanded the Meccan to "recite." In the original text Gabriel speaks of God as the one who has "created Man of a blood-clot," emphasizing the miraculous power of God in human reproduction. In Nicetas's quotation, God creates man "from a leech,"[19] an early example of the derogatory way in which many Islamic ideas and teachings would be described by Christians. The origin of the error again lay with the translators Nicetas used, but he should have known better.

THE VIEW FROM THE WEST

THE VENERABLE BEDE: ISLAM AND WORLD HISTORY

The Venerable Bede was the first major Western writer to report on Islam as a religion. Settled in northern England in the monastery of Jarrow, Bede looked out over the North Sea toward western Europe to see a land largely wasted by barbarian invasions. The Roman empire had long since fallen, and no ordered society had taken its place. Local rulers, many no more than tribal chieftains, dispensed what law and justice existed. Brigands and bandits threatened travelers, trade was severely limited, and people did well merely to survive. As Bede surveyed the Continent, he witnessed the Islamic advance across Africa, through Spain, and into France. His famous *History of the English Church and*

---

[18] Sahas, *John of Damascus,* 77.
[19] Meyendorff, "Byzantine Views of Islam," 122.

Its People (731) contains only one sentence about these events: "At this time, a swarm of Saracens ravaged Gaul with horrible slaughter; but after a brief interval in that country they paid the penalty of their wickedness."[20] Since the invaders were too far away to affect the British Isles, Bede seems to have had no need to elaborate on them in his history of England.

In his commentaries on the Bible, the British monk said a great deal more. He had no books or writings from or about Islam, but he did possess the Christian scriptures and he saw them as able to reveal the movement of God's providence within history. Like John of Damascus, Bede found the origin of the Arabs in the Genesis account of Abraham and Ishmael. Taking a literal reading of the text, he understood Arabs to possess the traits Abraham had attributed to Ishmael: "a wild ass of a man," whose hand was to be "against every man and every man's hand against him," who "would dwell over against all his kinsman" (Genesis 16:12). Here was the story of the Arabs' beginning, with a behavior he thought he saw in his own day. Thus he charged that Muslims were "enemies of the church" and "hateful to God."[21] By linking the Genesis prophecy to events on the Continent, Bede gave the Arabs and Islam "a niche in Christian history," to use the words of R. W. Southern.[22] They were fulfilling the prophetic texts of Genesis.

Western writers in the Carolingian era a century after the Venerable Bede reported little additional information on Islam, and they wrote without the rancor that came later, probably because Islam was not the military threat to northern Europe that the Germanic tribes were at the time. Southern notes, "[I]n the cosmic struggle of Good and Evil the Saracens had a relatively humble role."[23] The estimate of the Latins on that point would soon change.

REPORTS FROM SPAIN

In a Spanish source dating probably from the early 800s, we begin to hear the bitterness and exaggerations that would increasingly characterize Western accounts of Islam. The work is an anonymous biography of Muhammad entitled the *History of Muhammad*. Here one reads that Muhammad, who was orphaned early, married a widow "in accordance with some barbaric law," and later became an "avaricious usurer." Having heard Christian sermons in his travels, Muhammad refashioned them and thereby became "the wisest of all

---

[20] Venerable Bede, *A History of the English Church and People,* trans. Leo Shirley-Price, rev. R. E. Latham, rev. ed. (Harmondsworth, England: Penguin Books, 1968), 330. A tantalizing statement. The reference would seem to be to the Battle of Tours-Poitiers in 732/733, but Bede published his history in 731. Bede reports as omens of the event that in 729 "two comets appeared around the sun, striking terror into all who saw them" (ibid.).

[21] Benjamin Z. Kedar, *Crusade and Mission: European Approaches toward the Muslims* (Princeton: Princeton University Press, 1984), 6.

[22] R. W. Southern, *Western Views of Islam in the Middle Ages* (Cambridge, Mass., and London: Harvard University Press, 1962), 17.

[23] Ibid., 18.

among the irrational Arabs." He claimed that a golden-mouthed vulture that was the angel Gabriel visited him in a vision, and so he began to pass himself off as a prophet. He succeeded in weaning some of his people away from idols, and then turned to war, defeating the Greek army in Syria and capturing Damascus. The *History* says that he fabricated various "psalms," some about humans and some about animals (a few of the *suras* of the Qur'an carry animal names), and set out a law that allowed him to marry the divorced wife of one of his followers. He predicted that he would rise three days after his death, but that did not happen. Instead, dogs devoured part of the body and the followers buried the rest. The biography ends: "It was appropriate that a prophet of this kind fill the stomachs of dogs, a prophet who committed not only his own soul, but those of many, to hell."[24]

These quotations exhibit much that would become typical of Western accounts. The book's purpose is to defame Muhammad by presenting him as a man of base motives who was deceived by false visions and given to war and selfish pleasure. The prediction of the resurrection is of course a parody on Jesus, a complete fabrication, just as the story of the vulture is a parody on the Holy Spirit. In the far distance, behind this brief outline, one can discern the rudiments of the actual story now so distorted as to be a false portrayal of the Prophet, but the text reveals more about its author than about Muhammad. For this author, there can be nothing good in Muhammad, and he takes pains to convince his readers of this truth. It is of interest that the *History* says nothing about Arianism or Christian heresy, both of which, even if in error, would have at least been in the category of historical background rather than fancy. Muhammad here is simply a false prophet and an evil man.

HISTORY, ESCHATOLOGY, AND MARTYRDOM: THE MARTYRS OF CORDOBA

A more radical view of Islam, which linked the movement to biblical eschatology, appeared in Spain in the ninth century. The Iberian peninsula, by then ruled largely by Muslims, would soon become the locale of the majority of the conversations between Christians and Muslims (and Jews as well), conversations that proved strikingly important for the West. In the ninth century, however, Christians were still learning to adapt to the restrictions of the Islamic regime, whereby they paid the poll taxes of non-Muslims, were prohibited from public displays of the Christian faith, and, on pain of death, were forbidden to blaspheme Muhammad or the Qur'an.

In the 850s some fifty Spanish Christians attacked Islam publicly and suffered martyrdom at the hands of Islamic authorities for their violation of

---

[24] Quotations from Kenneth Baxter Wolf, "Christian Views of Islam in Early Medieval Spain," in *Medieval Christian Perceptions,* ed. Tolan, 94.

Islamic law. Paul Alvar, a layman of Cordoba and a contemporary of the group, provided some of the ideas that resulted in the martyrdoms. Eulogius, a some-time titular bishop of Toledo and later a martyr himself, in writing about this event, explained that his group was challenging Muslim law on the basis of Matthew 24:14, the statement of Jesus that the end of the age would not come until the gospel had been preached to all the world. Benjamin Kedar points out that this action was not so much preaching as it was an act of defiance against Muslim authorities, and that even so, in a manner of speaking they "assumed the office of apostle . . . to the Saracens,"[25] because they intended to hasten the arrival of the Last Day. Alvar applauded their efforts and advocated both preaching to the Muslims and waging holy war against them, the first so to propose.

The layman Alvar and the bishop Eulogius had been concerned that their fellow Christians, isolated as they were from the main body of Christendom and living under Islam, were succumbing more and more to Arab culture. Not only were Iberian Christians speaking Arabic rather than their Christian Latin, but they were forsaking commentaries on the Latin Bible and works of Christian theology and taking up Arabic poetry and literature. Like the Venerable Bede, the two leaders turned to the Bible for instruction, and they read therein not just Genesis with its reports of the beginnings of Arabs but the prophetic visions of the future with their dire warnings of the end-time, particularly as adumbrated in Daniel 7.

When Alvar read Daniel's prophecies of the four ungodly kingdoms, he, like Augustine before him, recognized the last of these to be Rome, which, as he read it, was to be followed by barbarians. A ruler would then arise and defeat three kings. Alvar saw Muhammad as this ruler, who, he said, had subdued the Greeks, the Franks, and the Goths. On the basis of the reference to "a time, two times, and half a time" in Daniel 7:25, Alvar calculated that the end of the world would come in the 860s (counting each "time" as seventy years for a total of 245 and using 622 or 618 as the beginning of Islam). A fact that helped clinch this dating was the anonymous biography of Muhammad mentioned above, which reported that the Prophet had died in the year 666 of the Spanish era, the number of the Beast in Revelation 13:18.

These Spanish Christians, struggling as they were under Islamic rule, saw in these biblical prophecies sure signs of their deliverance. Convinced of the rightness of their ideas, they took the radical step of martyrdom, apparently as a way of hastening the end of the age. Their goal was not to convert Muslims—although they probably would have approved such an outcome—but to act within the framework of the apocalyptic ideas of Alvar and Eulogius. Bede had used scripture to understand the past; these Spaniards attempted to use it to create the future, namely, the apocalyptic and eschatological events they read about in scripture. The theme of eschatology introduced by Alvar would appear

---

[25] Kedar, *Crusade and Mission,* 17.

again in the West in circles as diverse as the radical prophet-preachers of the First Crusade and Martin Luther, and some modern-day supporters of the state of Israel.

Courageous and bold as they were, these Spanish Christians knew little of Islamic teaching, preferring the unreliable Latin accounts of Muhammad to the authentic knowledge they could have gained from their Muslim neighbors. As Southern writes: "They were fleeing from the embrace of Islam: it is not likely that they would turn to Islam to understand what it was that they were fleeing from."[26] This pattern of teaching and writing about the Islamic faith without consulting Islamic authorities would continue.

The conflict these Christians had with Islam portended the future for Christian–Muslim relations in the Iberian peninsula, a pattern that contrasted sharply with the relatively peaceful interrelations of Jews and Muslims. The difference was that Christians and Muslims had competing truth claims, both saying that their views of divine things were correct and others were in error. Jews, while holding to the truth of their own views, rarely charged others with falsity.

---

[26] Southern, *Western Views of Islam,* 26.

4

Islam in the Eyes of the Medieval West

A "Deformed Image"[1]

The existence of Islam was the most far-reaching problem in medieval Christendom. It was a problem at every level of experience. As a practical problem it called for action and for discrimination between the competing possibilities of Crusade, conversion, coexistence, and commercial interchange. As a theological problem it called persistently for some answer to the mystery of its existence: what was its providential role in history—was it a symptom of the world's last days or a stage in the Christian development; a heresy, a schism, or a new religion; a work of man or devil; an obscene parody of Christianity, or a system of thought that deserved to be treated with respect? . . . The existence of Islam made the West profoundly uneasy.

—R. W. Southern[2]

John of Damascus and his Greek-language colleagues responded to Islam with a series of misunderstandings, false interpretations, and accusations that did much to advance the claims of Christendom but did nothing to come to terms with the fundamental religious and theological claims of Islam or the integrity of Islamic faith and life. Western Christians did no better. Added to Christendom's problem, both in the East and in the West, was the significant military threat that Islamic forces posed, particularly in the East, and the advanced social and economic life that grew up within Islam, a culture that was far superior to the West. All of this could do little but create envy and embarrassment to Europeans. Arabs had developed an urban society, sophisticated

---

[1] Norman Daniel says that he wrote to "delineate" this "deformed image" (*Islam and the West: The Making of an Image* [Edinburgh: University Press, 1960], 8).

[2] R. W. Southern, *Western Views of Islam in the Middle Ages* (Cambridge, Mass., and London: Harvard University Press, 1962), 3-4.

and powerful, that overshadowed an agricultural West still struggling to recover from the barbarian invasions. Meanwhile, "Islam resisted both conquest and conversion, and it refused to wither away."[3] Latin Christians certainly had reason to be defensive toward this new upstart faith, and defensive they were.

Muhammad and his religion remained virtually unknown in any detail in the West until the twelfth century, when crusaders met Muslims in the Holy Land, and Christian scholars in Spain and Sicily began receiving classical manuscripts and knowledge from their Muslim and Jewish colleagues. Once the Crusades were under way, knights, travelers, merchants, and pilgrims brought stories about Islam back from the Holy Land. Even though most of these were inaccurate, they did make the name of Muhammad well known so that Christians were forced to respond to him and to his religion.

The situation between Christians and Jews was different. In the early centuries Christian theologians made their peace, such as it was, with the continued presence of Judaism. Jews had rejected Jesus, but they had an ancient faith—their revelation preceded Jesus and was used by him. When Christians incorporated the Hebrew scriptures into their Bible, they co-opted much of Judaism into Christianity. Thus, for several centuries, so long as Jews confined themselves to the Hebrew scriptures and Jewish tradition, Jews lived fairly safely within the Christian domain. But the sixth-century Justinian Code threatened that security. It removed the statute of the earlier Theodosian Code that granted legal existence to Jews; it banned Jews from the practice of law, prohibited their holding Christians as slaves, narrowed their property rights, and barred them from certain public functions. In addition, the code sought to legislate Jewish worship by elevating Greek and Latin scriptures over Hebrew, eliminating the oral tradition (the Mishnah), and ordering excommunication and death for any who denied the resurrection. While these restrictions were rarely enforced, they set the tone for the future, and in the eleventh century violent persecution broke out against the Jews.

In contrast, Jews within Islamic areas usually fared well. The city of Baghdad, until the time of its fall, boasted a large Jewish community, and a visitor in 1170 reported twenty-three synagogues and ten rabbinical schools. Jews managed even better in Islamic Iberia, where they served as merchants, bankers, civil servants, teachers, and scholars, even though relegated to a second-class status by Islamic law. But the privileges they enjoyed under Muslim rulers later evaporated when they came under Christian rule, and their very presence was outlawed by the tragic decree of King Ferdinand and Queen Isabella in 1492 that ordered Jews either to convert, leave, or suffer death. The edict resulted in the loss of a valuable and productive middle-class leadership, which limited Spain for centuries.

Because virtually no Muslims lived within Christendom during the early centuries of Islam, laws to control them were not necessary. Such laws would

---

[3] Ibid.

come after the Christian Reconquest of Spain, which brought Muslims under Christian rule. There was need, however, in all of Christendom for a response to Muslim doctrines and to Islamic claims about Muhammad, but creating this was no easy matter.

At first, Christians saw Islam as a Christian heresy, but if it was a heresy, it had no independent revelation and should come under the authority of the church. But when Christians concluded that the religion of the Saracens originated outside the biblical revelation and the Christian tradition, neither arguments against heresy nor arguments against Judaism served. Medieval masters needed new arguments to refute Islam, and these were hard to develop within a culture whose learning rested heavily on tradition. One answer to this dilemma was to attack Muhammad the person.

THE CASE AGAINST MUHAMMAD

Before the mid-twelfth century Western Christians had available to them virtually no authentic written sources on Islam, and those who wrote about Islam relied largely on what the popular mind heard and repeated. In the early part of that century Guibert of Nogent, who penned a history of the First Crusade, admitted that he had only common opinion as his source for information on Muhammad. Unable to affirm the trustworthiness of this material, Guibert covered himself by saying, "It is safe to speak evil of one whose malignity exceeds whatever ill can be spoken."[4] This simple prejudgment allowed writers to say virtually anything about Islam so long as it was uncomplimentary. Unfortunately, Guibert's view dominated Western reporting about Islam in the medieval period, even after Muslim materials were available to them.

Occasionally, however, correct information did seep through. Writers more familiar with Muslim sources credited Muhammad with destroying idol worship and in some cases recognized that he preached the worship of the one God. But in the main the Christian accounts of Islam were exaggerated and often entirely false.

Essential to the Christian campaign against Islam was the defamation of Muhammad. Although Muslims did not consider him divine, they did claim him as the Messenger of God, the human source of revelations that were divine, and thus his character became fair game for Christian attack. Christian writers presented him as a lecher, a man of violence, untrustworthy, and a deceiver who passed off his own thoughts as the revelations of God. One account even reported that Muhammad had been a cardinal in the Roman church who, frustrated over his inability to attain his ambitions, fled to Arabia where he founded the false religion of Islam.

Medieval Christians, both early and late, charged that Muhammad possessed no signs of a true prophet—he performed no miracles, he offered no predic-

---

[4] Ibid., 31.

tions, and he lived an unworthy life, all of which contradicted the claim of prophethood. They pointed to the wound Muhammad received at the Battle of Uhud, the second battle with the Meccans, claiming that this incident proved him to be only an ordinary mortal. Norman Daniel summarizes the matter: "Muhammad was both wicked and human, and these two points seemed almost equally important."[5]

Christians delighted in the fact that the Qur'an reported no miracles by Muhammad, because they knew that later Muslim tradition said he performed some. Focusing on the perceived discrepancy between the Qur'an's rejection of miracles and the Muslim tradition that told of them, a Christian tract attributed to San Pedro Pascual (d. 1300) argued that Muslims made Muhammad a liar, because they claimed miracles of him while the Qur'an denied them. And there were plenty of Muslim traditions to cite. Muslim tales spoke of an ox that talked to Muhammad, a fig tree that bowed before the Prophet, and a leg of lamb that warned him that it was poisoned. One of the most popular of these stories reported Muhammad splitting the moon. The account is loosely based on a Qur'anic text that may have originally been metaphorical: "The Hour has drawn nigh: the moon is split" (54:1). But the full form of the story developed outside the Qur'an, probably after Muhammad's time. Christians ridiculed all of these stories.

In rejecting Muhammad's miracles, Christians ignored what Muslims called the "Standing Miracle" of Islam, the Qur'an, whose compelling cadences were unknown to them. Even after Westerners had access to a Latin translation, they could not experience the emotional power of the book in the original Arabic, and reading a translation only soured them the more. They argued that the book did not appear like the Bible—there were no narratives of salvation history, no parables to interpret, and no great passages of soaring prophecy. In part they objected to the form of the Qur'anic materials. The traveler and sometime missionary Ricoldo of Monte Croce (d. 1320) complained that the names of several *suras,* such as "Ant," "Spider," or "Smoke," were unsuitable for an inspired text, and that phrases were unnecessarily repeated: "may He be praised," "there is no god but God," and so on, phrases that the Arabic style enjoys saying over and over. He reversed the Islamic claim that neither human nor angels could produce such a book, arguing that they certainly would not because the book was full of lies and blasphemies.

Then there was the matter of revelations that focused on specific situations or persons, for example, the instruction to his wives:

> O Prophet, say to thy wives: "If you desire
> the present life and its adornment, come now,
> I will make you provision, and set you free with kindliness.
> But if you desire God and His Messenger
> and the Last Abode, surely God has prepared

---

[5] Daniel, *Islam and the West,* 96.

for those amongst you such as do good a mighty wage."
. . . [W]hosever of you is obedient to God and His
Messenger and does righteousness, We shall pay her
her wage twice over; We have prepared for her a generous provision.
(Qur'an 33:28-30)

The revelation that allowed Muhammad to marry Zaynab was cited even more often. Although the Bible has instances of revelations addressed to specific situations, medieval critics could not admit that such accounts in the Qur'an might be authentic. "For the Muslim, a revelation that responded to the circumstances of a particular moment was normal, whereas to the Christian mind such a thing seemed to be its own condemnation."[6]

MUHAMMAD'S CHARACTER

That Muhammad was a poor and unlettered man Westerners knew well. They said that as an illiterate, he had to be taught religion; he could not have gained it himself. They also ridiculed his low birth. In Arabia, such a charge was not serious, for Arabs valued upward mobility in society, but Western Europe thought otherwise. The critics said he was a man of arrogant ambition, who climbed the ladder of success through marriage. Using the economic and political power he gained from Khadija to advance himself, he turned to religion and his false claims of prophecy to authenticate his selfish grab of power. According to Islamic tradition, the sequence was the reverse: his prophetic work preceded his political career.

Little in Muhammad's story offended the Latins more than his sexual behavior. A man of almost unlimited sexual appetite, they said, equal to thirty or forty ordinary men. Further, while limiting his followers to four wives, he took perhaps a total of nine for himself. The case of Muhammad's securing a special *sura* approving marriage to his daughter-in-law Zaynab was too much. Here they saw Muhammad covering his lust with the claim of a special divine revelation. As to Muhammad's other marriages, the Christians did not know, or could not admit, that most of these unions were for political purposes, a common practice in his society. Some were entered into to help women left destitute, and several were not consummated. Nor did they credit Muhammad with the years of his monogamous marriage to Khadija.

They also criticized Muhammad's allowing Muslim men as many as four wives. In a context of caring for orphans, in this case women left without family to support them, Muhammad said:

If you fear that you will not act justly
towards the orphans, marry such women

---

[6] Ibid., 31.

> as seem good to you, two, three, four;
> but if you fear you will not be equitable,
> then only one, or what your right hands own,
> so it is likelier you will not be partial. (Qur'an 4:3)

The Prophet's mandate was in fact a restriction on polygyny, hardly a statement favoring laxity, but Christian critics did not know this. Tending to believe the worst, they saw only sexual excess. Nor did they know that few men availed themselves of the privilege of multiple marriages, thinking simply that if polygyny was the rule all males would follow it. Thus a consistent Christian charge was licentiousness, both in Muhammad's personal life, and in the freedom he gave to his followers.

In these disagreements two religious and social systems show themselves to be at odds with each other because of differing views of revelation and marriage. Muhammad's life and his alleged revelations simply did not meet the Christians' definitions. Difference could mean only falsity and illegitimacy. As to marriage, Christians held monogamy to be the divine norm, and monogamy for life with no divorce. This ideal was buttressed by the even higher ideal of celibacy in Christian priesthood and monasticism. The result was a view that marriage, even monogamous marriage, was at best a concession to weak humans, who, as Paul said, could not restrain their passions. Marriage was the lower way, and any violation of the strictures on marriage was a major violation of God's law. Christians possessed no categories for understanding the Muslim law of multiple marriage with the privilege of divorce.

Then there was Muhammad's use of war in establishing the Islamic movement, and particularly his allowing, even ordering, the execution of opponents in the struggles within Medina and the conquest of Mecca. They cited the assassination of the Jewish poet Ka'b ibn al-Ashraf, who left Medina and went to Mecca, where he composed verses urging the Meccans to rouse themselves against Muhammad. Upon the poet's return to Medina, the Prophet ordered him killed. What Muhammad saw as justice toward a traitor and rebel, his critics in the West saw as another example of a violent man. Muhammad's actions in devastating the recalcitrant Jewish clans in Medina brought forth the same complaints, in this case perhaps more understandably. Aware of the Islamic military conquests as they were, Christians argued that since Muhammad had no miracles to prompt faith, he turned to war. The two factors of sexual license and the use of war were cited again and again as the great evidences that Muhammad was an imposter, not an authentic prophet.

The Latins' objections to Muhammad's sexual behavior and his prosecution of war were at least based on truths, even if embellished, not on fabrications. The dispute was over the interpretation and evaluation of those facts. Muhammad did have numerous wives, and he did order executions. One could have appealed to the Old Testament on both matters. Several patriarchs and worthies of early Israel had multiple wives, and the great prophets, Moses, Elijah, and Elisha, all figured in warfare and killing. But this comparison would not have impressed the Christians, because those heroes belonged to an earlier dispensation, and Christians had the person of Jesus in mind as a model for comparison with Muhammad.

Nor, in regard to force, did they consider how the Christian movement had used it in Europe and would apply it in the Crusades. While Christianity in its first three centuries spread its message peacefully, the grand union of religion and society that formed medieval Europe practiced violence and war aplenty in support of its religion, sometimes in requiring newly conquered peoples to convert, and sometimes in forcing wayward subjects to conform. Christians who criticized Islam for violence omitted all this from their comparisons and criticisms.

REPORTS BASED ON FANTASY

A great number of Christian reports on Islam came from fantasy and calumny. That Muhammad had the sexual potency of thirty men, that his goal was to develop a permissive sexual ethic instead of restraining an already permissive one—these charges were common at the popular level, and were false. Then there is the fanciful yarn about a vulture that brought revelations to Muhammad. More common was the story of a dove, or even more popular, the account of a calf or bull (or a camel) that carried the holy Qur'an to Muhammad between its horns.

Some of these anecdotes came from legends and folktales popular in certain Islamic circles, and some were invented by Islam's critics. In neither case did Christians attempt to consult with knowledgeable Muslims to confirm the truth of things they said or learn how thoughtful Muslims evaluated them. Christians passed down a negative evaluation from the beginning. Norman Daniel observes, however, that things might have been the same without the inventions:

> It is very interesting that the facts were so often invented, or else falsified, or just exaggerated; but had they not been so, it is certain that the most sober relation of Muhammad's life would have caused Christians to say that no true prophet could conduct his personal life as Muhammad did his. In this matter there is little common ground between Christianity and Islam.[7]

MUHAMMAD THE ENEMY

Latin Christians said that Muhammad foisted onto his followers a religion full of lies and falsehoods. He denied the crucifixion of Jesus, he claimed that

---

[7] Daniel, *Islam and the West*, 102. Daniel believes that stories like these originated among Christian Arabs (p. 13).

both Old and New Testaments had been corrupted, and he rejected the author-ity of the Christian priesthood—these charges were true and they were of course too much for the Christians to swallow. Because Islam rejected Jesus as Christians saw him, Christians concluded that Muhammad and his followers were the enemies of Christ.

At that point a circle in the reasoning appears. Because the enemy of Christ would be someone very unlike Christ, it was essential that the Christian pro-gram demonstrate how different Muhammad was and thus portray him as a great blasphemer who used religion to justify his violence and sexuality. As to the claimed revelations, Muhammad either fabricated them or gained them dur-ing seizures. Aisha had said that the visitations left him weak with sweat as though he had been in a severe trance. The reports of epilepsy, however, come from outside Islam.

In an age when circumstances of death were held to reveal what a person was, the stories Christians knew of Muhammad's death further debased the claim that Muhammad was a prophet. They were unaware that he died a natural death in the arms of his beloved Aisha and was buried at his home, or that an impressive mosque was raised over the tomb. They thought he had been eaten by pigs or dogs; or smothered while in an epileptic seizure and then eaten by pigs; or murdered by a Jewish woman who fed him poisoned lamb; or killed by a Jewish woman who fed his body to pigs save for his left foot that she kept, claiming that angels had carried the rest of the body away. Christians some-times used the references to swine to explain the Islamic prohibition of pork. Another fanciful account had Muhammad's body in an iron coffin that was raised into the air by lodestones his followers attached to the "temple" in Mecca. At some point the adage about the mountain coming to Muhammad entered the tradition, totally without Islamic foundation. These stories were told and retold, more often to entertain than to inform. The more serious writers usu-ally knew better, but wherever these tales were told they served to undermine Muhammad's authority.

IDOLATRY

While informed reporters on Islam knew that Muslims were monotheists and that Muhammad had eliminated idolatry, not all writers were so aware. The *Song of Roland*, the famous twelfth-century poetic account of Charlemagne's incursion into Spain, alleges Muslim idolatry. The poem tells of three golden idols the Saracens had in a grotto, notably not an impressive temple or mosque. The images were of Muhammad, Apollo, and Tervagant, the latter two under-stood as devils. Angered because these deities could not prevent Charlemagne's victory, the wife of the Saracen king and some of his warriors rushed to the crypt and tore down the statues. When the angry Muslims threw the idol of Muhammad into a ditch, dogs bit and trampled it, a tale reminiscent of the fate of Queen Jezebel in 2 Kings 9. Meanwhile, Charlemagne's soldiers are said to have entered the "synagogues and mosques" of Saragossa and smashed "the statues and all the idols" so that "no sorcery or false cult will remain."[8] Following this iconoclasm, Charlemagne ordered the Saracens who opposed him "to be taken prisoner, burned, or put to death." The poem relates that over a hundred thousand were forcibly baptized, save for the queen who was led captive to France, for "The King wishes her to become a convert out of devotion."[9]

The *Song* gives a dramatic account of Charlemagne and his army and the death of his nephew, Roland, Duke of Brittany, but is ill informed on the history. The Frankish king went into Spain at the request of a Muslim ruler who had asked him for aid in his defense against another Muslim, and the force that attacked him at Roncesvalles was composed of Basques, not Muslims.[10]

This story, written some three hundred years after the event, is more fancy than fact, but its value lies in showing that its authors could be so misinformed about Islam as to portray Muslims as idolaters. (Nor does the author hesitate to report compulsory baptisms.) Later and more knowledgeable Christians would have an understanding of Islam closer to the truth. Even so, the early view of John of Damascus and Constantine Porphyrogenitus that the famous chant *"Allahu akbar"* revealed Muslims calling on pagan deities continued. The Latins even added a confirming point, namely, that Friday, the Muslim holy day, had long been associated with the worship of Venus.

ISLAMIC PRACTICES

Although many Christian writers knew of the Ka'aba and the stories of its establishment by Abraham and Ishmael, some thought it was still a house for idols, particularly of Venus, and thought Muslims went there to worship Muhammad. They knew the Muslim custom of prayer five times a day, but the converted Jew Pedro de Alfonso (d. 1110) claimed that the number was a compromise the clever Muhammad made between three times in Judaism and seven times in Christianity. Mark of Toledo, who prepared a Latin version of the Qur'an shortly after 1200, said that Christian churches had been turned into mosques where "wicked men devote supplications to the execrable Muhammad."[11] An eyewitness, the Dominican Ricoldo of Monte Croce, was impressed with the devotion of their prayers, or in his words, "the pretence of devotion."[12]

Ramadan, the Muslim holy month of fasting, came in for criticism as well. Muslims did not fast at all, the Christians said, for at night they gorged themselves and even embarked onto a sea of sexual license and gratification. "Their

---

[8] *The Song of Roland: An Analytical Edition,* ed. Gerard J. Brault, vol. 2 (University Park, Pa., and London: Pennsylvania State University Press, 1978), 223 (stanza 266, lines 3662-65).

[9] Ibid., 225 (stanza 267, lines 3669-74).

[10] Hugh Goddard, *A History of Christian-Muslim Relations* (Edinburgh: Edinburgh University Press, 2000), 81.

[11] Daniel, *Islam and the West,* 211.

[12] Ibid., 214.

fasting is of such a kind that they fast all day, and all night they really do not stop eating, drinking and copulating," as Pedro de Alfonso said.[13] Again two religious systems present themselves, the one understanding fasting as a severe discipline over numerous days for the few, the spiritually robust, the other practicing fasting in a day-long discipline for all, manageable by any ordinary person—these were different fasts for different purposes. Christians, seeing the difference, concluded that the Muslim form was insincere, a mockery, a hypocrisy, rather than recognizing another discipline at work.

The same problem emerged in regard to Muslim ablutions before prayer, namely, the washing of hands, face, and feet. A pale imitation of Christian baptism, Europeans said, again suggesting insincerity in the practice. Some thought Muslims designed their flowing garments as copies of Christian monastic habits. As to the Muslim call to prayer, it was seen to replace the Christian ringing of bells. In Norman Daniel's description, "Islam was always a reflection, often a muddied reflection, of what was familiar at home."[14] "Home" was the norm; departure from "home" was error, hypocrisy, insincerity. The Latins made little effort to get behind the Muslim practices and find out how Muslims saw and intended them. "On both sides it was the extent of the disagreement, not of shared beliefs, on which men concentrated their attention."[15] Differences counted; similarities were ignored.

POSITIVE WORDS ON ISLAM

In spite of these criticisms and castigations, a few Christians, principally visitors to Islamic areas, did find occasion to praise Muslims. Ricoldo of Monte Croce traveled in the Near East and lived among Muslims for twenty years or so. He marveled at the behavior of Muslims toward each other—far better, he said, than Christian behavior toward other Christians. Muslims practiced Christian virtues while Christians did not. "We were astounded how in so false a religion could be found works of such perfection."[16] They did not steal or kill or rape, and they treated each other and their visitors with great courtesy and civility, while in Christendom murder and thievery were rampant. In these ways he praised Muslims, doubly so in fact, for he thought their religion should have brought a lower state of behavior than among Christians. Despite being one of the few medieval writers who knew and talked with Muslims at first hand, Ricoldo shared the same negative evaluation of Islamic doctrine as his colleagues, but his biases came from the real differences between the two religions, not from fanciful and false stories. Because Islam was not Christianity,

---

[13] Ibid., 222.

[14] Ibid., 227.

[15] Ibid., 194.

[16] Quoted from Ricoldo's *Itinerarium* by Daniel, *Islam and the West,* 196.

it was false; because it rejected specific Christian doctrines, it was evil—
Ricoldo's reasoning was direct and clear.

Crusader chroniclers praised the virtue of the great Muslim commanders, such as Saladin and Baybars, both of whom treated the Christian prisoners more charitably than Christians had treated Muslims. Of the Mameluke leader az-Zahir Baybars (Mamelukes were a military corps, once slaves, who became a ruling power in Egypt), who worked perhaps more than any other to destroy the Latin state in Palestine, the thirteenth-century Dominican William of Tripoli said: "He detests and hates wine and prostitutes. . . . He requires his subjects to live justly and in peace, and protects the Christians who are subject to him, and especially the monks who are on Mount Sinai."[17] Some wondered if the virtues of some Muslims signified their nearness to Christian conversion.

On balance, however, Christian tradition was developing the view that Islam was at best a heresy, at worst a demonic religion. Not only had it brought military defeat and threat to Christians; it aimed to seduce and deceive, and thus bring its converts to perdition. This gloomy view was virtually unanimous, even when firsthand information became available.

---

[17] Daniel, *Islam and the West,* 201.

5

The Western Counteroffensive

The Reconquest of Spain and the Crusades to the Holy Land

Perhaps it is not so remarkable that much of the world of the crusaders is still in evidence. They altered their world and ours with a crusading movement that had incomparable popular appeal and which lasted almost 700 years and touched the lives of countless millions in Europe, Asia, North Africa and the Middle East.

—Malcolm Billings[1]

The year 1050 can serve as a dividing point for this study since changes then began to come quite rapidly. Spain and Portugal were still in the hands of the Moors, but Muslims in both Iberia and North Africa were torn by conflicts as the once united caliphate divided among new, smaller caliphates and governors who struggled with and against each other. The Middle East was still Islamic, of course, but less Arab and more Turk and divided off from the western branches of Islam. The Christian Eastern empire, now much reduced in size, faced a new and serious threat in the powerful and aggressive Seljuk Turks. Relations of the Eastern Church in Byzantium with the Western Church headed by the bishop of Rome were at an all-time low, portending the formal break that came in 1054.

The Eastern emperor, attempting a defense against the Turks, knew that he needed outside help, and the spectacle of a Europe free of barbarian invasions offered the prospect of assistance for his beleaguered empire. The help he requested he received in the form of crusader armies. Thus it was that the West began a military response, a counterattack, against the territory of Islam, and it

---

[1] Malcolm Billings, *The Cross and the Crescent: A History of the Crusades* (New York: Sterling Publishing Co., 1987), 232.

did so both in the East in Crusades for the Holy Land and in the West in the campaign to reconquer the Iberian peninsula.

THE RECOVERY OF SPAIN AND PORTUGAL

The seventh- and eighth-century Arab and Berber takeover of Spain left only one Christian area, a small Visigothic state called Asturia in the northwestern part of the peninsula. When Charlemagne entered Spain in 778, he did so not to aid the Asturian Christians but to assist a Muslim ruler caught in a dispute with other Muslims. When called home to quell a Saxon uprising in the north, Charlemagne retreated, taking what prisoners he could, but on his way out of Spain the rearguard of his column was ambushed by Basques, and Charlemagne's nephew, Roland, and many others died in the fighting. *The Song of Roland,* the French epic cited above recounts an embellished form of the story. Some years afterward Charlemagne returned to organize a Christian citadel in the Spanish March alongside the Pyrenees, but nothing was done to dislodge the Muslims. Asturia remained an isolated Christian refuge.

By the eleventh century, however, Christian rulers in southern France were strong enough to attack the Spanish Moors,[2] who had become greatly weakened through internal divisions. In 1018 a Norman army entered Spain, and in 1033 forces from Burgundy came as well. Soon Christian rulers in northern Spain entered the fray themselves. In 1085 Alfonso VI of León captured Toledo, the largest city in Spain. It had been the Visigothic capital of Spain before the Arab-Berber conquest and had since become the intellectual center of Andalusia (as Muslims called the peninsula), if not of Europe. Toledo was noted for the study of advanced astronomy, mathematics, horticulture, and philosophy, as well as for important conversations among Jews, Christians, and Muslims. The loss of this important city was a great blow to the Muslims.

The Christian advance slowed for a time, but as the Moors fell into further internal strife and even internecine war in the mid-twelfth century, the Christians resumed their attacks. The great city of Cordoba fell in 1236, Valencia in 1238, and then Seville in 1248. In 1469 when the marriage of Ferdinand and Isabella united Aragon and Castile, the fate of the rest of the peninsula was sealed. When Christian forces took Granada in January 1492, all of Spain was united under the Spanish crown and the almost eight-hundred-year rule of Muslims in southwest Europe came to an end.

In that same year the Spanish monarchs issued their famous decree against Jews, ordering them to convert and receive baptism, go into exile, or face execution. Most Jews fled, some to North Africa and others to Turkey, where Muslim rulers allowed them a freedom Christian rulers refused. Yet others emigrated to the Netherlands, where Christian laws were more moderate.

---

[2] "Moors," a common term for Muslims in Spain and Portugal related to the word "Morocco."

Ten years later Ferdinand and Isabella issued the same decree for Muslims, though it was applied only sporadically for some time. These harsh decrees on Jews and Muslims, enforced by the Spanish Inquisition, ensured the christianization of Spain, but the price of uniformity was high: both Jews and Muslims were an important resource for the Spanish rulers. Their skills in crafts and commerce and finance plus their substantial contributions in taxes were a significant factor in the financial stability of the Spanish administration. Philip Hitti estimated that perhaps as many as a half million Muslims were either killed or expelled, a number that may have grown as large as three million by the end of the process in the early seventeenth century when the last of them left. He noted that Spain "became the conspicuous exception to the rule that wherever Arab civilization was planted there it was permanently fixed."[3]

While Western Christendom was advancing south on its western borders, the Islamic Seljuk Turks and their successors the Ottomans were advancing northward on Europe's east, creating a dramatic shift of respective power bases. Christendom was expanding in the west and shrinking in the east while Islam was doing the reverse. The threat from the Seljuk Turks brought the Eastern empire into a major crisis that prompted the Christian Crusades.

THE CALL FOR CRUSADE AGAINST THE HOLY LAND

If the Reconquest of Spain was Christendom's most successful attempt to recover lands from Islamic control, the Crusades against the Holy Land were the least successful and the most costly. In attempt after attempt—by 1217 there had been five major Crusades—popes, monarchs, nobility, knights, and common people as well, sought to create Christian kingdoms in Syria and Palestine and thus restore to Christendom the holy sites of the Bible and early Christian history that had been lost to the Arabs in the seventh century. The attempts succeeded for a time, but failed in the end.

The occasion for Crusade came from a request in 1095 from the emperor Alexius Comnenus I of Constantinople to Pope Urban II for aid against the Seljuk Turks. Urban, in a famous sermon at Le Puy, France, November 27, 1095, just after the Council of Clermont had adjourned, tells of Alexius's plea. One account reads in part:

> A grave report has come from the lands around Jerusalem and from the city of Constantinople. . . . A people from the kingdom of the Persians [the Seljuk Turks], a foreign race, a race absolutely alien to God . . . has invaded the land of those Christians, has reduced the people with sword, rapine and flame and has carried off some as captives to its own land, has cut down

---

[3] Philip K. Hitti, *The Arabs: A Short History,* 5th rev. printing (Chicago: Henry Regnery Co., 1949), 201. Hitti places the final order for the expulsion of Muslims in 1609.

others by pitiable murder and has either completely razed churches of God to the ground or enslaved them to the practice of its own rites.[4]

Emperor Alexius had addressed Pope Urban directly in spite of the official split between the two great branches of the church some forty-one years earlier, a division created when the bishop of Rome in the West and the patriarch of Constantinople in the East mutually excommunicated each other. The description of Turkish persecution of Christians in the pope's sermon is highly exaggerated, whether by the emperor or the pope we do not know, but even so, the situation of Eastern Christians in general and Byzantium in particular was desperate, and rumors of the supposed violence doubtless spread among the Christians quickly. The fact is, Seljuk Turks from western Asia had swept through the Near East, had taken Jerusalem in 1073, moved into Anatolia, and were beginning to threaten the capital itself. Alexius knew that his forces could not withstand the Turkish onslaught for long and that he needed to strengthen his defenses against them.

Pope Urban's sermon was not the first discussion of Western military support for the East. Urban himself had probably considered it for years, and the idea had been discussed at a church council the preceding March. Now, however, the pope had in hand a direct request from the emperor for aid from the Latin Christians, and thus Urban announced his appeal.

FACTORS BEHIND THE CRUSADES

A CALL TO RESTORE THE HOLY LAND TO CHRISTIANS

The request from Emperor Alexius brought to Western Christians the exciting prospect of liberating from Islamic control the city of Jerusalem with its sacred tomb of Christ and the Church of the Holy Sepulcher. They thought of the Holy Land as a Christian land, not Muslim, nor even Jewish. Medieval Christians read the New Testament almost exclusively, not the Old, and they had little appreciation for Palestine as a land promised to Jews, understanding that idea to have died when the Jewish nation refused to accept Jesus as Messiah. Jews were seen as Christ-killers, and the idea of a Jewish interest in the Holy Land was nonexistent. But, eight hundred years later, when Jewish Zionists would launch a campaign to reclaim the Holy Land for a Jewish state, Jewish leaders would do so with Christian support.

For medieval Christians, however, Palestine was where the Savior had lived and walked and the church had been founded. In the Third Crusade, King Richard I of England would call upon his troops to "restore the kingdom of Israel," not to Jews, of course, but to Christians. For Muslims, infidels as Chris-

---

[4] Billings, *Cross and the Crescent,* 18.

tians saw them, to possess the land of the Savior was a wrong that had to be righted. Defending Constantinople from Turkish attack was important, but the overriding theme in the crusader movement was restoring the land to Christians, its true owners. A millennium later Arabs and Muslims would use the same argument in reverse against the state of Israel, claiming that they, the Muslims, needed to reclaim the same land, long part of the *dar al-Islam*, from Jewish Zionists.

An Opportunity to Reunite East and West

The letter from Emperor Alexius to Pope Urban II shows that in spite of the division of the church in 1054 the ideal of one church had not died, and communication between the two great divisions, East and West, Greek and Latin, was still possible. While this reunion was probably not uppermost in Urban's mind, he certainly would have seen the invitation as an opportunity to improve his own position. If he could rescue the Byzantine emperor, the emperor might return the favor and recognize the supremacy of the Roman pontiff, and then the rift between the two great divisions of the church would be healed and the pope's supremacy established. A successful Crusade might also help heal the breach between Pope Urban and the counterpope, Clement III, a division that resulted from the great dispute between Pope Gregory VII and Emperor Henry IV some twenty years before.

A Need to Protect Pilgrims

A need to protect pilgrimage routes to the Holy Land also figured in the plan. With the end of the barbarian invasions in the tenth century and the stabilization of the Latin lands of western Europe in the following century, the already long-standing Christian custom of pilgrimage to the Holy Land increased markedly, so that each year not only dozens but hundreds of pious Christians made their way to Palestine in acts of penance, devotion, and prayer. Florence of Worcester, a late-eleventh-century chronicler, tells that in one case —the year was 1060—a band of some seven thousand Christians with bishops in the lead set out on their pilgrimage journey only to be attacked by Saracens looking for gold. The number is doubtless exaggerated, but the story was still circulating in 1095 along with other such accounts that would certainly have inflamed the zeal of any who heard them.

A Way to Control Rowdy Knights

A Crusade might also serve to bring the knights of France under control. Fighting among them had gotten out of hand, so much so that some historians say the period from 1020 to 1030 was the most violent in French history. The great Cluny monastery from which Urban had come had instituted two major reforms to restrain this violence, the Truce of God to prohibit fighting on holy days and certain other days of the week, and the Peace of God to protect non-combatants from attack. Urban had called the Council of Clermont to deal with these very problems. Now he was appealing to the knights of France and the Latin West to take up a holy Crusade.

The proposed Crusade offered the nobles, particularly those of France, a solution to the problem of violence among their subjects: send the knights abroad where their fighting energies could be put to good use, namely, the relief of Byzantium and the recovery of Jerusalem. The populace would be free of their marauding, and they would be aiding fellow Christians in distress and reclaiming places holy to Christians. Noting the irony in all this, Karen Armstrong observed: "there would be the Peace of God in the West and the War of God in the Middle East."[5]

GOLD AND GLORY

The famous slogan of the later European explorers to the Americas of "gold and glory" had not come into being, but the principle had. Palestine offered the possibility of new farmlands at a time when land was at a premium in Europe. In addition, death on Crusade, at least in battle, was held to erase all one's debts for sin and to bring immediate entrance into paradise. Whether Pope Urban announced such at Clermont is uncertain, but respondents to his call believed he had, and in time he did announce a plenary indulgence for any who went on Crusade.

THE SIGNIFICANCE OF THE SERMON

No sermon, with the possible exception of the apostle Peter's sermon on Pentecost Day, has brought such momentous consequences to Christendom as Urban's sermon that day in an open field near Le Puy. The chroniclers say that the crowd answered, "God wills it," a slogan Urban often used himself. Nobles, knights, merchants, craftsmen, and peasants by the thousands responded to the call. They sold or leased their lands, settled their families, and set out for the Holy Land on a costly journey full of severe difficulties and dangers.

Considering the situation in western Europe in the preceding centuries, this was an astonishing development. After the fall of the Roman empire, Europeans struggled simply to survive, as their lands suffered repeated invasions and internal turmoil. Goths, Suevi, Vandals, Angles, Saxons, Vikings, and others had come, one after the other, century after century. Carolingian monarchs, Charlemagne in particular, had brought a brief period of order and organization in the eighth and ninth centuries, but that stability faded under the attacks of Norse

---

[5] Karen Armstrong, *Muhammad: A Biography of the Prophet* (San Francisco: HarperSanFrancisco, 1992), 247.

and Magyars in the 800s and 900s. Western Christians, busy with the problems brought by these new invaders, had little time to concern themselves with Islam.

By the eleventh century conditions had changed. The barbarian invasions had ceased, society was better organized, and trade and travel had resumed. Latins could now think about other areas of the world than their own, and their thoughts turned to the Holy Land.

THE NATURE OF CRUSADE

JUST WAR; HOLY WAR

Urban's call instigated a dramatic shift in the Christian doctrine of warfare. Christian theory allowed Christians to engage in war through a doctrine of just war, a view usually traced back to Augustine, who favored Christians' bearing arms in certain situations.[6] On this view, even though warfare was an activity of the fallen, sinful world, Christians could fight under certain conditions. They needed a just cause or reason (self-defense, for example), an appropriate leader (the legitimate ruler), and a just end in view (righting a wrong, not self-aggrandizement). Given those conditions, plus the use of just means, warfare was permissible, and could even be necessary.

Urban's summons for Crusade brought two changes. First, he was calling not simply for a just war but for a holy war, whereby participants in this campaign were to "take the cross" as pilgrims with the prospect of spiritual rewards of the highest order. What the pope called for was similar to the second or "lesser" form of Islamic *jihad*, namely, combat and battle, in contrast to the "greater struggle" for self-control and obedience to God. One wonders if Urban was influenced in any way by Islamic *jihad*, but the cases are not the same. While both crusaders and Muslim warriors believed that their death in holy battle would guarantee them a heavenly reward, the authority for this belief was different. For Muslims it was the Prophet himself. For Christians the authority was probably less clear, since it is not certain that the pope promised such a reward, even though the crusaders believed he had. Furthermore, Christians already had the clear pattern of pilgrimage to the Holy Land, even though combining war with pilgrimage changed the pattern considerably.

Second, this war was called by the bishop of Rome, the spiritual head of the church, not by a secular monarch or prince. The spiritual leader of the church was now taking on a military responsibility. Urban was able to do this in part

---

[6] St. Martin, a fourth-century Roman officer who converted to Christianity, offered an opposing view: "I am a soldier of Christ. I must not fight" (quoted by James Reston, Jr., *Warriors of God: Richard the Lionheart and Saladin in the Third Crusade* [New York and London: Doubleday, 2001], 10-11).

because his predecessor, Gregory VII, had brought the papacy to a new level of power and influence over secular rulers, and because earlier popes had both blessed and called for warfare on occasion. But no earlier pope had called for Crusade, for warfare on this scale or with a purpose so vast.

In a nod to the just war tradition before him, Urban had two "just" reasons for his proposal. First, he was responding to a plea to help fellow Christians seeking to defend themselves from a powerful adversary; and, second, the Holy Land, which had been under Christian rule for centuries, was now occupied by Muslims, a wrong, as Christians saw it, that needed to be made right. The first case appeals to the principle of defense, or in this instance, aiding another in self-defense. The second case is less clear, because by Urban's time the Holy Land had been in Muslim hands for four and a half centuries. But the land where the Savior himself had lived had been Christian before that, and sup- porters of the pope claimed that Muslims had taken it unjustly.[7] Indeed, as the Crusades developed and support for them grew, the recovery of the Holy Land was more and more the basis for the holy war. St. Bernard, the noted bishop of Clairvaux, a major figure in announcing the Second Crusade, called upon the faithful to "defend their Lord in his own land."[8] Furthermore, Bernard saw only two possible outcomes, the conversion of the Muslims living there, or their extermination.

In the 1270s the Dominican Humbert of Romans, a major theorist of the Crusades, maintained that they were a just war par excellence, fought on divine authority. Adding to earlier claims, he said that the church was commissioned to fight heretics and rebels, and the Islamic people were both. The entire Islamic nation was culpable, and hence the wars were fully justified. Indeed, some would finally say that the essence of crusading was "to slay for God's love." In Bernard's words, "A Christian glories in the death of a pagan [i.e., Muslim] because Christ is glorified."[9] Muslims within Christendom were to be tolerated, since in time they might be converted, but war against Muslims out- side Christendom was justified. Once again, in these ideas Christian theorists developed a view of the world rather like the Islamic distinction between the *dar al-Islam* and the *dar al-harb*: for Muslims, Islamic areas and non-Islamic areas; for Christians the area of Christendom and areas outside Christendom.

Thoughts of violence in religion are repulsive to modern minds, but that era had little such sensitivity. Both sides were guilty. Christians would defame, besmirch, and destroy Muslim mosques. Muslims would do the same to Chris- tian churches.

---

[7] Pope Innocent IV added that he, as successor to the former rulers of Rome, had jurisdiction over what had been part of the Roman empire (Jonathan Riley-Smith, *What Were the Crusades?* [Totowa, N.J.: Rowman & Littlefield, 1977], 20).

[8] Norman Daniel, *Islam and the West: The Making of an Image* (Edinburgh: University Press, 1960), 109.

[9] Ibid., 113.

PILGRIMAGE AND CRUSADE

Crusaders "took the cross" as regular pilgrims did, often wearing a cross sewn on clothing. Documents that survive detailing the arrangements for their journey strongly resemble those prepared by pilgrims. Crusade became a pilgrimage to propitiate one's sins, the burden of which was the great and dominating problem for piously oriented people of the Middle Ages. Taking the cross and going on Crusade would relieve these warrior-pilgrims of the temporal penalties for their sins, and while the pope himself may not have offered the distinction of full martyrdom if they died in the cause, most crusaders thought that was the case, as did many who wrote about them.

Urban exempted from his call to take the cross Spaniards already fighting to regain lands from Islamic control and gave them the right to an indulgence for their fighting like the one for his Palestinian crusaders. The strategic import of these two campaigns was to attack Islam with a pincer movement, advancing on Islamic territory from both the west and the east. The military response of Christendom to the Islamic world was under way.

THE SEQUENCE OF THE CRUSADES

The major Crusades were eight in number. The First Crusade covered the years 1095-1099. Crusaders conquered Jerusalem and established the Latin states. This was the most successful of the eight. The Second lasted from 1147 to 1149 and was undertaken by the largest army of any Crusade. Because of poor decisions and internal squabbling, however, it accomplished almost nothing. and lost Jerusalem.

The Third in 1188-1192 was an unsuccessful attempt to retake Jerusalem after its capture by Saladin. The Fourth, 1201-1204, turned into an attack on Constantinople, the capital of the Christian Eastern empire and was perhaps the most tragic of the Crusades. The Fifth Crusade, 1217-1221, launched against Egypt, resulted in the entrapment of the crusading army and a truce with the Muslims. In the Sixth Crusade, 1228-1229, the German emperor Frederick II won Jerusalem back through a negotiated truce, the climax of a brief Crusade. In the Seventh, 1248-1254, the forces of the French king (St.) Louis IX were defeated in Egypt, and he was captured and later ransomed. In 1270 in the last of the eight Crusades, King Louis sailed to Tunis, where he died. His army returned to Europe.

THE RESPONSE TO THE CALL

After Urban preached his sermon, there were stirrings aplenty. Thoughts of plenary indulgence, of reclaiming the Holy Land, and of getting farmlands in Palestine danced in the heads of many. Urban pressed his case with a lengthy journey across France the following year urging Christians to take up the cross in this holy Crusade. He was joined by other leaders announcing this call—bishops, monks, and self-styled prophets—until a virtual fever seized France and parts of Germany.

But crusading was not cheap. The warriors-to-be mortgaged land, sold possessions, and turned their farms over to others to manage for them. One estimate has it that the crusaders needed an amount four times their annual income to pay for the journey. Popes were soon reduced to taxation efforts to assist in the financing. Malcolm Billings observed: "It is not generally known that income tax began as a means of raising money for [the Crusades]."[10]

The core of the movement was composed of knights, the military elite of Europe, aided by their assistants: cooks, armorers, clerics, aides, smiths, and women to attend to their various needs. Nobles led the Crusade, but no kings enlisted. Men and women by the thousands soon dropped their work, settled their families with relatives or friends, sewed the red cross on their breast,[11] took up arms, and left for the Holy Land. But before the Crusade proper was under way, an early misguided effort was made by a less than worthy group.

A CALAMITOUS BEGINNING

Urban's intent was to recruit warrior knights for his enterprise, not just anyone who wanted to go, but as news spread and enthusiasm increased, Urban lost control of the personnel enlisting in his Crusade. Self-appointed prophet-preachers announced that this war against Muslims was part of the events of the Last Day, and they soon assumed a leadership the pope had not counted on.

Their ideas sprang from a popular book called *Revelation* (not the Revelation of the New Testament), which claimed, falsely, to be from Methodius, a fourth-century martyr and saint. Composed in seventh-century Syria just after the Arab invasions, *Revelation* had been written in the style of a prophecy that could comfort Christians suffering from the Islamic conquest. After tracing the early history of the world, the book skips to its "prophecy" about the Ishmaelites—Arabs who would come out of their desert fastnesses and conquer Christians, seducing them into their false faith. At this point this seventh-century work presents as prophecy events that had already taken place, what one writer calls "a chronicle written in the future tense."[12] *Revelation* says that

---

[10] Billings, *Cross and the Crescent,* 12.

[11] Norman Cohn notes that this was the first use of a badge by an army in postclassical times, and the beginning of what became military uniforms (*The Pursuit of the Millennium: Revolutionary Millenarians and Mystical Anarchists of the Middle Ages,* rev. ed. [New York: Oxford University Press, 1961, 1970], 64).

[12] Benjamin Z. Kedar, *Crusade and Mission: European Approaches toward the Muslims* (Princeton: Princeton University Press, 1984), 29, citing Paul J. Alexander.

invasions by the Ishmaelites would be a sign of the Last Day and that God's great resolution of human history would follow soon thereafter.

The work was never popular in the East, but a Latin translation was often used in the West, and in the hands of the *prophetae* it turned many of the poor into crusaders. Lay preachers offered messianic and visionary descriptions of the great new age that lay ahead and promised rewards for the poor in the Holy Land, which would become a virtual paradise for them. None of this came from the pope or his officials, but in the countryside, villages, and cities popular preachers belabored these themes, deriding Islam as the dreaded incarnation of evil that would persecute the saints before the Last Day. These messages carried great power, even more perhaps than the strong words of Pope Urban.

As a result, the first stage of the Crusade was led by misguided fanatics, lay prophet-preachers whose followers unleashed terrible violence and carnage as they journeyed to Palestine. The worst of these *prophetae* was a self-appointed preacher named Peter the Hermit, who gathered around him a ragtag army of poor people and malcontents from northern France and Germany and set out toward the Holy City in what historians have called the Peasants' or People's Crusade. Peter bred among his followers a passion to kill infidels, and the first "infidels" they saw were Jews.

Relations between Christians and Jews had been strained for some long time. Beginning in the early fourth century, church councils had legislated to restrict the associations Christians could have with Jews. Synagogues had often been attacked, and Jews were not only criticized for having rejected Jesus but charged with responsibility for his death: "Christ-killers" they were called. Seeking to keep the laws of the Pentateuch, Jews lived a separate life, working and marrying among themselves, and had been relegated to a second-class status in Christian society. Furthermore, since Christians were forbidden by canon law to loan money at interest, they went to Jews to borrow money, and bitterness grew against Jews because of their collection of interest. Violence against the Jews became a simple way of wiping out these loans and seizing Jewish wealth, a measure King Edward I took later in 1290 when he banished Jews from England and seized their property for the crown. By the time of the preparations for the First Crusade, western Europe had a great deal of anti-Jewish sentiment on which troublemakers could call.

Peter, aided by Count Emich of Leiningen and other anti-Semitic preachers, inflamed his followers with a fiery message of vengeance toward nonbelievers. Impatient to wait for Muslims in Palestine, they set upon Jews, first in Lorraine and then in the Rhine valley, looting, killing, burning homes and synagogues, and sometimes forcing baptisms. Their vengeance on Jews was only increased by their belief that, because Jews were led by demons, killing them would hasten the End of the Age.

The worst attacks occurred in episcopal cities along the Rhine valley. The bishops of Cologne and Mainz attempted to restrain the terror, but their success was limited. "Twelve Jews were murdered at Speier, 500 at Worms, 1,000 at

Mainz, 22 at Metz."[13] In the case of Mainz, a group of Jews barricaded themselves in a barn, only to be burned alive as fanatics torched the building. No one
knows how many were killed altogether in these terrible outbursts, but the number was certainly in the hundreds, and some estimates run into the thousands.
Later Crusades would repeat these atrocities. Karen Armstrong observed: "The
lure of a Christian Jerusalem thus helped to make anti-Semitism an incurable
disease in Europe."[14] The terrible pattern of *pogroms* against Jews had begun
and would eventually lead to the Holocaust of Nazi Germany.

The unruly band's behavior within the Eastern empire was no better. They
robbed and stole to support themselves, creating havoc and fear wherever they
went. But their faith remained, strengthened by reports of a vision of the heavenly Jerusalem ready to descend to earth. They suffered major losses in fighting and illness as they traveled through southeastern Europe, and by the time of
their arrival at Byzantium they were little more than a "corps of vagabonds."[15]
They were hurriedly ushered out of Byzantium by the authorities and sent on
their way (the month was August 1096). Clad in tatters and rags, and driven by
a vengeance and ferocity that alarmed even the Turkish soldiers, these early
crusaders looted, raped, and killed indiscriminately as they passed through the
countryside, but their campaign ended when their ranks were decimated by the
professional Turkish cadres. The few who survived retreated to join the second
wave of the First Crusade, the Crusade proper. Meanwhile, Peter, their erstwhile leader, forsook his followers and returned to France. He later joined the
official crusaders in Syria but finally returned to the Low Countries, where he
died.

THE FIRST CRUSADE

By 1096 the crusading effort was more organized, the visionary hopes had
faded, and a professional fighting force of some seven thousand knights set out,
accompanied by the entourage of attendants needed to supply and support the
heavily armored warriors. They were led by several nobles, including Godfrey
of Bouillon, and his two brothers, Baldwin of Flanders and Eustace of Boulogne.
Bishop Adhémar of Le Puy, the first to volunteer at Clermont, was papal legate.

When the crusaders arrived in Syria, one column turned aside to attack
Edessa, in Armenia, which they took and held. The balance of the force
besieged Antioch, which they captured easily with the aid of a traitor within the

---

[13] Paul Johnson, *A History of Christianity* (New York: Atheneum, 1980), 245.

[14] Karen Armstrong, *Jerusalem: One City, Three Faiths* (New York: Alfred A. Knopf, 1996), 272.
Edward H. Flannery reports that the practice of remembering Jewish martyrs, Jews who gave their
lives "to sanctify the name," began following these cruelties (*The Anguish of the Jews: Twenty-Three
Centuries of Antisemitism* [New York and Mahwah, N.J.: Paulist Press, 1985], 93).

[15] Cohn, *Pursuit of the Millennium*, 65.

city. A sizable Turkish army that had come to relieve the city retreated, but the Franks did not pursue. The crusaders next surrounded the small city of Maara, a town without a major military force. The inhabitants surrendered, believing that the Franks would keep their word to spare them all if they surrendered. But the Franks reneged and subjected the entire town to a massacre. Even worse— and both Muslim and Christian sources testify to this almost unbelievable horror—the crusaders cooked and ate some of their captives, boiling the adults in pots and roasting children on spits over a fire. Muslims saw a barbarism here they had never imagined, and never forgot.

In June 1099, the army of crusaders arrived in Jerusalem. Bishop Adhémar had perished the preceding August in an epidemic during the siege of Antioch, but it was said that he appeared to a priest in a vision and instructed the crusaders that if they repented, fasted, and walked around the city barefoot, they would prevail. Some said they saw the good bishop fighting with them in the battle. On July 15 they breached Jerusalem's walls and entered it in victory. Once in the city, the crusaders massacred virtually every person they found, Muslim and Jew (Christians had been sent out of the city earlier by the governor), sparing only a few of the city's leaders. The chroniclers claimed that blood ran in the streets ankle deep. As soon as the slaughter ended and while the streets were still clogged with bodies of the slain, the knights gathered in the Church of the Holy Sepulcher for High Mass to give thanks for their victory. The few inhabitants who had been spared were assigned the grim task of burying the dead. Urban II, who initiated all this, did not learn of the victory; he died a fortnight later before the news of the victory could reach him.

Reports of the massacre spread among Christians and Muslims alike, and both were horrified. At first the Muslims had not been alarmed by the Latin incursion, thinking of it as "another factor in the tangled politics of the time,"[16] but the Jerusalem debacle caused them to change their view, and they determined that the Franks had to be driven out. Later, when more moderate Latins attempted to create an accommodation with the Muslims, the memory of the massacre stood in their way. Nor did the crusaders behave any better toward their fellow Christians: they expelled all non-Latin priests from their churches, tortured orthodox Christians to reveal the location of the true cross of Jesus, and created new difficulties for nonorthodox Christians, who had fared well under Muslim rule.

The initial horror that Christians felt soon faded and pride took its place, views of many falling into line with those of Raymund, one of the Crusade's leaders:

This day, I say, will be famous in all future ages, for it turned our labors and sorrows into joy and exultation; this day, I say, marks the justification of all Christianity, the humiliation of paganism, the renewal of faith. "This

---

[16] Steven Runciman, *A History of the Crusades,* vol. 1, *The First Crusade and the Foundation of the Kingdom of Jerusalem* (Cambridge: Cambridge University Press, 1968), 287.

is the day that the Lord hath made, let us rejoice and be glad therein," for on this day the Lord revealed himself to his people and blessed them.[17]

Just as the Islamic invasions had been read by Christians as acts of divine judgment, so these victories were taken to be signs of divine providence. A great event, the greatest since the crucifixion according to Robert the Monk, it surely was an omen that the Last Days were at hand with the final battles against evil and the Antichrist.

As soon as order was restored and Frankish rule over Jerusalem secure, many crusaders returned home. Those who remained established Latin states, dividing the areas among the principal leaders. They built castle-fortresses for their defense and organized their life much as it had been in France, living relatively separate from their Muslim subjects. Existence for the Franks was difficult and precarious at best, residing in a foreign land and ruling a potentially rebellious population.

Usamah, a Syrian emir and chronicler of the time, reports that the longer a crusader stayed, the more likely he was to become tolerant and give up his "barbarian ways," barbarian in the eyes of the Muslim chronicler. He recounts an incident in which a newly arrived crusader maltreated a Muslim pursuing his prayers, only to be seized by another crusader who, having been there some time and familiar with Muslims, admonished the first man to respect the prayers of the Muslim.

But the Frankish system of using the method of ordeal to establish guilt and innocence was not at all pleasing to Usamah. He tells how he observed such a trial when a Frank sought justice for an offense he had received. Rather than calling witnesses to testify before a judge in a formal trial, the Franks allowed the man to challenge the accused to a duel. The latter, rather than risk his own life, employed a surrogate, who after a terrible and bloody fight, ran a lance through the prostrate accuser, whose body was then hung from a tree. Usamah could not believe the horror and brutality he had witnessed in the name of justice. In such cases Islamic *shari'a*, a sophisticated system of law and justice, would have required witnesses, evidence, and a formal hearing. In the Frankish system of ordeal Usamah saw only barbarism.

THE SECOND AND THIRD CRUSADES

But the struggle for Palestine was not over. Islamic forces recovered the city of Edessa in 1144, prompting the Latins to organize another Crusade. Trumpeted by Bernard of Clairvaux, the Second Crusade (1147-1149) had three arms: one against Muslims in Portugal, the second against Slavs in eastern Europe, and the third against Muslims in Syria and Palestine. Jews of the

---

[17] Armstrong, *Jerusalem*, 274.

Rhineland suffered once again from the crusaders, and Bernard hurried from Flanders into the Rhineland to call a halt to the massacre.

This second crusading army, the largest the Latins had created, accomplished nothing in Palestine. Quarrels among the leaders, bad decisions, and defeats at the hands of Muslims all conspired to make the second Palestinian campaign a dismal failure. As a result, the spirits of the Muslim world revived. Meanwhile the Crusade in Portugal succeeded. In 1147 Lisbon fell to a multinational Christian force, breaking the Moors' rule in Portugal.

The days of the Latin states in Syria and Palestine were now numbered. In a revived *jihad* a new Islamic leader arose, Saladin by name (*Salah-al-Din*), a Kurd who led an army assembled from a variety of groups, most of them professional soldiers. Not only did Saladin's military and leadership skills surpass those of the earlier Islamic leaders, but he succeeded in uniting the various Muslim groups whose internal divisions had weakened them in the First Crusade. Angered by the tactics of one Reynald of Châtillon, who had twice violated truces negotiated by Saladin and had even attempted a campaign against the holy city of Mecca itself, Saladin vowed revenge on the Christian leader. He gained it in July 1187, at the Battle of Hattin, where the crusaders, exhausted by a lack of water, were decisively defeated. While permitting most of the captured Franks to be ransomed, Saladin allowed members of the Sufi order (a branch of Islam devoted to the practice of mysticism) the privilege of beheading the captured Templars and Hospitallers, knights who belonged to two new military orders. Saladin executed Reynald himself.

After reducing several other sites on the coast, Saladin moved his force to Jerusalem, which fell to him on October 2, 1187. Saladin ordered no executions—all the inhabitants were spared. Because he took the city through a negotiated surrender, the laws of medieval warfare would have prohibited vengeance, a principle the crusaders violated at Maara, but the Muslims kept at Jerusalem. Not all got away free, however, for many were sold into slavery. Saladin allowed the Syrian Christians to retain their churches and encouraged Jews to return.

Saladin's capture of Jerusalem prompted a Third Crusade (1188-1192), the first to be formed under lay and secular auspices with political interests paramount. The leaders were Frederick Barbarossa of Germany, Philip II of France, and Richard I, the Lionheart, of England. The fleet that carried Richard and Philip numbered some 219 vessels, 39 of them war galleys. Richard's first effort was at Acre. Already under siege for three years, the city fell four weeks after his arrival. Richard, remembered in fiction as kind and generous, was in fact ruthless. When Saladin delayed in fulfilling some of the terms of surrender, Richard ordered the execution of two thousand Saracen prisoners, to the horror of both his troops and later historians. Their final crusader victory was at Jaffa, where Richard and a handful of knights waded ashore and pushed back defenders several times as numerous. Richard performed enough of such feats of valor and strength to make him immortal even among the Turks. Even Saladin respected Richard more than any other of his several Western opponents. The

Muslim ruler sent him two fresh horses during one of the battles, and once said: "If I should be fated to lose the Holy Land, I would rather lose it to Melec [King] Ric than to any other."[18]

But Richard failed in his major goal, the conquest of Jerusalem. One reason was Saladin's military skill and his success in getting the Muslims to overcome their earlier divisions. The other factor was divisions among the Western leaders, particularly the failure of the French to support and fight as well as they could have.

The larger conflict finally ended in a virtual draw, and Saladin agreed to a three-year armistice with Richard that granted Christians access to Jerusalem and its holy sites. Several crusaders entered the city, but not Richard. If he could not go as conqueror, he would not go at all.

Although Richard did not take Jerusalem, the city came back into Christian hands for a brief time in 1229 in the Sixth Crusade through a negotiated truce between the German emperor Frederick II and the Sultan of Egypt, al-Kamil. When Richard's nephew, another Richard, this one the earl of Cornwall, sailed to the Holy Land in 1240, he confirmed the treaty Frederick had made, gaining additional concessions in the process, including additional areas in Galilee. Three years after Earl Richard sailed for home, however, the city came back into Muslim hands. In this case the Muslims were Turks who swept down from the north and took Jerusalem from the crusaders, who were unprepared for such an attack. The tragic defeat of a large crusader force shortly thereafter at a battle near Gaza spelled the virtual end of any significant European military presence in the Holy Land.

Jerusalem would not come under Western control again until General Edmund Allenby and his British troops captured it from the failing Ottoman Empire in 1917, six and a half centuries later. In that victory Allenby, a British commander, accomplished what Richard I, a British king, could not.

OTHER CRUSADES

Of all the Crusades to the Middle East, the Fourth was the most tragic. Announced in 1198 by Pope Innocent III and supported in great part by the commercial interests of Venice and other Italian port cities, the Crusade was planned as an attack upon Egypt and the Ayyoubid dynasty, which ruled Egypt and Palestine at the time, but the campaign was diverted to Constantinople and turned into a war against Eastern Christians. In 1204 crusaders sacked the great city, pillaging, killing, raping, and even desecrating the high altar of Hagia Sophia, the famous church of Justinian. They justified their attack on the grounds that their head, the bishop of Rome, was not subject to the patriarch of Constantinople and that their mission was to replace a usurper to the Byzantine

---

[18] Barbara W. Tuchman, *Bible and Sword: England and Palestine from the Bronze Age to Balfour* (New York: Ballantine Books, 1984), 68.

throne with the legitimate emperor. Commercial motives and the desire of the warriors for booty dominated, and the spoils were considerable. "The whole of western Europe became enriched with the treasures exported from Constantinople; most of the western European churches received something from 'the holy relics' of Constantinople,"[19] though perhaps no church received as much as the Cathedral of San Marco in Venice. The four bronze horses that grace the entrance to the cathedral today are copies of originals taken from Constantinople that are now stored away for safe-keeping. Numerous trophies, including precious icons, a magnificent reredos behind the high altar of San Marco, and rare chalices in alabaster, onyx, gold, and silver display the wealth and splendor taken from the capital of the Eastern empire. If the division of Eastern and Western churches in 1054 began the separation of the two halves of Christendom, the memory of this frightful event among Eastern Christians ensured a continuation of the division for centuries to come. An especially unfortunate result was the destruction of many of Byzantium's defenses, leaving the city vulnerable to the attacks of the Ottoman armies in the fifteenth century. The Fourth Crusade showed the Western Christians in the worst light possible.

Attempts at other Crusades were failures. Worst was the Children's Crusade in the early thirteenth century, which was begun in 1212 by a French shepherd lad named Stephen, who claimed to have been visited by Christ in a vision. He gathered a host of followers, mostly young, as he made his way to Paris to inform King Philip of his plans. Another group set out from Cologne. Records of these events are sketchy, late of composition, and contradictory, but they tell us enough to conclude that none ever reached the Holy Land. Some turned off to support Crusades against heretics in Europe; some died in shipwrecks in the Mediterranean; others are said to have reached Egypt, where they were sold into slavery. While the numbers in the reports are highly inflated (thirty thousand with Stephen, seven thousand in another troop, etc.), it is clear that this part of the Crusade movement involved a considerable number of people.

King Louis IX of France led two Crusades, 1248-1254 (the Seventh) and 1269-1272 (the Eighth). On his first Crusade Louis invaded Egypt, but he was defeated at Mansura and taken captive for four years. The Crusade of the Shepherds in 1251 was led by the so-called Master of Hungary. Composed of poor folk, many of pastoral background but with many unsavory hangers-on as well, the group was at first welcomed in Paris by Queen Blanche, King Louis's mother. Their rowdiness and violence brought a crackdown that scattered the group. Some continued their attempt to reach the Holy Land, but they failed to get out of France.

The end of any significant European presence in the Holy Land came with the fall of Acre in 1291, a year after King Edward I expelled the Jews from England. Withdrawal of the Latins from the rest of the Near East followed. By

---

[19] A. A. Vasiliev, *History of the Byzantine Empire, 343-1453* (Madison: University of Wisconsin Press, 1952), 462.

then, relations between Christians and Muslims had become so embittered that some Muslim rulers began persecuting native Christians, enforcing conversions to Islam even though forced conversions are a violation of Islamic law. Here and there Christians were prohibited from serving in Muslim civil service, as many had done for centuries. Jonathan Riley-Smith says, "Thus the crusades, one of whose declared aims was to bring aid and succour to the native Christians of the East, had the long-term effect of irretrievably weakening their protected status within Muslim society."[20]

Later events added to the enmity. In 1365 King Peter I of Cyprus landed a sizable force at Alexandria, which fell to him within forty-eight hours. A ruthless massacre followed, of Christians and Jews as well as Muslims, and, after looting the city of all they could carry, Peter's ships weighed anchor and sailed away. The results were grim. Prices for exports from the East shot sky high in Europe; the Mameluk rulers of Alexandria instituted a persecution of Christians as a reprisal; and the Holy Sepulcher in Jerusalem was closed for several years. By 1400 the crusading movement had lost its force, and the Crusades were for all practical purposes at an end. Minor attempts would still be made: a naval Crusade against Smyrna in 1472; a Spanish landing in North Africa in 1492; a successful attack on Tunis ordered by Emperor Charles V in 1535. Even Christopher Columbus entertained thoughts of yet another Crusade. But these brought no lasting results. By the seventeenth century, Palestine had become primarily a center for European trade with Asia, and its character as a Holy Land had diminished, particularly for Protestant Europe, which put no stock in pilgrimages to Jerusalem. The theme of a Holy Land would be revived in the Zionist movement of the twentieth century, this time as a land for Jews.

RESULTS OF THE CRUSADES

The Crusades brought mixed results. Christians, already divided East and West, were now wider apart than ever. Little direct knowledge of Islam was gained, although general awareness of Islam and its great prophet, Muhammad, prompted Latin scholars to begin a study of Islamic texts. Contacts for commerce and civic affairs were numerous, but direct cultural contact was minimal. Missionary attempts to convert Muslims were few and far between, and not particularly successful.

On the positive side, trade was opened, and that proved to be a boon to Arabs, Turks, and Westerners alike—particularly the Venetians, who had the sailing ships and wealth to undertake such commerce. This trade brought to Europe goods from the East, the treasures of the Orient—spices, jewels, and silks. These came to Europe over trade routes that Islamic rulers and merchants controlled, a situation that would become more and more objectionable to

---

[20] *The Oxford Illustrated History of the Crusades,* ed. Jonathan Riley-Smith (Oxford and New York: Oxford University Press, 1995), 242.

Westerners and would finally lead to the search for a sea route to Asia. But at the time, the Crusades did little more than deplete Western resources, both material and human, and perhaps much of the West's moral idealism as well.

The Crusades were the Western response to the Muslim *jihad* of the seventh century and something of a mirror image of Islamic *jihad* as well. In a way both attempted to "right wrongs" through warfare, and warriors on both sides believed in an immediate entrance into paradise if killed in the campaign. Neither required the conquered to convert to the victor's faith, but allowed the practice of the earlier religion to continue, even if in a second-class status, though conversion to Christianity was later required in Spain. Both established formal rules and laws to limit mixing with the conquered population, and both levied a special tax on members of the other religion.

In respect to violence and unnecessary carnage, the Christian side had the worse record, the case of Jerusalem being the most glaring example, though Islamic commanders sometimes ordered mass executions as well. Christian rhetoric often spoke of the need to "kill Muslims," whereas Muslim rhetoric rarely, if ever, rose to that level. Save for the Muslim allowance of religious freedom for the heterodox groups within Christianity—an important boon to be sure—neither brought immediate blessings to the conquered.

The Crusades made the West aware of how vast Islam was, and of its dominance over the West's trade with Asia. But within a few centuries the West would become a power center itself. Its mastery of the seas would challenge Islam's control of Western commerce, and eventually European colonialism would carry the West's industrial and commercial power around the globe, engulfing the world of Islam.

6

Translating Islam

Peter the Venerable and
the Spanish Connection

> *It required a measure of both originality and heroism on the part of Peter the Venerable to initiate the study of Islam in Europe. Although the Islamic empire was hewn out of Christian lands to a very large extent, "the Christian world was slow to recognize Islam for what it was . . . an independent religion of considerable appeal."*
>
> —James Kritzeck[1]

By the mid-twelfth century Christians of Western Europe found themselves in a new situation in respect to Islam. The Reconquest of Spain was well under way, and Frankish crusading armies were campaigning in the Holy Land. In Spain and in the Levant, Christian rulers governed Muslim subjects for the first time, and the number of Christians who lived alongside Muslims was increasing. Thus, two situations presented themselves to Christian authorities: the possibility of preaching directly to Muslims for conversion to Christianity, and a concern for defections by Christians to Islam.

The problem of defections to Islam had existed since Islam's conquest of Christian territories. Many Christians who lived under Islamic rule had converted, partly because conversion brought them social, economic, and political advantages they lacked as Christians. But none of those advantages held within Christendom; indeed, the reverse would be the case because converts to Islam would be persecuted, and so concern about defections to Islam within Christian areas proved to be misplaced. Medieval Christians joined various heretical and schismatic movements, but not Islam. Even so, clerical leaders thought instruction in the evils of Islam would be important.

---

[1] James Kritzeck, *Peter the Venerable and Islam* (Princeton: Princeton University Press, 1964), 15, quoting Gustave E. von Grunebaum, *Medieval Islam* (Chicago: University of Chicago Press, 1946), 12.

More relevant was the presence of Muslims under Christian rule, who now became prospects for conversion to Christianity. Foremost among the Christian leaders who took note of this new circumstance was the noted abbot of Cluny monastery, Pierre Maurice de Montboissier, better known as Peter the Venerable.

By Peter's time the small reform monastery founded in 910 at Cluny, France, had blossomed into a huge organization with some six hundred branch monasteries and ten thousand monks. From its houses had come popes (Urban II, for instance), cardinals, and counselors to emperors and kings, as well as a continuing campaign for strengthening the moral and spiritual life of the church. Cluny's plan to contain medieval violence with the Truce of God, which prohibited fighting on holy days, and the Peace of God, which defined who could be combatants, were mentioned earlier. Peter now undertook a publishing enterprise that marked a new stage in the Latin West's encounter with Islam, namely the translation of Muslim materials.

When the idea of such publications first occurred to Peter is uncertain, but in 1142 he journeyed into Spain to inspect Cluny's branch monasteries and to confer with the Spanish emperor Alfonso VII. There he saw at firsthand Christians and Muslims living side by side and recognized the problems and opportunities this new development could bring. While in Spain the abbot met Peter of Toledo, a skilled translator of Arabic, and commissioned him to render into Latin the *Apology* of al-Kindy, "perhaps the most celebrated of the early Christian Arab apologetical works."[2] The book, commonly called by its Arabic name, *Risalah*, was probably written in the East in the tenth century. It consists of two letters, the longer of which is a Christian statement denouncing Islam. Peter of Toledo found additional scholars to help him translate three other Arabic-language tracts from Islamic authors plus the Qur'an itself.[3] Peter's project was apparently the first organized attempt in Western Christendom to collect reliable information on Islam since Charlemagne in 799 asked his education aide, Alcuin, to procure a document that told of a disputation between one Felix and a Saracen.

Toledo, along with Cordoba and Seville, had become by this time a major site for scholarly work among Jews, Muslims, and Christians, and particularly for translating Arabic- and Syriac-language manuscripts into Latin. Toledo's Bishop Raimondo had established a school to undertake these translations, the first such school in Europe. The leading translator of the materials they used had been prepared by Hunayn ibn-Ishaq (Joannitius), a Nestorian Christian mentioned earlier. He is said to have translated from Greek into Syriac and

---

[2] Kritzeck, *Peter the Venerable,* 32.

[3] Bernard Lewis observes that Christians and Muslims had the same religious vocabulary, in addition to sharing the same language in cases where both spoke Arabic. This commonality made the task of translation relatively easy, a situation that did not exist with Persian, Turkish, and the Indian languages. Thus, disputations among Muslims, Christians, and Jews were easy to arrange (*Islam and the West* [New York and Oxford: Oxford University Press, 1993], 5-6).

Arabic Galen's works on science and anatomy (the latter of which survive only in Arabic, the Greek he used having been lost), Hippocrates, Plato's *Republic*, and Aristotle's *Categories, Physics*, and *Magna Moralia*. These writings and more from the ancient world had been lost to Western Europe through the destructions wrought by the barbarians, but they had been kept alive in the Greek language in Byzantium and then in Arabic (and/or Syriac) in Islamic centers such as Baghdad. Now they became available to Latin-speaking Christian theologians and philosophers in the West. Included were marvelous texts on mathematics, astronomy, and medicine, not to mention philosophy and history. In this remarkably open setting in Spain, Arabs both Muslim and Christian, and Jews as well, were fueling the intellectual furnaces of the Christian West. According to James Kritzeck, "There was no intellectual center in Europe that was not touched in some way by, that did not owe some debt to, the school of Toledo."[4]

By 1143 Peter's translators had completed his project, and they forwarded the finished manuscript to him, a handsome original of which rests today in the Bibliothèque de l'Arsenal in Paris. Foremost among the "Toledan Collection," as the documents are often called, was the Qur'an translated by Robert of Ketton, an Englishman noted for his work in astronomy and mathematics and aided in Peter's project by a Muslim scholar named Muhammad. That Ketton could recruit a Muslim to assist him is surprising in light of the Islamic prohibition against translating the Muslim holy book. Robert's translation rearranged the *suras* and tended to put positive words and statements into superlatives, thereby sometimes changing the force of the expressions. The work is partly a paraphrase, but it gave Westerners for the first time a way to examine the themes of the Qur'an. Pleased with his work, Ketton wrote Peter: "I have uncovered Mohammed's smoke so that it may be extinguished by your bellows."[5]

The *Fables of the Saracens*, the first translation in the Toledan Collection, was an excellent choice for Peter's project in spite of its suggestive name, because it contained material otherwise almost entirely unknown in Europe, both legends and facts about Islam. The other two Muslim tracts in the Cluny anthology, the *Book of the Birth of Mahumet* and the *Doctrine of Mahumet* were less constructive. The former contained material that was trivia at best with little information of an accurate sort, and the latter lacked a good Muslim pedigree of authorship, the traditional Arab method of authenticating a written source.

In these three works one reads stories of the miracles and wonders that had become popular in Muslim life. For instance the *Book of the Birth of Mahumet* tells of a donkey that proclaimed of Muhammad, then five years old: "This is the seal of the prophets, the lord of the messengers, better than those who went

---

[4] Kritzeck, *Peter the Venerable*, 54.
[5] Ibid., 65.

before, a friend of Almighty God."[6] The reader may recognize the parallel between this story and tales of Jesus in the noncanonical Christian Gospels. In both cases, Christian and Muslim, such material was somewhat on the margin of the main tradition, but it was known and used nonetheless. One may also read of a mystic light that surrounded Muhammad, a theme present also in *The Fables of the Saracens* and often met elsewhere in Islamic lore. These stories and traditions had become common in Muslim tradition, and they were certain to draw the fire of Christian scholars.

The last title in the translations, al-Kindy's *Apology*, consists of two pieces, *The Letter from a Saracen* and *The Reply of a Christian*. Al-Kindy, the Christian, claims to be a convert from Islam but was probably a lifelong Oriental Christian in Syria familiar with Islam. The structure of the book is an imagined debate between a Muslim named al-Hashimi and the Christian al-Kindy. The Muslim protagonist speaks first, explaining to al-Kindy what the latter can gain if he converts to Islam: he can have as many as four wives, he can divorce at his pleasure, and he will find favor in the courts of the Muslim rulers. One can hear overtones of the Christian criticisms of Islam in al-Hashimi's overture, indicating that the author was probably a Christian, not a Muslim.

Al-Kindy's arguments against Islam are fairly standard. He begins by attempting to set his Muslim friend straight on the doctrine of the Trinity. To the author's credit, he understands both the Muslim objections to trinitarian doctrine and the Muslim view of Jesus. On other matters he repeats the usual Christian criticisms of Muhammad's militarism, his multiple marriages, and his inability to work miracles, all of them proofs, he claimed, that Muhammad was not a prophet. Al-Kindy charges that Muslim warriors were hypocrites because they joined a military effort for material gain and heavenly reward. He claims that the pilgrimage to Mecca is idolatrous, and that holy war is "the work of Satan."[7]

Dissatisfied with the al-Kindy piece, Peter wanted a new apology against Islam based on the primary works he now had in the Latin language. He proposed to Bernard of Clairvaux that Bernard should write it. When Bernard failed to do so, Peter wrote the apology himself and entitled it *A Summary of the Entire Heresy of the Saracens*. He placed it at the head of the Toledan Collection as an introduction.

With the help of his new sources, plus the *Chronicon* of Theophanes, Peter was able to write with a greater accuracy than his predecessors. He correctly described the Muslim objection to the Trinity, presented the Islamic view of Jesus, gave an accurate dating for Muhammad's life, and repudiated a popular view that Muhammad was somehow connected with the troublesome views of Nicholas, a "deacon" named in Acts 6 and according to Christian tradition an alleged arch-heretic. But errors continued. He claimed that Muhammad turned

---

[6] Ibid., 88.
[7] Ibid., 105.

to religion in order to save his failing political ambitions, a charge known to be false. He alleged that the Prophet approved gluttony, seemingly unaware that Muhammad's practice was the reverse, and he continued the view of John of Damascus that Muhammad was once a Nestorian Christian, the heretical group that favored the humanity of Jesus over against his divinity. And his dating of the conquests of Asia and Africa is incorrect.

Words of derogation continue. Muhammad was "a barbarian among barbarians," an "idolater among idolaters"[8] inspired by Satan. Of the Muslim writings published in his Toledo Collection, Peter says: "In no way could anyone of the human race, unless the devil were there helping, devise such fables as the writings which here follow."[9]

Peter could write in remarkably conciliatory tones, however. His *Book against the Sect or Heresy of the Saracens* opens with this beautiful and oft-quoted introduction:

> It seems strange, and perhaps it really is, that I, a man so very distant from you in place, speaking a different language, having a state of life separate from yours, a stranger to your customs and life, write from the far parts of the West to men who inhabit the lands of the East and South, and that I attack, by my utterance, those whom I have never seen, whom I shall perhaps never see. But I do not attack you, as some of us often do, by arms, but by words; not by force, but by reason; not in hatred, but in love.[10]

Peter did not eschew violence altogether, however. He supported the Crusades but added an interesting criticism: by failing to evangelize Muslims the crusaders squandered an opportunity to convert them. As he saw it, military and political goals were not enough to justify Crusade. As to the excesses of the Crusades, Peter wrote to King Louis VII: "*God does not will* [italics added] cold-blooded murder or outright slaughter."[11] The italicized words parody "God wills it," the cry of Pope Urban's audience at Clermont upon hearing his call to Crusade.

In his publishing project Peter had the two purposes in mind, namely, to discourage Christians from becoming Muslims, and to encourage Muslims to convert to Christianity. Both would turn out to be idle goals. To paraphrase Bernard Lewis's sage and insightful observation: in time Christians decided that preventing conversion to Islam was not necessary and that converting Muslims was impossible.[12]

In the end, Peter's assessment of Islam, like that of his predecessors, was entirely negative. Islam was a major threat to Christendom, militarily and reli-

---

[8] Ibid., 127.
[9] Ibid., 147-48.
[10] Ibid., 161.
[11] Ibid.
[12] Lewis, *Islam and the West,* 13.

giously, and like the earlier Christian heresies, it was the work of Satan. His attempt to refute the evils of Islam was more creditable than those of his predecessors, since he had the good judgment to collect authentic Islamic materials. That was a major step in the history of Christian–Muslim relations. But his work had value only to Christians. No Muslim would have been interested in his arguments since they were based on Christian presuppositions and could have only one result, the denigration of the Islamic faith. His sources were limited, but more adequate sources would probably not have changed the outcome of his judgment, since like the earlier writers on Islam, he proceeded from an absolute stance that credited the Christian religion with truth and Islam with falsehood. That prior commitment determined the final outcome. His work was a tour de force for the Christian community.

7

Christian Attempts to Convert Muslims

Peaceful Missions and Conversion by Force

The history of Europe's relations with Islam begins with an enigma: Did a Roman pontiff attempt, some twenty years after the death of Muhammad, to convert Muslims to Christianity?

—Benjamin Kedar[1]

The first evidence of reaching across the divide between the two religions in order to convert is a report of an Islamic approach to Christians. A Muslim source says that the Prophet Muhammad once sent letters and rich gifts to the emperor Heraclius of Byzantium, to the emperor of Persia, and to the rulers of Abyssinia and Egypt inviting them to profess Muhammad as a prophet, although the missives apparently did not ask for conversion to Islam as later letters would. The source for this account is quite late and of dubious reliability. If the view of some Western historians is correct that Muhammad intended his religion only for Arabs and not for the whole world, there is additional reason to doubt the report's authenticity. Others surmise that if the report is true, Muhammad may have been attempting to forestall any Meccan attempt to enlist the support of these rulers for the Meccan cause.

The next account tells of an approach in the other direction, namely, that Pope Martin I (r. 649-653) wrote certain Muslim authorities commending the Christian faith to them. The report appears in a document Pope Martin is said to have written after the emperor ordered him abducted to Constantinople, where he was charged with treason and exiled to the Crimea. Martin reigned in

---

[1] Benjamin Z. Kedar, *Crusade and Mission: European Approaches toward the Muslims* (Princeton: Princeton University Press, 1984), 3.

the period when the Byzantine emperor still had considerable power in Italy, and Martin's opposition to several of the policies of Emperor Constans II had brought the latter's ire down upon him. In a letter written after his abduction Martin, "intimates that his enemies accused him of dispatching to the Saracens letters, money, and 'a so-called *tomus* [instructing them] in what manner they should believe.'"[2] While at this distance such an overture might seem perfectly proper, the circumstances would make such a letter seem unlikely, since at the time the Byzantines were still smarting under the loss of much of their territory to early Arab expansion and a direct approach to the Arabs by the pope in Rome could have appeared to the Byzantine authorities as an act of betrayal. In any case Martin denied that he wrote the Arabs. Benjamin Kedar concludes that, uncertain as the report may be, one cannot rule out Martin's having written such a letter.[3] The report is interesting, even if clouded over with speculation. More important is Kedar's observation that "more than three centuries will pass before an attempt at Muslim conversion will again be alluded to in a European source, and more than five centuries before Europeans will launch a systematic missionary effort among the Muslims."[4]

This glaring lack of interest in converting Muslims occurred at the very time when European Christians were assiduously christianizing numerous other groups on their northern and northeastern borders. Interesting too is the fact that Charlemagne seems to have given no thought to a missionary effort among Muslims during his military campaign in Spain, even though he forced Saxons of northern Germany to convert and for a time considered liberating Iberian Christians from Saracen rule. Another case is Willibald, the famous missionary to the Germans, who in 720 traveled as a pilgrim to Jerusalem, where he doubtless encountered numerous Muslims, but his detailed account of the journey reveals no interest in converting them.

We can probably attribute this lack of Christian missionary interest to the severity of Islamic law, which can still be a factor in such activities. The *shari'a*, the legal code of Islam, mandates the death penalty for criticism of the Prophet and the Qur'an and orders the same penalty for Muslims who leave Islam for another religion. On both sides, that of the missionary and that of his prospective convert, the risk of missionary work was formidable, as it still is in some Muslim areas today.[5]

The harshness of these rules may offend modern sensibilities, but medieval Christendom adopted a similar policy from the twelfth century on, when Christian authorities named heresy a capital offense. The case of the Cathars, a

---

[2] Ibid. The words in brackets are Kedar's.

[3] Ibid., 3-4.

[4] Ibid., 4.

[5] Mission undertakings with Muslims in Christian lands may have been more successful. St. Ramón of Peñaforte claimed that a school he founded in twelfth-century Spain converted some ten thousand Muslims, many of them well educated (Norman Daniel, *Islam and the West: The Making of an Image* [Edinburgh: University Press, 1960], 120).

heretical group in thirteenth-century France, is a good illustration of these severe restrictions. Cathars were a large and powerful religious group whose numbers increased enough to take over entire towns. To put them down the Christian authorities attacked them in an internal Crusade. The historian Paul Johnson cites a contemporary report of the attack on Cathars in Beziers:

> In 1209, Arnold Aimery exulted to the Pope that the capture of Beziers had been "miraculous"; and that the crusaders had killed 15,000, "showing mercy neither to order, nor age nor sex." Prisoners were mutilated, blinded, dragged at the hooves of horses and used for target practice.[6]

Violent actions like this were based on the principle just discussed, that defection from the true faith was punishable by death. These constraints were (and sometimes are) in settings where the democratic principles of human rights and equality before the law that are familiar and fundamental to Western societies were (and sometimes are now) not in effect.

THE MENDICANT ORDERS: FRANCISCANS AND DOMINICANS

Organized missionary activity among Muslims began with the two great mendicant orders, the Franciscans and the Dominicans. Founded in the early thirteenth century, both worked for the conversion of Jews and Muslims in Spain, North Africa, and the Holy Land. Dominicans focused on training missionary monks and established several schools for the study of Arabic, thereby implementing Peter the Venerable's century-old vision of preaching to Muslims, although they advocated continuing the Crusades alongside preaching.

ST. FRANCIS OF ASSISI

St. Francis of Assisi's short trip to Egypt is perhaps the best known of these missionary efforts. In 1219 the saint traveled there to witness to the sultan al-Kamil, who was engaged in fighting the crusaders of the Fifth Crusade, a journey he had attempted twice before. In doing so Francis was following in the steps of Jacques of Vitry, who, as bishop of Acre, had begun preaching to Muslims in 1217 and, like Francis, thought that the goal of Christians should be to reach the whole world for the gospel.

Details of Francis's meeting with the sultan are few. It is reported that he crossed over enemy lines, apparently during a pause in the fighting while proposals from the sultan were under consideration in the Christian camp. He was received warmly, delivered his message, and returned safely. One account says

---

[6] Paul Johnson, *A History of Christianity* (New York: Atheneum, 1980), 252.

that the sultan told Francis that Christians should abstain from invading Saracen lands since they had been taught by their God not to return evil for evil.

Although Francis was unsuccessful in gaining converts in the sultan's camp,[7] there are other accounts of conversions to Christianity (and also of some conversions to Islam). Indeed, reports from Damietta, Egypt, indicate a considerable interest among those crusaders in converting Muslims. Francis's own effort became an oft-repeated subject in artistic depictions of the saint, from Giotto on. The saint's compatriot in founding mendicant orders, St. Dominic, also planned to preach to Muslims, but he died before he was able to do that.

Francis is associated also with the desire for martyrdom in missionary work, a theme he presented in the first draft of his *Rule* for the Franciscan Order, in which he supported martyrdom with quotations from the Gospels. In the years 1219-1220 five Franciscan friars followed his counsel. They vigorously criticized Muhammad and Islam, first in Muslim Seville and then in Morocco. Four friars did the same in Jerusalem in 1391, a Muslim city at the time—all nine gained martyrdom. It is notable that Islamic authorities were slow to administer the sentence in a few of these cases and apparently tried to discourage their missionary visitors from forcing the issue. Both groups of friars, like the earlier martyrs of Cordoba, quoted scripture before the authorities, in this case Mark 16:15-16. The Marcan text, after advocating preaching "to every creature," concludes: "he that believeth not shall be damned."[8] Benjamin Kedar wonders if the friars, knowing that the possibility of conversion was small, might have intended to secure the condemnation of their Muslim hearers if their preaching failed to bring conversions.[9]

WILLIAM OF TRIPOLI

William of Tripoli, a thirteenth-century Dominican based in a monastery in Acre, worked in both the West and the East and authored the valuable *Tract on the Standing of the Saracens and of the False Prophet Muhammad, and of Their Law and Faith*. He seems to have known Arabic well enough to read the Qur'an in the original, as well as Arabic-language commentaries on the text, and was one of the few non-Arab Christians to appreciate the moving style of the Qur'an's language. His biographical accounts of Muhammad parallel the older ones, though he lessens considerably the fabulous and imaginative. He noted instances where Christianity and Islam agreed, citing passages on Jesus and

---

[7] The pious and legendary *Little Flowers of St. Francis* provides a different ending to the story. Here the sultan, acknowledging that his conversion would bring his execution along with that of Francis and his company, says he will convert later. Francis promises to send two friars to baptize him, and, after Francis dies, they arrive and baptize the converted sultan just before his death (*The Little Flowers of St. Francis and Other Franciscan Writings,* trans. Serge Hughes [New York: New American Library, 1964], 91-92 [chapter 24]).

[8] King James Version.

[9] Kedar, *Crusade and Mission,* 126.

Mary from the Qur'an and the *hadith,* quoting from the Qur'an at length and quite accurately. He seems to have once appeared before Pope Urban IV in 1263 to plead for help for the crusaders in Palestine. Believing that the Muslims were about to convert to the Christian faith, he felt that more fighting was not necessary.

RICOLDO OF MONTE CROCE

The most prominent of the mendicant missionaries was Ricoldo from Monte Croce in Tuscany (d. 1320), also a Dominican. His laudatory description of Islamic morals and behavior was noted earlier. A significant author on Islam, he introduced his *Refutation of the Law Set Down by Muhammad for the Saracens* with this description of Muhammad:

> During the time of the Emperor Heraclius there came forth a man named Muhammad—a devil and a first-born child of Satan he was—[who stood] against the truth and against the Christian church, [a man] drowning in carnal indecency who dealt in [the] black arts. With the prompting and help of him who is a liar and the father of all lies, he put forth a law full of lies and untruths that appeared as though it had been spoken by the very mouth of God. He named that book the Alcoran [Qur'an], that is, the Summa or Collection of the divine commands.[10]

Ricoldo joined the Dominican Order in 1267 in the Cloister of St. Maria Novella in Florence. A gifted preacher of rather independent stripe, he embarked on a journey to the Middle East shortly after 1280, and for some two decades he traveled in Egypt, Palestine, and Iraq with the twin purposes of learning about Islam and converting Muslims. He succeeded in the first goal, but not in the second. His *Itinerarium*, the report on his travels, was one of the more important books on Islam created in the medieval West.

He began by visiting the Holy Land, where he saw many sacred sites: the house in Cana where Jesus turned water into wine, the cave where Joseph's brothers hid him before selling him to the Midianites, the place of the Annunciation to Mary, and so on. From there he went north across Syria, and then east through Mesopotamia, then into Persia, returning finally to Baghdad. The once-great capital was ruled by Mongols and in decline from its former glory, but it was still a major center of Muslim learning. While in Baghdad, Ricoldo heard of the fall of Acre and the loss of its Dominican monastery. The event shook Ricoldo deeply and he wrote about the tragedy with considerable feeling.

Ricoldo's arguments resemble earlier ones. The Qur'an is a conglomeration of earlier heresies on the Trinity and the incarnation. The Qur'an cannot be

---

[10] My translation of Martin Luther's German rendering of Ricoldo's *Refutation of the Alcoran* (*Confutatio Alcorani*) (*D. Martin Luthers Werke, Kritische Gesamtausgabe,* vol. 53 [Weimar: Hermann Böhlaus Nachfolger, 1920], 276). Luther calls him "Richard."

God's law, since it is confirmed by neither Old or New Testament. One new theme appears, namely, the Muslim claim that Jesus' promise in John 15:26 to send the Paraclete can be read as a prediction of Muhammad. Based on a statement in Qur'an 61:6, Islamic tradition holds that the term *paraklētos* in the Gospel of John is a Greek term that mistakenly represents what Jesus really said and that his original word is closely related to the name Muhammad.[11] This is an instance of the corruption that Muslim tradition claims has entered into the Christian text. Without going into these details, Ricoldo rejects the argument. The Qur'an's style and poetic power are no evidence of divine inspiration, he says, since God did not use those means to communicate his revelation. In fact, the Qu'ran is self-contradictory, teaching in one place that Jews and Christians can be reckoned as just, but in another saying they can be justified only if they follow Qur'anic law. Muhammad worked no miracles and appealed to the sword instead. Muhammad's unworthy lifestyle, the rituals of Islam, and Islamic ideas of paradise all deny a divine origin of the religion. Muhammad is not the seal of the prophets, nor is Mary a daughter of Abraham or a sister of Aaron—references that are read metaphorically in Islam. Nor does God need a wife in order to have a son. As to the Qur'an, it offers a law of murder and death. Even the nonchronological order of the *suras* in the Qur'an suggests that the book is not from God. (Save for the first, the *suras* are arranged by order of length from longer to shorter.) Muhammad is the forerunner of the Antichrist, and the author of the Qur'an is not God but the devil. Muhammad, an arrogant, ignorant, and illiterate man, sought to lord himself over the Arabs and then claimed that his epilepsy was the way God gave the divine revelations to him. Ricoldo also criticized the story of Muhammad's night journey to the throne of God. All of these objections belong to the standard medieval canon of criticisms of Islam.

In Ricoldo's travelogue, the *Itinerarium*, he repeated his arguments that the doctrines of the Qur'an are Christian heresy, but, as already noted, he praised Muslim piety and morals.

> Who will not be astounded, if he carefully considers how great is the concern of these very Muslims for study, their devotion in prayer, their pity for the poor, their reverence for the name of God and the prophets and the Holy Places, their sobriety in manners, their hospitality to strangers, their harmony and love for each other?[12]

Of the many writers on Islam in the Middle Ages, he was one of the few who got to know Muslims by living in an Islamic society, an experience that caused

---

[11] "The classic explanation by some Muslims of this foretelling of Muhammad by Jesus is that Ahmad = Perikleitos = Parakletos (and Ahmad, of course, is said to equal Muhammad)" (Daniel, *Islam and the West,* 335 n. 18; also Abdallah Yusuf Ali, *The Holy Qur'ān: Text, Translation and Commentary* [Brentwood, Md.: Amana Corp., 1983], 1540 n. 5438).

[12] Daniel, *Islam and the West,* 196.

his otherwise narrow bigotry to moderate somewhat. Save for Spanish cities like Toledo and the Norman kingdom of Sicily, lengthy personal contact with the followers of Islam was a factor missing from Christian–Islamic relations, and would continue to be for centuries.

THE MASTER: RAYMOND LULL

The most remarkable of the medieval missionary advocates and missioners was Raymond Lull (ca. 1233-1315), a poet, philosopher, theologian, and mystic from Majorca, and third-order Franciscan, that is, one who lived in the world without the full vows of the Franciscan Order. In the course of his career his thoughts and proposals on relating to Islam ran the entire gamut of medieval Christian positions, from peaceful witnessing, to apologetic and debate, to military Crusade. Benjamin Kedar wryly observes, "his may well be the most effective presentations of *most* of the opinions then current"[13] (italics added). Lull authored some two hundred books and tracts in three different languages— Latin, Catalan, and Arabic—established a school for missionaries, attempted a visit to the Egyptian sultan, and went to North Africa three times, where he died. His advocacy of a peaceful approach to Islam through preaching was passionate, and he recognized that such preaching could result in martyrdom.

> I see many knights who go to the Holy Land beyond the sea, wanting to conquer it by force of arms, and in the end they are all brought to naught without attaining their aim. Therefore, it seems to me O Lord, that the conquest of that Holy Land should not be done but in the manner in which You and Your apostles have conquered it: by love and prayers and the shedding of tears and blood.
>
> As it seems, O Lord, that the Holy Sepulcher and the Holy Land beyond the sea should preferably be conquered by preaching rather than by force of arms, the holy monk-knights should go forward, O Lord, buttress themselves with the sign of the cross, fill themselves with the grace of the Holy Spirit, and go preach to the infidels the truth of Your Passion, and shed for Your love all the water of their eyes and all the blood of their bodies, just as You have done out of love for them![14]

Lull was not the first to plead for a peaceful approach to Saracens, nor the first to advocate martyrdom, but his arguments were the most eloquent. In the same work, however, Lull recognized that force may sometimes be necessary to bring about conversions, accepting the principle that preaching is not the only way. At the Council of Vienne (1311-1312) he successfully proposed that the authorities establish schools of language for training in Arabic, create an order of

---

[13] Kedar, *Crusade and Mission*, 190.
[14] Ibid., 190-91.

Christian knights to conduct Crusade, and commission the writing of polemical works to refute the errors of the infidels.

In one of his works, Lull argued, as had Pope Innocent IV before him, that the pope must send well-trained preachers, fluent in the language of their hearers, but if the infidels resist preaching, Christian authorities should wage war against them to make them more amenable to the words of the gospel. The argument that the resistance of infidels to preaching was a legitimate basis for war was common among theorists of Christian warfare. Its similarity to the Islamic justification for *jihad* is striking.

In yet another work, a novel, Lull shifted his view. In his imagined story, an emissary of the sultan approaches the pope and argues that it is odd that the pope, a representative of Jesus, a man of peace, should choose to follow the way of the Prophet in using arms against the Holy Land instead of simple preaching. In his story, the pope implements this peaceful approach, but when the hearers do not heed, he turns to force, the policy of the popes Gregory IX and Innocent IV. Lull seems to return again and again to the justification of Crusade in the service of missions. While in his eighties, Lull set out for Tunis, in Kedar's colorful words, to "hurl at the Saracens the not-inconsiderable force of his intellect," and perhaps to seek martyrdom.[15] He died on that journey but whether in martyrdom is unknown.

CONVERSION BY FORCE OF ARMS

Nowhere did the fusion of a conviction of absolute truth with the use of absolute power find a clearer manifestation than in the policies of restriction and, finally, exclusion and threat of death that were placed upon Jews and Muslims from the thirteenth century on. Initially the purpose was to bring about the conversion of these non-Christians. When this course was not successful, the authorities moved to more extreme measures, including killing.

Conversions to Christianity were compelled earlier in Charlemagne's campaign against the Saxons of northern Germany, a campaign that proved successful, at least on the surface. A second case is in *The Song of Roland*, discussed earlier, which tells of Charlemagne's ordering Muslims to convert, but that report, written in the twelfth century, is spurious, not factual. But twelfth-century accounts are not all imagination, for that was when the church itself began calling for force to bring pagans and infidels into the faith. The great Bernard of Clairvaux is an example. When Christian forces moved against the Wends, a Slavic people in northeastern Europe, Bernard urged the Christian warriors to take up the cross and, in words encountered earlier, "utterly annihilate or surely convert" the pagans, fighting "until, God helping, either that [pagan] rite itself or that nation be annihilated."[16] Bernard's contemporary,

---

[15] Ibid., 199.
[16] Ibid., 70.

Pope Eugene III, exhorted the forces of his day to a similar end, warning them not to allow the Wends to remain in their paganism in exchange for bribes (an interesting problem in itself).

As Crusade followed Crusade, interest in converting Muslims of the Holy Land increased until by the Fifth Crusade in the 1200s conversion was said to be the main purpose. But in actual fact, the practice of conversion by force was not implemented, even though Christians did from time to time mount preaching efforts. Some conversions resulted, especially among the slaves of Christians for whom converting could be especially attractive since Christian baptism could make them eligible for emancipation—Christians were not allowed to hold other Christians as slaves. In fact, the number of slaves seeking conversion in the crusading kingdom became so large that their Christian masters finally instituted measures to limit the practice. Here and there a few free Muslims in the Holy Land converted on their own, but by and large, the pattern under the crusaders was the same as elsewhere: Muslims chose to keep to Islam.

As the Reconquest of Spain proceeded and the Crusades achieved their early successes, more and more Muslims came under Christian rule. Legislation against Muslims began to appear in greater frequency, and not against Muslims alone but against Jews as well. The Lateran councils of 1179 and 1215 increased the restrictions on contacts between Christians and their Jewish and Islamic neighbors: trading with Jews and Muslims, eating with them, and caring for their children were all prohibited. Pope Gregory IX's advocacy of force for the conversion of Muslims was mentioned earlier. In 1227 Gregory ordered distinctive dress for non-Christians, forbade the Muslim public call to prayer, and prohibited Jews and Muslims from appearing on the streets during Christian festivals. Jews were expelled from England in 1290 and from France in 1394. By 1301 Charles of Anjou, king of France, had expelled the Muslims from Sicily, and in 1492 King Ferdinand and Queen Isabella did the same for Jews in their land, and then followed with an order for the expulsion of Muslims in 1502, although the banishment of virtually all Muslims from Spain did not occur until 1609. Not all of Europe acted this severely toward non-Christians, and in the long run Jews were to suffer more than Muslims since there were more of them and they lived all over Europe. But the pattern was clear—non-Christians lived within medieval Christendom at the pleasure of Christians, always as second-class citizens and often as a persecuted minority.

8

Bridges from Christendom to Islam

Examples of Cooperation

At Perpignan in the far south of France two chapels . . . face the entrance to the courtyard of the Kings of Majorca. [Around two alcoves in one runs an abstract design.] It is the writing of another language, another world, turned by the ignorant into a meaningless combination of horizontal and vertical blocks. The language is Arabic, and the words, . . . probably contained the crucial phrase: la ilah illa 'llah wa Muhammad rasul Allah— "There is no god but God, and Muhammad is the Messenger of God."
—Michael Brett[1]

In the midst of the continual controversy and struggle that Christendom carried on with Islam, there are several instances of bridges across the chasm that separated the two civilizations. Although few in number, and shaky and impermanent in character, they are of considerable importance. The most significant were in Spain and in the Norman kingdom of Sicily and southern Italy. Both flourished only briefly, but they imparted a value far beyond their years.

THE PHILOSOPHERS AND ISLAM

The translating work commissioned by Peter the Venerable in Spain was significant but nothing like the work in the century and a half that followed, when scholar-translators turned into Latin much of the thought and knowledge of the classical world long lost to the West. Save for some few texts preserved in Ireland, the rich manuscript collections of Western libraries had been destroyed in

---

[1] Malcolm Billings, *The Cross and the Crescent: A History of the Crusades* (New York: Sterling Publishing Co., 1987), 232.

the barbarian invasions. But now, in the twelfth and thirteenth centuries, primarily in the Spanish cities of Toledo and Cordoba, and in Sicily, Jewish, Christian, and Muslim scholars brought to the Latin-speaking world philosophy, science, geography, medical treatises, astronomical tables, and mathematics the West had not seen for centuries. This material from ancient Greece was still alive in the Byzantine world, and much of it had been translated into Syriac and Arabic in Baghdad and elsewhere, and now Muslims began sharing these works with Jews and Christians in remarkable settings of understanding and trust. Henri Daniel-Rops remarks, "It was mainly due to Arabian influence that Greek thought was rediscovered."[2] Effects of these materials can be traced in virtually every area of intellectual activity, with the result that medieval Europe exploded in a new burst of knowledge and learning. Montgomery Watt, noting how the disparagement of Islam has prompted Westerners to ignore this contribution to Europe observed: "Today an important task for us as western Europeans, as we move into the era of the one world, is to correct this false emphasis [on Europe's direct dependence on Greece and Rome] and to acknowledge fully our debt to the Arabic and Islamic world."[3] Muslims were bringing intellectual resources to Europe that would fire the imaginations of Western scholars and thinkers. In a comment of rather stark grimness, Karen Armstrong observes that this cooperative intellectual undertaking in the West took place while Christian crusaders "were butchering Muslims in the Near East."[4] The West could be positively schizophrenic in its treatment of Muslims.

A CONVERT FROM JUDAISM

Pedro de Alfonso, the Christian convert from Judaism named earlier, once observed that he had "been nurtured among the Muslims."[5] In the light of all the negative, derogatory things Christians had been saying about Islam, his statement is noteworthy. Alfonso lived in Spain at a time when Muslims, Jews, and Christians conversed, debated, and studied with one another, relatively free of the religious coercion and bitterness that came later. His was the age of the great Muslim philosopher Averroës (ibn Rushd, 1126-1198) and the famous Jewish thinker Moses Maimonides (1135-1204). Averroës lived and taught in Cordoba and then Seville. Maimonides was born in Cordoba but fled to

---

[2] Henri Daniel-Rops, *Cathedral and Crusade: Studies of the Medieval Church, 1050-1350,* vol. 2, trans. John Warrington (Garden City, N.Y.: Doubleday, 1963), 22.

[3] William Montgomery Watt, *The Influence of Islam on Medieval Europe,* Islamic Surveys 9 (Edinburgh: University Press, 1972), 84.

[4] Karen Armstrong, *Muhammad: A Biography of the Prophet* (San Francisco: HarperSanFrancisco, 1992), 29.

[5] Quoted by Thomas E. Burman, "'Tathlîth al-waḥdânîyah' and the Twelfth-Century Andalusian-Christian Approach to Islam," in *Medieval Christian Perceptions of Islam: A Book of Essays,* Garland Medieval Case Books 10, Garland Reference Library of the Humanities 1768 (New York and London: Garland, 1996), 14.

Morocco to escape persecution and later taught in Cairo. Christian philosophers, among them Albert the Great, called the Master of Cologne, and Thomas Aquinas at the University of Paris, drew from this deep well of philosophical knowledge and inquiry, though both wrote to criticize Averroës's philosophical ideas.[6]

Alfonso developed a defense of the Christian doctrine of the Trinity for Muslims, arguing that the belief could make sense even in Islamic theology. Muslim theologians had long distinguished elements that were essential to the character of God from elements that were not essential. Islam also speaks of the ninety-nine names of God, each of which identifies a quality of the deity. Alfonso claimed that these ninety-nine could be reduced to three, which three he identified as power, knowledge, and will, equating these in turn with the three persons of the Trinity. The medieval theologians Peter Abelard, Hugh of St. Victor, and Thomas Aquinas later used the same language. One can be certain that Alfonso convinced no Muslims with his argument, but he represents an attempt to conceive a synthesis and an agreement rather than just a fight. The synthesis was on Christian terms, of course, a pattern to be repeated by Nicholas of Cusa.

THOMAS AQUINAS

Of the Christian scholars and theologians who used these newly translated texts, the greatest was St. Thomas Aquinas (ca. 1225-1274), who adopted the philosophy of Aristotle in his explanation of Christian theology. He represented engagement with Islam in two ways. First, in developing his theology he drew upon the Islamic philosophers themselves, as well as on the translations of Aristotle. Second, he wrote about Islam, joining the lengthening tradition of Christian writers arguing against it.

Trained first at the new University of Naples established by the emperor Frederick II, Aquinas not only read Aristotle but owed an especially large debt to Averroës, the greatest of the Muslim Aristotelians. In Averroës, Aquinas found a philosopher who offered new and refreshing insights into the great philosophical and religious themes. Here, in a subtle but direct way, elements from Islam entered Christian theology, not as doctrines or specific beliefs but as philosophical ideas and principles that traced back to the Greek master, Aristotle. Thomas's great exposition of the Christian faith, his *Summa theologiae,* is built in great part with those philosophical principles.

Aquinas wrote on Islam in his *Summary against the Gentiles* and his *Reasons of Faith against the Saracens, Greeks, and Armenians.* The *Summary*

---

[6] Karen Armstrong notes how revered were ibn Rushd (Averroës) and the other great Muslim philosopher, ibn Sina (Avicenna), in the Middle Ages and how despised Muhammad was. Dante placed the two Islamic philosophers in Limbo with the worthies of the classical world, but Muhammad in the Eighth Circle of Hell with Christian schismatics (*Muhammad,* 29).

against the Gentiles (literally "nations," probably meaning Muslims) is said to have been written at the urging of an early-twelfth-century canon lawyer and advocate of missions Ramón of Peñaforte. Anton Pegis, a modern editor of Aquinas, says that this work was "a manual of Christian doctrine written for the use of missionaries,"[7] though a reader of the book will recognize quickly that the Angelic Doctor, as he was later called, had missionaries of a quite sophisticated intellectual level in mind. His *Reasons of Faith*, composed in the 1260s at the request of a cantor in Antioch, Syria, was the only polemical work composed by a member of a mendicant order for Latins living in the crusader East. An indication of the value of these works is seen in the fact that both were translated into Greek by Demetrios Cydones, a Greek convert to the Catholic Church who also translated Ricoldo's *Refutation* into Greek.

Although Aquinas used the traditional Christian arguments against Islam (its alleged violence and sexual license, and Muhammad's lack of miracles), the fundamental problem he saw with Islam was its lack of authority, an authority that miracles could have provided. Beyond that premise most of Thomas's arguments are philosophical. One hears little debate over classical Christian and Muslim doctrines. In one matter Aquinas is distinctive, namely, the question of the Christian scriptures, where he allowed Muslims some flexibility of interpretation: Norman Daniel observes that he was the single exception to the medieval practice of insisting that Muslims accept at face value the witness of Christian scripture.[8]

Aquinas wrote for missionaries working with Muslims who lived under Christian rule, and he rejected the view that the use of force was appropriate for converting Muslims. Force could be used to restrain the attacks of infidels on the Christian faith, but not to coerce faith, "because to believe is a matter of the will."[9] Educated Christian leaders were the best means of defending against error and mounting missionary efforts. Aquinas said, however, that the case of heretics and apostates was different: having once professed faith, they may be coerced, "that they may fulfill what they have promised, and hold what they at one time received."[10]

The classical and Islamic works that Aquinas and other Western thinkers and scholars acquired came to them because of the climate of trust and communication that existed for a time in Spain and Sicily. But that climate did not hold. Further, by the middle of the thirteenth century Western scholars began getting materials directly from the Byzantine Christians, and the transmission of classical learning from Arabs to Latins was no longer necessary. By then the

---

[7] Anton Pegis, ed., *Basic Writings of Saint Thomas Aquinas,* vol. 1 (New York: Random House, 1944), xlix.

[8] Norman Daniel, *Islam and the West: The Making of an Image* (Edinburgh: University Press, 1960), 55, and 336 n. 25.

[9] James Waltz, "Muhammad and the Muslims in St. Thomas Aquinas," *The Muslim World* 66, no. 2 (April 1976): 92.

[10] Ibid.

Reconquest of Spain was well under way, and both clerical and secular authorities were beginning to enforce Christian norms on non-Christians more strenuously. The earlier pattern of communication among the several religions began to wane, against the time two centuries later when the Christian confession would be mandated in Spain for both Jews and Muslims. Indeed, the opportunity for collaboration had already begun to end when Pope Gregory IX promulgated a policy of forced conversion of Muslims.

SICILY AND SOUTHERN ITALY:
COOPERATION AND FORCED CONVERSION

The work of translation in the Norman kingdom was not as extensive as in Spain, but it was significant. More distinctive, however, was the Norman court, with its open intercourse among Jewish, Christian, and Islamic scholars. The period was brief, but no other instance of communication among these three traditions equals it.

As early as 652 Arab forces landed in Sicily, though they did not fully occupy the island until 831. From Sicily, Arab troops ventured into Italy on several occasions and in 846 briefly reached the outskirts of Rome. For the better part of two centuries, southern Europe experienced repeated attacks from Arabs, thereby contributing to the Western attitudes of intolerance toward Islam. Until the Norman conquest of the island in the eleventh century, Islamic rule prevailed with its standard pattern of controlled toleration of Christians and Jews.

When Sicily came under Norman rule in the eleventh century, the initial policy of the new Christian rulers was to eliminate Islam. The twelfth-century Norman court operated somewhat differently, however, and opened itself to contact with Jews and Muslims. Count Roger I, who completed the Norman conquest, allowed Muslims to live as an autonomous community with freedom of worship, as did his son, Roger II. The latter dressed like an Arab and was called by his critics "a half-heathen king." In Roger II's court worked abu-Abdullah Muhammad ibn-Muhammad al-Idrisi, the most distinguished cartographer and geographer of the time, a Hispano-Arab Muslim, who constructed for his monarch "a celestial sphere and a disk-shaped map of the world, both in silver."[11] On the other hand, this same Roger II ordered an invasion of North Africa and for a time ruled an area from Tripoli to Tunis. His army in Italy included Arab warriors. His grandson, Frederick II, sometime emperor of the Holy Roman Empire, inherited the Kingdom of the Two Sicilies, which included the island of Sicily proper and southern Italy. Like his grandfather before him, Frederick had an interest in science and employed the skills of Arab scientists to help him pursue the study of natural history. A patron of Arab

---

[11] Philip K. Hitti, *The Arabs: A Short History,* 5th rev. printing (Chicago: Henry Regnery Co., 1949), 209.

scholarship and himself fluent in Arabic, he had numerous manuscripts translated from Arabic into Latin. Perhaps his greatest monument is the University of Naples, which he established in 1224, the first university in Europe founded with a definite charter.

The Norman court was a meeting place for Latin, Greek, and Arabic, as scholars versed in these languages worked together in a setting marked by freedom and respect. All three languages were spoken in the Norman court, which for a time served as a bridge over which Muslim and Christian scholarship traveled with ease, and Jewish scholarship as well.

The policy of toleration that Muslims enjoyed under the Normans was confined largely to the court. The Muslim population at large often had to conform to strict controls, and occasionally groups were expelled when they refused to convert to Christianity. Pressure for conformity increased during Frederick's reign when in 1233 Pope Gregory IX instituted his program of forced conversion of Muslims. Two factors lay behind the pope's policy: the problem of controlling the Muslim population in the newly reconquered Christian territory in Spain, and Pope Gregory's need to implement the authority that popes had begun to claim over secular rulers. In both cases ecclesiastical control over the people of Western Europe was tightened. The policy brought Frederick and Gregory into conflict over the emperor's treatment of the Muslim inhabitants of Sicily.

When the island fell to the Normans, the population of perhaps one-half million was evenly divided between Arabic-speaking Muslims and Greek Christians, but within a few years the Norman program of "conversion, persecution, and emigration had reduced the Muslim population by about ninety percent."[12] In order to resolve an internal disturbance, Frederick resettled a group of Muslims to Lucera, a relatively unpopulated site in Italy where they would be isolated and easier to control, though much nearer to Rome. He granted them religious freedom and a degree of self-government in return for their labor in making the once-vacant land productive, an economic benefit for both Muslims and the emperor. In the process the Arabs apparently occupied some of the unused Christian churches—or so Pope Gregory claimed, charging dire sacrilege. As a Christian ruler, Frederick had sworn numerous oaths to the pope not only to uphold the church but to protect it and its members. He was duty-bound to prevent occurrences such as violation of the churches, and failure to do so was a violation of the "right order of Christendom."[13] As the conflict intensified, the pope began to threaten Frederick with excommunication. The practical-minded Frederick saw his action in Lucera as justified by his own authority as emperor and the demands of the situation. But the pope saw Frederick's behavior as defiance of the divine authority of the papacy.

In 1233, not ten years after the resettlement of Frederick's Muslims, Gregory

---

[12] Phillip Lomax, "Frederick II, His Saracens, and the Papacy," in *Medieval Christian Perceptions of Islam*, ed. Tolan, 177.

[13] Ibid.

ordered the emperor "to terrorize his Saracens into conversion."[14] While Pope Gregory's stated purpose may have been flawed, his rhetorical language was not. Warning Frederick of his impending excommunication, Pope Gregory wrote:

> Behold the ramparts of Babylon are built from the ruins of Jerusalem and schools for the sons of Hagar from the stones of Zion. Buildings in which the divine name is honored are forced to become places where the damnable Muhammad is adored. . . . [T]he flocks of the faithful depart from the Lord's fold, and the Hebrews are so oppressed by the Egyptians that it is as though they are subject to their rule.[15]

Frederick claimed that the report about the destruction of Christian churches was a "persistent fable." Gregory's fear in this situation was considerable. Not only had Frederick established an infidel Muslim colony virtually at the door of Rome itself (the pope knew well of the earlier Arab invasions of Italy), but Frederick's independence threatened the papal claims to authority over Christendom. Ultimately the pope excommunicated him twice, and it was with Frederick that charges of corruption in the papacy and the call for its reform began.

Pope Gregory claimed that the emperor, in addition to denying the virgin birth and other cherished Christian doctrines, had remarked that Moses, Jesus, and Muhammad were all "tricksters [who] cunningly and deceitfully seduced the whole people of their own times, in order to dominate the world."[16] Perhaps Frederick said this, perhaps not, but given the acrimony that existed between the two, one tends to discount the charge.

Frederick initiated several attempts at conversion of Muslims, with modest success, and probably thought that the relatively small Islamic population in Lucera would eventually move into the Christian faith, but he did not force them to do so. The Muslims did not convert, however, even after Frederick's death.

On Pope Gregory's orders, Frederick reluctantly led the Sixth Crusade to the Holy Land and negotiated the return of Jerusalem into Christian hands in 1229, but the surrender was almost a fluke. When Frederick arrived in Palestine, he found that Jerusalem had no city walls. Al-Mu'azzam Isa, sultan of Damascus, who made the Holy City his residence for a time, feared that crusaders would retake the city and massacre its inhabitants once again and reasoned that if the city were made defenseless, there would be no violence. Thus he ordered the walls torn down, leaving the city helpless. The Muslim population departed, knowing they could not be defended if attacked, and the city was reduced to little more than a village.

Meanwhile, al-Kamil, the sultan of Egypt, had a falling out with al-

---

[14] Ibid., 184.

[15] Ibid., 185-86.

[16] Norman Daniel, *The Arabs and Mediaeval Europe* (London: Longman, 1975), 160.

Mu'azzam and, knowing he could not defend the city, was ready to give it up. When Frederick suggested that he do just that, the sultan agreed. On February 29, 1229, the two princes signed a treaty at Jaffa.

> There would be a truce for ten years; the Christians would take back Jerusalem, Bethlehem, and Nazareth, but Frederick promised not to rebuild the walls of Jerusalem. The Jews would have to leave the city, but the Muslims would retain the Haram [the ancient Temple Mount]. Islamic worship would continue there without hindrance and the Muslim insignia be displayed.[17]

The city remained in Christian hands until 1244, when it was captured and devastated by an army of Khwarazmian Turks fleeing the Mongol invasion of their lands in Central Asia.

Both Christians and Muslims were irate over the truce between al-Kamil and Frederick, Muslims because the city had been surrendered to Christians without a fight, Christians because they considered it blasphemy to make a treaty with infidels. Frederick had achieved a Pyrrhic victory at best. Nonetheless, he named himself king of Jerusalem. When he could get no priest to crown him because he was excommunicated, he entered the Church of the Holy Sepulcher and placed a crown upon his head himself. His behavior at the Temple Mount, the Islamic Holy Sanctuary, further antagonized the crusaders. He beat a priest whom he saw carrying a Bible there, and when he learned that the *muezzin* had been ordered not to announce the Muslim calls to prayer, he ordered them reinstated. His critics said that his conduct was inappropriate for a Christian prince, and crusaders at Acre even tried to murder him. Frederick had negotiated a truce, but the agreement did little more than reveal the bitterness on both sides. By this time it was impossible for amicable and peaceful relations to develop between Christians and Muslims in the Holy Land.

Frederick was a complex man, a mix of sheer practicality, imaginative foresight, and considerable independence, and stories of his free-wheeling behavior abound, although a goodly portion of them are probably exaggerations, if not outright legends. In contrast to Pope Gregory, who thought in terms of Western Europe and Christendom and evaluated leaders according to their orientation toward Christianity with the pope as its head, Frederick looked toward the world of the Mediterranean and treated other rulers in a more evenhanded way. Gregory expected his subjects to act in terms of the Christian ideology and papal alliances. Frederick behaved practically, relatively free of ideology. The openness that Frederick sometimes exhibited was a pattern that was not to last. The forces of exclusivism and oppression were to increase.

---

[17] Karen Armstrong, *Jerusalem: One City, Three Faiths* (New York: Alfred A. Knopf, 1996), 302.

9

The Renaissance

Thoughts of Rapprochement and Dialogue

You and we . . . believe in and confess one God, admittedly in a different way, and daily praise and venerate him, the creator of worlds and ruler of this world.

—Pope Gregory VII to the Hammadid ruler
Nasir ibn 'Alnas, ca. 1076[1]

Yet all, Christians, Jews and Muslims, adore one God, Creator of heaven and Earth, and all believe that they will be saved without doubt.

—Unknown medieval Christian author[2]

An important shift in attitude toward Islam came in the Renaissance. Three fifteenth-century authors—a Spanish Franciscan named John of Segovia, Pope Pius II, and Nicholas of Cusa, a bishop and cardinal of the church—and one sixteenth-century writer, Theodore Bibliander, a Protestant theologian in Zurich, developed views that recognized legitimate religious values in Islam. Criticism remained, but for the first time Christians thought of formal discussions with Muslims for the purpose of finding common ground between the two religions.

While these theologians were contemplating their lofty thoughts, Christendom's military situation was worsening, as Islamic armies moved deeper and deeper into eastern Europe. The Turkish victory over the Serbs at Kosovo (at the "Field of the Blackbirds") in 1389 annihilated Serbian nobility and secured Ottoman control of the Balkans, and in 1453 Turkish forces conquered the East-

---

[1] Norman Daniel, *The Arabs and Mediaeval Europe* (London: Longman, 1975), 251. The pope cites John 1:9, 1 Timothy 2:4, and Qur'an 1:1. Gregory says not only that they believe in the one God, but that God has "inspired" the king's heart and "illuminated" his mind.

[2] Norman Daniel, *Islam and the West: The Making of an Image* (Edinburgh: University Press, 1960), 43.

ern capital, Constantinople, attacking from both north and south, by land and by sea. Belgrade fell in 1518 and Hungary in 1526. When Bibliander published his impressive collection of materials on Islam in 1543, only fourteen years had passed since the army of Suleiman the Magnificent had besieged Vienna, threatening the very heartland of Europe. Suleiman withdrew from Vienna— winter was approaching and his supply lines were overextended—but Turkish armies returned later, and both their land and sea forces remained a threat to western Europe for over a century.[3]

Meanwhile, the internal life of western Europe was changing rapidly: the Renaissance recovery of the literary treasures of Greece and Rome, sea voyages, first down the coast of Africa, then to the Americas, and then to India, the astronomical theories of Copernicus, the changes brought by the Protestant Reformation. These developments and more were revitalizing the people of western Europe. The work of these four theologians spans all of these events.

JOHN OF SEGOVIA

The first to suggest a new approach to Islam was the Franciscan John of Segovia, a scholar and cleric committed to the campaign for church reform that had wide support in the early fifteenth century. In the 1430s Segovia participated in and wrote the history of the Council of Basel, which attempted, albeit unsuccessfully, to reform the late medieval church and bring a better sense of responsibility and honor to the papacy. He also committed himself to the study of Islam and lamented the lack of knowledge of that faith among Christians, including the fact that a copy of the Qur'an was difficult to find.

Recognizing that Ketton's twelfth-century version of the Qur'an lacked the accuracy that Renaissance scholarship demanded, he sought to sponsor another Latin translation, but could find no Christian in all of Europe who knew the Arabic language. How different this was from ninth-century Spain, when Paul Alvar complained that Andalusian Christians had forsaken Christian Latin for Muslim Arabic. The Reconquest and christianization of the Iberian peninsula had succeeded so well that Arab culture had been left behind, even for many Muslims. Segovia had to settle for a Muslim jurist from Salamanca, but his translator withdrew before the project was finished and Segovia's desired translation was never completed, though he later produced a Latin version of a Spanish translation of the Qur'an on his own. Segovia wanted to know whether the Qur'an was the Word of God or not, but the canons of Renaissance scholarship would require a careful analysis of the text to resolve that question, a project that would be attempted later by Nicholas of Cusa, also called Nicholas Cusanus.

---

[3] The fact that these thinkers could look upon Islam with tolerance and understanding at a time when armies of Muslim warriors posed a significant threat to Europe is impressive.

Segovia's thoughts went further. In a letter to Nicholas he argued that Christendom's difficulties with Islam could not be settled by combat. Founded on war as Islam had been, warfare might be appropriate for Muslims, he said, but violence created evil effects, nor was military action against the Turks likely to succeed. Christianity did not begin in warfare, and it could not responsibly adopt fighting as its strategy. Segovia believed that the controversy between Christendom and Islam could be settled only through peaceful means, a view represented earlier by Raymond Lull.

Missionary work was peaceful and both mendicant orders, Dominicans and Franciscans, had undertaken missionary endeavors. Segovia recognized, however, that the Christian mission effort had met with little success and was not the answer he sought. In Benjamin Kedar's incisive words: "Mendicant missionizing in Muslim countries was much more conducive to filling heaven with Christian martyrs than the earth with Muslim converts."[4] Muslims simply did not adopt Christianity on the basis of evangelical preaching. Segovia was perhaps the first to grasp this point.

Segovia suggested to Cusanus another approach, namely, a conference of Muslim and Christian leaders. Such a conference might result in conversions to Christianity, but if not, it could accomplish other worthy goals, among them the avoidance of war, and perhaps the creation of some useful understandings. He discussed his ideas with two Muslims, one a soldier and the other an ambassador from Granada, but he died soon after his letter to Nicholas, and no conference emerged.

NICHOLAS OF CUSA

Nicholas Cusanus, a man of prodigious accomplishments, was the first Christian writer to search for a way of comprehension that found truth in other religions. A churchman committed to reforming the church from corruption, he too was an active member of the Council of Basel. A philosopher, he composed major philosophical works in the Neoplatonic tradition. As a Renaissance scholar, he used the new methods of historical criticism to demonstrate that the so-called *Donation of Constantine*, a famous document the papacy had used to support its claim for its political and territorial possession of Rome and the papal states, was a forgery. Pope Innocent IV had used the *Donation* to justify *de jure* papal authority over infidels. Through calculations based on his studies in astronomy, Nicholas developed a reform of the Julian calendar that gave a correct date for Easter. He did all this scholarly work while serving as bishop and cardinal, establishing a hospital in Kues (Cusa) on the Mosel River in Germany, and repeatedly accepting major assignments from the pope, including the task of leading negotiations for a hoped-for reunion of the Catholic and Eastern churches.

---

[4] Benjamin Z. Kedar, *Crusade and Mission: European Approaches toward the Muslims* (Princeton: Princeton University Press, 1984), 155.

ON THE PEACE OF FAITH

Cusanus took up Segovia's idea in *On the Peace of Faith* (*De pace fidei*[5]), probably his best-known work. It is a fictional account of a conference such as the one Segovia had proposed, a setting that Nicholas used to argue for a recognition of elements common to all religions. Writing a few weeks after the fall of Constantinople to the Ottoman Turks, the cardinal opened his book by brooding over "those deeds that were reported to have been perpetrated at Constantinople most recently and most cruelly by the King of the Turks, . . . a persecution that was raging more fiercely than usual on account of the difference of rite between the [two] religions."[6] In this book Nicholas's protagonist prays that God will restrain this violence, whereupon he is shown a vision in which representatives from the major religious and ethnic groups of the world gather in the heavenly realm before the saints Peter and Paul and the Word of God in the presence of the Almighty, in order to find the harmony that lies underneath the various religious traditions. The Almighty has heard the moans of the many who suffer from religious persecution and is determined to bring about a solution. In this heavenly setting the various representatives enter into conversation to discover what they have in common. James Biechler and Lawrence Bond, editors and translators of the book, observe that Nicholas's book "is probably the first Christian work which attempts to come to grips in a concrete way with the problem of world religion using an approach along lines other than [overt] conversion or mission."[7]

In the congress of religions that Nicholas imagines are gathered European Christians ranging from Englishmen in the west to Bohemians and Greeks in the east, plus participants that are Jewish, Arab, (Asian) Indian, Chaldean, Scythian, Persian, Syrian, Turkish, Tatar, and Armenian. The apostles Peter and Paul and the Word speak on behalf of Christianity. The group is brought together "with the charge from God that 'by the common consent of all humanity all diversity of religions be brought together peacefully to one religion to remain inviolable from now on.'"[8] When the Tatar asks how the great variety can be unified, Paul answers that the key is faith. Rites are signs of faith, and while rites can change, the faith expressed through them can remain the same. Nicholas's formula for this is "one religion in a variety of rites" (*religio una in rituum varietate*).[9]

---

[5] While "Peace of Faith" is a literal translation, other renderings bring out more of the nuances in Nicholas's Latin phrase, as, e.g., "On Interreligious Harmony," from James E. Biechler and H. Lawrence Bond, *Nicholas of Cusa on Interreligious Harmony: Text, Concordance, and Translation of De Pace Fidei*, Texts and Studies in Religion 55 (Lewiston/Queenston/Lampeter: Edwin Mellen Press, 1990). The title of this work by Cusanus is sometimes called *De pace seu concordantia fidei* (*On the Peace or Harmony of Faith*).

[6] *Nicholas of Cusa's "De pace fidei" and "Cribratio Alcorani,"* translation and analysis by Jasper Hopkins, 2nd ed. (Minneapolis: Arthur J. Banning Press, 1994), 33.

[7] Biechler and Bond, *On Interreligious Harmony*, 33.

[8] Ibid., xiii.

[9] Ibid.

The Word leads the conversation, and point by point he gains the assent of the participants to the main tenets of Christian doctrine. Segovia had proposed an open-ended dialogue without the goal of conversion; Cusanus imagined a different scenario—conversations that would lead, if not to conversion, at least to the approval of Christian doctrine.

As Cusanus opens the address to God, he says that even though humankind began as one with a single faith, it divided into a multitude of people with a diversity of religions. He acknowledges the prophets and kings God sent to communicate his truth, but he says that people erred in taking these messages to be the exact words of God himself rather than the words of humans speaking on God's behalf. Claiming their own form of faith to be absolute, they have quarreled with and condemned other communities for having a different religion. While all religions possess authentic revelations from the one God, their adherents have failed to recognize the relative nature of these revelations, and, having made them absolute, they cannot see the truth in other religious traditions. But the one transcendent God is beyond these limited human visions. Cusanus, a mystic in his theology, says in words of prayer, "You [O God] . . . are the one who is seen to be sought in different ways in different rites, and you are named in different names; for as you are [in Yourself] You remain unknown and ineffable to all."[10] At the earthly level the various professions of faith seem contradictory and therefore exclusive of each other, but at the divine level they agree, for in God these seeming contradictions are reconciled. Humans may divide, but the transcendent unites. At the conclusion Cusanus holds that Christ is present in other religions, even if unrecognized, and that the underlying unity among the religions is to be found in the truths of Christianity.

In his claim that all religions reflect the Almighty, Cusanus departed from the path of strict Catholic orthodoxy that usually saw little if any truth in other religions. His thoughts recall the more liberal side of Christian tradition, such as the second-century Justin Martyr, who said that all who knew and lived by the divine Reason or Word or Truth (the Logos of John 1:1-14) should be accounted as Christians, even if atheists, or the third-century biblical scholar and theologian, Origen, who believed that at the end God would call back unto himself all of his creatures in a final "restoration" of his creation.

The case of Islam is central to Nicholas's argument. By emphasizing the theme of monotheism, citing the sometimes exalted statements about Jesus in the Qur'an (both traditions often looked to the other's scripture for proof texts supporting their own view) and identifying various elements common to Islam and Christianity, the Word brings the imagined Islamic speaker into an acceptance of the Christian doctrines. He cites passages in the Qur'an that parallel references in the Bible. In this book, Nicholas takes specific Islamic practices such as prayer and holy lustrations to be agreeable parallels to Christianity in contrast to the medieval tradition of branding Islamic practices as false, pale

---

[10] Hopkins, *"De pace fidei"* and *"Cribratio Alcorani,"* 35.

imitations of true Christian practice. Cusanus argued that beneath the surface of Islam one can discern an outline of the Christian faith, which, if drawn out and developed, can allow Christianity to fulfill the other religion. As earlier noted, Cusanus sees Christ present in other religions, even if unrecognized—"Christ is the one presupposed by all who hope to attain ultimate happiness."[11]

While holding that the earthly contradictions among religions are reconciled in the transcendence of God, Nicholas also suggested that those differences can be resolved on earth given a proper reading of Christian doctrine, and his little book was an attempt to do that very thing. The *una religio* in which all religious rituals are one is in fact the *religio Christianitas*. Each religion carries within it an undisclosed bud that if brought into the light can blossom into the full Christian confession.

THE *CRIBRATIO*

Cusanus also authored a book on Islam, but in it he pursues a different course. Entitled *The Sifting of the Qur'an* (*Cribratio Alkorani*) and dedicated to Pope Pius II, the book is an attempt to implement Segovia's proposal to analyze the Holy Qur'an. Nicholas wrote his *Cribratio* in late 1460 or early 1461, fewer than ten years after the fall of Constantinople to the Ottoman Turks, and some seven years after *On the Peace of Faith*. By then he had investigated Islam for some time.

Cusanus first obtained Ketton's Latin Qur'an at the Council of Basel in 1432, where he met John of Segovia. In 1437 Cusanus saw an Arabic copy of the Qur'an in Constantinople, while there on his assignment for renewing ties between Rome and the Eastern church. Pope Pius II, knowing of Cusanus's interest in Islam, requested that Nicholas write a refutation of the errors of Islam, and his work on the Qur'an is that book. While one finds elements here of the generous-minded approach of *On the Peace of Faith*, by and large the *Sifting* is a scathing denunciation of the Qur'an, its Prophet, and Islam.

Cusanus's analysis of the Qur'an repeats many of the earlier views on Islam. He says that the Muslim holy book was formed from three sources: Nestorian Christianity, Jewish teachers, and "corruptions" that Muslims introduced after the Prophet's death. While noting the Qur'an's positive statements about Jesus and its clear monotheism, Nicholas returns almost enthusiastically to the calumnies that preceded him: the Qur'an is full of lies, it leads to moral turpitude, and if inspired by a supernatural spirit, the spirit was Satan, not a spirit from God. Muhammad used his claim to divine revelations selfishly to satisfy the appetites of the flesh, and both Muhammad's career and the Islamic movement were characterized by violence ("you reduce all [matters] to the sword"[12]).

---

[11] Ibid.
[12] Ibid., 161-62.

Examples of Cusanus's harshness that arose through errors in the translation of the Qur'an can be excused, but most of his denunciations derive from the writers already reviewed—Peter the Venerable, the *Apology* of al-Kindy, and Ricoldo, among others. But the worst of the old accusations are absent: the legends of a cow carrying the Qur'an to Muhammad, or his body being devoured by swine—these fall away in favor of correct information. The correct facts are read as an indication of insincerity and unworthiness. When placed beside his *On the Peace of Faith*, his *Sifting of the Qur'an* is disappointing. The "peace" proposed in the former is lacking in the latter.

One may wonder what accounts for this shift from the tolerant attitude in his work on peace. Was it the continuing military advance of the Islamic Turks into Europe with the violence such warfare brings? He wrote *Peace* immediately after the fall of Constantinople and the *Sifting* some seven years later. Was it the opportunity he now had to study the Qur'an in intense detail? Or did Nicholas in fact hold both views: the broadly based conviction that Islam, like all religions, contains a great deal of God's truth, but that at the same time in its fully manifest form it contains much that is to be considered despicable? The answer is probably the latter: the truth present in Islam is compromised by the falsehoods and errors that distort it, and the latter are to be condemned.

Even so, *On the Peace of Faith* was the first Christian writing based on the clearly stated principle that the various religions contain common elements that could provide a basis for conversation and understanding. Cusanus's conviction of the superiority and finality of the Christian revelation marks him as a traditional Christian theologian, but his proposal in *De pace fidei* to move beyond polemical arguments in order to develop a common understanding marks him as a notable innovator.

THE WORDS OF A POPE: PIUS II

A third Renaissance treatment of Islam is a letter from Pope Pius II to the Turkish sultan, Mahomet II. Elected pope in 1458, Aeneas Silvius Piccolomini was a respected Italian humanist who took to himself the name Pius II. John of Segovia, in the last month of his life, wrote Piccolomini, then a bishop and cardinal, on the subject of Christendom's relation to Islam, arguing that the cardinal was wrong in advocating a new Crusade against Islam. He reminded the soon-to-be pope that Muslims were far more numerous than Christians (not true now, but true then) and that in war numbers usually won the day. In words like those he gave to Cusanus, Segovia told the cardinal that "the gift of Christ to the Church was peace, not war."[13]

---

[13] R. W. Southern, *Western Views of Islam in the Middle Ages* (Cambridge, Mass., and London: Harvard University Press, 1962), 99.

Approximate boundaries
of EurAsian religions,
circa 1450

Predominantly Christian

Predominantly Islamic

Predominantly Hindu

Predominantly Buddhist

Buddhist, Confucian, Taoist

Unshaded land areas remaining
to traditional religions

Piccolomini sent no reply to Segovia, but as Pope Pius II he acted on Segovia's suggestion two years later, drafting an eloquent letter to Mahomet II, the Turkish commander who had conquered Constantinople. With splendid language and fine reasoning, he commended the Christian faith to the Ottoman ruler. Although the West probably faced a superior power in the Ottoman Turks, Pius nonetheless boasted of the West's strengths—Germany, France, England, Poland, Spain, and Italy—to suggest to the Turkish sultan that conquering Europe would be no simple matter. More to the point, however, the pope proposed that Mahomet become a Christian. In an argument more political than spiritual Pius enumerated to Mahomet the advantages of such a conversion (reminiscent of arguments the Muslim al-Hashimi gave earlier to the Christian al-Kindy in favor of Islam). Pius said that with nothing more than a little water—the water of baptism—Mahomet could become "the greatest and most powerful and most famous man of [his] time." "We will call you the emperor of the Greeks and of the East. The land which you now occupy by force you will then hold by right, and all Christians will reverence you and make you their judge."[14]

Turning to the religious questions themselves, Pius pointed out his understanding of the common ground between the two religions. R. W. South summarizes Pius's argument:

There are many points of agreement between Christians and Mosle God, the creator of the world; a belief in the necessity for faith; a f of rewards and punishments; the immortality of the soul; the con of the Old and New Testaments; all this is common ground. We about the nature of God.[15]

The thoughts of Pius II parallel what Pope Gregory VII wrote to in the eleventh century, and echo Nicholas's approach in *De p*

Pope Pius II is generally thought to have shown disdain t but his letter shows another side. Eloquent and clearly argue resents an attempt at reason, not military force. In the end quence and rationality were probably in vain—the letter sent. And if it was sent, received, and read, one can be cer commander was unmoved.

THEODORE BIBLIANDER

A century later, the Swiss theologian and Renai Bibliander contributed two things to the Christian co

---

[14] Ibid., 100.

[15] Ibid., 101. In Theodore Bibliander's *Alcoran*, discussed b some thirty-eight pages. A polite reply from Mahomet, of unce

Bibliander

impressive publication entitled in short form *The Alcoran*, a virtual library of Christendom's materials on Islam, and a description of the commonalities among the religions of the world. While Bibliander is primarily remembered as a Protestant reformer (he succeeded Ulrich Zwingli as teacher in the Protestant school of Zurich), his training lay in the Renaissance.[16] A gifted linguist who authored a Hebrew grammar, his study of language intersected with his theological work not only at the practical level of the biblical languages, but at the theoretical level of the nature of language, particularly the question of connections among the various human languages.

Cusanus pondered resemblances among religions; Bibliander puzzled over parallels among languages. In his study of Latin, Greek, Hebrew, Chaldean, Ethiopic, and even Arabic, he saw what appeared to be similarities close enough for him to think of a single origin, surviving traces he imagined of the one language all humans spoke before the Tower of Babel.[17] While language and religion are not the same thing, the apparent cognates in religious vocabularies intrigued him.

In 1548 Bibliander published his *Commentary on the Common Style and Way of All Languages and Literature with a Short Explanation of the Moral Life and Religion of All Peoples,* wherein he presented his theory, namely, that the discovery of a single underlying language could result in the uncovering of an underlying common faith. In support of the idea of a single faith he identified ten elements that were held by the religions he knew. These points included recognition of the spiritual nature of life, belief in the immortality of the soul, an affirmation of one God the Creator, the need for morality and piety, and, he added as the most important point, the idea that in every age God had given to humans a person to lead God's people, a leader who was to be obeyed as God himself. Like Cusanus, he believed that every religion had within it some legitimate knowledge of God. Further, he held that God's mercy extended to all and any who had not heard of Jesus would be saved, such as the pious pagans classical age (a view his predecessor Zwingli had also held), as well as men and women of Islam and Judaism, and other religious traditions as

er's *Alcoran* was his most important publication on Islam: Its full *Coran: The Lives of Muhammad, the Chief of the Saracens, and of s, Their Teachings, and the Qur'an Itself.* Published in Basel in er's book brought together most of the important materials sessed on Islam, including Ketton's Qur'an (the title, *Alcoran,*

[16] Bibl... surname.

[17] Against t...naissance-style Latin form of Buchman ("bookman"), his original German hold that the huma... guage. While not ho...language is entirely learned, some contemporary students of language Renaissance theologian...es within it from birth the rudiments and fundamental structure of lanporary linguistics. ...e Tower of Babel story, their conclusions resemble the ideas of this ...ist. I am grateful to Hunter Godsey for this information on contem-

translates literally "the Qur'an") and most of the Toledan Collection. Also included were Cusanus's book on the Qur'an, Pope Pius II's letter to Mahomet II, Ricoldo's *Refutation*, and a long tract against Islam by the sometime Byzantine emperor John VI Cantacuzene, written after he was deposed and had taken the monk's cowl. John of Damascus was here as well. About the only thing missing was the Islamic part of the *Apology* of al-Kindy. Bibliander had collected a virtual encyclopedia of Islam for sixteenth-century Europe.

Without the timely intervention of Martin Luther, Bibliander's *Alcoran* might not have been published at all. When the Basel town council learned what Bibliander's printer, Oporinus, was up to, they arrested the printer, confiscated the pages he had printed, and prohibited Oporinus from working on the book, fearing that the publication of Muslim materials would encourage interest in Islam among Christians. When Luther heard of this, he wrote the council and urged them to approve the printing, advising them that their fears were unfounded. He assured them that when people saw for themselves what Luther considered to be the lies and foolishness of the Muslims, they would reject Islam altogether. The council acceded to Luther's request, and the publication appeared in 1543, exactly four hundred years after the Toledan Collection of Peter the Venerable. A later edition was published in 1550.

CONCLUSION

R. W. Southern observed that in these thinkers one sees a vision toward Islam far superior to the views put forward before them, and to any for several centuries afterwards.[18] That is true, but while proposing dialogue, these Christian writers made no attempt to bring Muslim scholars into their discussions. The followers of Islam had no voice of their own here—one hears them only through voices imagined by their Christian opponents. The ideal of interreligious dialogue was not yet acted upon.[19] Such dialogues would be a long time in coming.

Even so, this was a striking moment in the rivalry between Christendom and Islam. The strident charges and claims of earlier Christian writers became muted, and a path of understanding was laid out. That was a significant accomplishment. Their proposals could be of only limited success, however, since the solution they offered subsumed Islam under Christianity so fully as to strip it of its real character. One cannot imagine a devout Muslim responding favorably to that part of Renaissance thinking.

---

[18] Southern, *Western Views of Islam,* 103.

[19] So-called "disputations" between Christians and Jews did take place, an oft-noted one in Barcelona in 1263. Usually stacked in favor of the Christian side, they did offer a semblance of communication, though such a semblance is certainly inferior to a full-fledged dialogue.

10

The Turks as a Sign of the End of the Age

Luther and de Susannis

The world runs and hastens so diligently to its end that it often occurs to me forcibly that the last day will break before we can completely turn the Holy Scripture into German. For it is certain from the Holy Scriptures that we have no more temporal things to expect. All is done and fulfilled: the Roman Empire is at an end; the Turk has reached his highest point; the pomp of the papacy is falling away and the world is cracking on all sides almost as if it would break and fall apart entirely.

—Martin Luther (1530)[1]

[The approved preachers] should in no way presume to preach or bring the news of the exact time of future evils, Antichrist's advent, or the precise day of Judgment. . . . Nevertheless, if the Lord shall have revealed to certain [preachers], by a special inspiration, particular future events, we do not at all wish to impede these men.

—Fifth Lateran Council (1516)[2]

MARTIN LUTHER

In Luther's day the military threat of Islam to Europe was severe. For the first time in centuries Muslim forces, Turkish armies this time, were moving

---

[1] "Luther to John Frederic, Duke of Saxony," the dedicatory epistle to Luther's German translation of Daniel (*Luther's Correspondence and Other Contemporary Letters,* vol. 2, trans. and ed. Preserved Smith and Charles M. Jacobs [Philadelphia: Lutheran Publication Society, 1918], 516-17).

[2] Kenneth R. Stow, *Catholic Thought and Papal Jewry Policy: 1555-1593* (New York: Jewish Theological Seminary of America, 1977), 251.

into European areas. Their presence reversed the long movement of the West against Islamic lands. Christian Crusades had taken Christian armies to the Holy Land, and talk abounded of yet another Crusade. The last of the Islamic strongholds in Spain fell in 1492 to Ferdinand and Isabella, and the entire peninsula was again in Christian hands for the first time since the eighth century.

But the tide was now running the other way. Constantinople, the great capital of the Byzantine empire and one of the greatest cities in the world, had fallen to the Ottoman Turks in 1453, and the Byzantine empire, the surviving remnant of ancient Rome, was no more. By then Turkish forces had already moved into the lower Balkans, and after their conquest of Constantinople they pushed farther north into Hungary. By 1529 the great Suleiman II, grandson of the conqueror of Constantinople, stood with his army at the gates of Vienna. If Vienna fell, the way into central Europe would be open and both Germany and France would be at risk. Suleiman already controlled most of the northern coast of Africa, plus the Balkans, two-thirds of Hungary, the sea lanes of the Mediterranean, and the Middle East all the way through Iraq. Now he seemed ready to add Europe to his domains.

As it turned out, Vienna was as far as he could reach, first in 1529 and again in 1532. Both times his armies retreated without taking the city. The threat of the Turks finally ended when Turkish forces "foundered under the walls of Vienna in 1683,"[3] but for a century and a half, and during the whole of Luther's lifetime, the outcome was uncertain.

Meanwhile, Europe was in political, military, and religious turmoil. In the 1520s the new Holy Roman Emperor Charles V was struggling to make his power secure. Conflicts with the papacy (Charles's troops sacked Rome in 1527), with Francis I of France (whom Charles bested in the contest for emperor), and difficulties with the Protestant rulers of northern Europe all plagued his reign. At times Charles wanted to mount a Crusade against the Turks, and popes encouraged this, but he could not muster sufficient support. In early 1529 at the Diet of Speyer (where the term "Protestant" was coined), Charles was represented by his brother, Ferdinand, king of Hungary and Austria, who asked the princes for troops to push Suleiman out of Hungary, but they offered only enough soldiers to defend their own territories in Europe, and certainly not enough to dislodge the Turkish forces.

Although most of the Reformers took note of the Turks, with the exception of Theodore Bibliander and his impressive book on Islam, only one, Martin Luther, gave substantial attention to the problem. John Calvin discussed the Turkish threat occasionally, but said very little about Islam itself, and he completely ignored Bibliander's important publication, which was printed at Calvin's own press in Basel. Desiderius Erasmus discussed Islam several times,

---

[3] Bernard Lewis, *The Middle East: A Brief History of the Last 2000 Years* (New York: Scribner, 1995), 237.

describing it as a mixture of errors coming from Judaism and heretical Christianity. He argued against converting Turks by force, but agreed that the Christians of Europe needed to defend themselves against their attack. Like Luther, he believed that Christians needed to repent to avoid the judgment God might bring upon them through the Turks. This was about all the Reformers said.

It was Luther who took the matter into hand. He composed three major tracts on Islam and several minor ones; he translated Ricoldo's *Refutation* of Islam into German; and, as already reported, he figured decisively in the publication of Bibliander's *Alcoran*. A Catholic monk turned university professor, Luther lived and worked relatively secluded within the forests of Saxony in northern Germany far from the sophistication of southern Europe. Thus his outlook on Islam was formed more by the medieval tradition than by the ideas of the Renaissance. He exhibited none of the broad philosophical approach of Segovia or Cusanus. Luther spoke as an evangelical Christian.

Luther's writings on Islam carry marked contrasts. He eschewed Crusade but recognized the need for war; he feared the attack of the Turks but virtually welcomed them as a divine judgment on the evils of Christendom. Hardly an ardent preacher of the Apocalypse, he saw the Turkish invasion as fulfilling the predictions of the apocalyptic writings. For Luther, the Turks were God's judgment on a Christendom that had allowed both papacy and church to become corrupt, and they could well be signs of the Second Coming of Jesus.

LUTHER'S EARLY STATEMENTS

Luther's first words on Islam came in 1518, when, defending his famous *Ninety-five Theses,* he argued that God was sending the Turks as judgment on the Christians, just as he has sent wars, plagues, and earthquakes. "None but a poor Christian would fail to recognize in these the lash and rod of God,"[4] he said, implying that the pope in Rome, spiritual leader of the Christian world as he was, could not see the obvious meaning in the Turkish threat. The surprise in Luther's words comes in his seeming opposition to the use of war for defense against the Turkish invaders.

> Many, however, even the "big wheels" in the church, now dream of nothing else than war against the Turk. They want to fight, not against iniquities, but against the lash of iniquity and thus they would oppose God who says that through that lash he himself punishes us for our iniquities because we do not punish ourselves for them.[5]

---

[4] Martin Luther, "Explanations of the Ninety-five Theses," trans. Carl W. Folkemer, in *Luther's Works* [hereafter *LW*], general editor Helmut T. Lehman, vol. 31 (Philadelphia: Fortress Press, 1957), 92.

[5] Ibid.

His criticism of this rush to war came back to haunt the young reformer in Pope Leo X's famous bull (from *bullum*, the wax seal on papal documents), *Exsurge domine* of June 15, 1520. In that pronouncement Leo threatened Luther with excommunication and quoted the German monk as saying, "To make war against the Turks is nothing else than to strive against God who is punishing our sins by means of the Turks."[6] The pope was attempting to portray Luther as a seditionist who advocated surrender before the Turks.

In time, however, Luther developed his own advocacy for war against the Turks. Christians could fight the Turks, he said, but first they had to repent and reform their lives and their church. Because the Turks were God's judgment on Christendom, Christians had to remove the reason for the judgment. When that was done, Christians could mount a war in their defense, and it would then be a just war. Both the holy book and the events of the day confirmed the need for reform, and if war were undertaken before adequate reform took place, the campaign would fail, since it would be against the very work of God. Luther echoed Maximus the Confessor, the seventh-century Byzantine writer who, writing about the first onslaught of the Muslims, said that the repentance of Christians could blunt the Muslim attack. Always the reformer, Luther called upon Christians and Christian leaders to change.

This fight must be begun with repentance, and we must reform our lives, or we shall fight in vain.[7]

God does not demand crusades, indulgences, and war. He wants us to live good lives. But the pope and his followers run from goodness faster than from anything else, yet he wants to devour the Turk. [In irony Luther observes] [t]his is the reason why our war against the Turk is so successful—so that where he formerly held one mile of land he now holds a hundred.[8]

But if Christians fight, they must do so with a conscience that has been cleansed by repentance and spiritual renewal.

Since the Turk is the rod of the wrath of the Lord our God and the servant of the raging devil, the first thing to be done is to smite the devil, his lord, and take the rod out of God's hand, so that the Turk may be found only, in his own strength, all by himself, without the devil's help and without God's

---

[6] The thirty-fifth article of *An Argument in Defense of All the Articles of Dr. Martin Luther Wrongly Condemned in the Roman Bull* (1521), in *Works of Martin Luther,* vol. 3 (Philadelphia: Muhlenberg Press, © 1930), 105.

[7] Martin Luther, "On War against the Turk," in *LW* 46:171.

[8] Martin Luther, "Defense and Explanation of All the Articles" (1521), *LW* 32:90.

hand. . . . If the Turk's god, the devil, is not beaten first, there is reason to fear that the Turk will not be so easy to beat.[9]

Luther's explanations, perhaps clear enough at this distance, did not work for all his readers. Even some of his supporters continued to think that if the Turks were the agents of God, opposing them would be opposing God. These twists and turns of Luther's mind illustrate well the difficulties a theologian can have in reading political and military problems through religious categories.

Luther held that the corruption of Rome was at the heart of the difficulties within Christendom. He complained that Rome taxed Christians and sold them indulgences on the pretense of using the funds to fight the Turks, but "not a *heller* of the annates [religious taxes] or of the indulgence-money or of all the rest is used against the Turks, but all of it goes into the bottomless bag."[10] Furthermore, he said, "They lie and deceive. They make laws and they make agreements with us, but they do not intend to keep a single letter of them."[11]

SPIRITUAL AND TEMPORAL AUTHORITIES

In *On War against the Turks*, written to Count Philip of Hesse just a few months before the Turks laid siege to Vienna, Luther tried to clarify all these points by explaining the difference between spiritual and temporal authority, and thus spiritual and temporal warfare. The distinction is a famous one in Luther's thought and a principle he says he had not yet understood when he first wrote on Islam. He said that spiritual authorities must fight spiritual battles with spiritual weapons, not physical weapons. The reverse is true for the secular authorities. In the affairs of princes and rulers, the rules of justice, not forms of religious confession, are to regulate war and peace. Thus, there should be no war between Christian and Muslim as such, only between the attacked and the attacker. By the same token, the conversion of Muslims can come only through spiritual struggle, not military force. He thus ruled out Crusades against Islam.

At the same time, Luther, like Ricoldo of Monte Croce and Peter the Venerable before him, believed that the religion of Islam was from the devil, a work of evil and unbelief. The Turks were virtual double agents, since as administrators of divine judgment they were serving God, albeit unwittingly, while in

---

[9] Luther, "On War against the Turk," 170. Desiderius Erasmus offered similar thoughts. "The most efficacious way of overcoming the Turks would be if they beheld that which Christ taught and examplified shining forth in our own lives" (quoted by George Huntston Williams, "Erasmus and the Reformers on Non-Christian Religions and *salus extra ecclesiam,*" in *Action and Conviction in Early Modern Europe,* ed. Theodore K. Rabb and Jerrold E. Seigel [Princeton: Princeton University Press, 1969], 328).

[10] Martin Luther, "An Open Letter to the German Nobility" (1520), in *Works of Martin Luther,* 2:85.

[11] Martin Luther, "To the Christian Nobility of the German Nation," trans. Charles M. Jacobs, rev. James Atkinson, in *Three Treatises: Martin Luther,* rev. ed. (Philadelphia: Fortress Press, 1970), 31.

fact they were servants of the devil, their true master. Both pope and Turk represented forces opposed to God: "Just as the pope is the Antichrist, so the Turk is the very devil incarnate. The prayer of Christendom against both is that they shall go down to hell, even though it may take the Last Day to send them there; and I hope that day will not be far off."[12] Nothing here argues for fighting Turks just because they are Muslims. Shortly after Luther wrote these words, Suleiman reached Vienna only to retreat after a brief siege. Luther thought the prayers of devout Christians had brought about the Turks' defeat.

Luther soon began to say more about the nearness of the Last Day, of which he believed both Turk and pope to be harbingers. The great events they portended would be difficult to endure. "Christians will be punished here on earth because of their sins and the innocent will be made martyrs."[13] Luther saw the dreaded days of the predicted evil powers of Gog and Magog just ahead, and even though those two incarnations of evil would be destroyed by fire from heaven, before that happened they would wreak havoc on Christians. Then, in a seeming turn from his earlier arguments, he charged that Christians must fight the Turks because they are of the devil and are enemies of God. "Whoever fights against the Turk should have no doubt that he fights against the Devil himself."[14] Luther seems to have urged a religious war in spite of himself.

Finally, Luther considered the possibility that Turkish armies would overrun Germany. If that were to occur, there could be Christian martyrs. Realizing that many could suffer imprisonment, he admonished his readers to memorize the Ten Commandments, the Lord's Prayer, and the Apostles' Creed, so that both minds and hearts would have the faith that would save them. He said that, if this dire tragedy should come to pass, one could know that the end of the age was near, and in that fact lay the Christian's final hope.

THE LAST PUBLICATIONS

Luther published his last materials on Islam while Turkish armies were gaining control of virtually all of Hungary, raising once again the specter of warfare in the West. Between 1539 and 1543 he republished two of his earlier writings, wrote a new small tract, and brought out his German translation of Ricoldo's *Refutation of the Qur'an*. Luther says he had read Ricoldo's work (Luther calls him Richard) as early as 1530, but that at the time he questioned whether Muslims could really believe what Ricoldo said they did. But when a copy of Ketton's Latin Qur'an came into his hands in 1541, he concluded that Ricoldo was right about the evils of Islam, and in 1543 Luther wrote a preface to one of the printings of Bibliander's *Alcoran*.

Luther offered no new interpretation of Islam. His thoughts were almost

---

[12] Luther, "On War against the Turk," 181.

[13] Martin Luther, "Army Sermon against the Turks," in *D. Martin Luthers Werke,* 30/2:170. My translation.

[14] Ibid., 173. My paraphrase.

entirely about the events of his own time—the Turkish menace and the corruption of papacy and church. Corrupt papacy, false church, invaders from the east were to him signs of the end of the age. In this apocalyptic view Luther stood in a line of interpreters that included the seventh-century Byzantine writer Sophronius, the martyrs of Cordoba, Peter the Hermit, and Joachim of Fiore, the Calabrian prophet who had earlier called the papacy the Antichrist and had predicted the early arrival of a great age of the Spirit.

THE TRADITIONAL CATHOLIC VIEW:
MARQUARDUS DE SUSANNIS AND THE *DE IUDAEIS*

Another eschatological view came to the fore in the sixteenth century from a rather unexpected source, a Catholic official, the Marquardus de Susannis, who prepared a compendium of papal legislation on Jews entitled simply *On the Jews* (*De Iudaeis*), published in Venice in 1558. Three years earlier Pope Paul IV had issued a bull that not only renewed all the earlier restrictions on Jews but added new ones, namely, "that all Jews live in an enforced ghetto, that they sell all their real property to Christians, and that they limit their commercial activity with Christians in the sphere of the necessities of life (i.e., food and clothing) to the selling of second-hand clothes."[15] This principle of restricted toleration of Jewry had a goal of converting Jews and committed the papacy to an ongoing preaching activity. Motivation for these restrictions came from Paul's prediction in Romans 11:26 that "all Israel" would come into the kingdom shortly before the Last Day.

In part three of *On the Jews* Susannis discusses Islam. After warning the rebellious Protestants that their campaign of reform was certain to fail, and after dismissing the question of the new lands in the Americas by saying that they will be easy to convert, Susannis discusses the Muslims, who he says are the only people left, along with the Jews, who had heard the gospel but had not converted. What is needed, he says, is preaching to Muslims. Employing well-worn and by now familiar arguments, he says that Muhammad adopted warfare to establish his religion since he knew that if his followers heard the Christian gospel they would choose it over Islam. Jesus defended his gospel with miracles, not force. The difficulty then was not with Muslims, who would convert if they heard the gospel clearly, but with their ruler, the sultan, who refused to allow Christian preaching. Susannis says that if Christians could convert the sultan, his war against the Persians would become part of the final cosmic struggle between good and evil at the Last Day. The Turkish leader's conversion would be a major event in world history. "What the sultan was to be promised, then, was not battlefield success, but the ultimate victory, the escha-

---

[15] Stow, *Catholic Thought and Papal Jewry Policy,* 3.

ton."[16] These ideas, which placed Islam within an eschatological setting, would lie dormant for several centuries, but would return this century, not so much in reference to Islam as in regard to Jews and their resettlement in the land of Israel.

---

[16] Ibid., 137. Protestant theologians had a parallel view toward Jews, namely, that the purified religion of Protestantism would be so alluring to Jews that they would convert and would thus hasten the Last Day in line with Paul's statement in Romans 11:25-26.

11

The Sea Explorers and Western Colonialism

Europe Outflanks and Overpowers the Islamic World

The whole complex process of European expansion and empire in the last five centuries has its roots in the clash of Islam and Christendom.
—Bernard Lewis[1]

Two themes dominate the first half of twentieth-century Muslim history: European imperialism, and the struggle for independence from colonial rule. Few events were more far-reaching and influential in the relationship of Islam to the West than the experience of European colonialism.
—John L. Esposito[2]

The Turkish empire of Suleiman the Magnificent was the pinnacle of Islamic power vis-à-vis the West. Later Turkish armies and navies continued to threaten, but they could not reach the level of success he had achieved, and the tide began to turn yet again. The dominant power this time was on the side of the Europeans, first through their sea explorations, which opened up the entire globe to them, then through the industrial revolution, which brought them machines and almost undreamt-of production, and finally through their conquest of nations and lands far away and the colonies they would plant there. If the Crusades remain a bitter memory among Muslims, a yet nearer memory, even more bitter, is that of European colonialism, as the statement of John Esposito quoted above suggests.

---

[1] Bernard Lewis, *Islam and the West* (New York and Oxford: Oxford University Press, 1993), 17.

[2] John L. Esposito, *The Islamic Threat: Myth or Reality?*, 3rd ed. (New York and Oxford: Oxford University Press, 1999), 45.

The intellectual responses of Christians to Islam in the late Middle Ages and Renaissance that brought a more favorable attitude to the religion of Islam were small changes compared to the events of the following centuries that brought the European powers into a virtual hegemony over the lands of Islam. Utilizing sea paths opened up through the explorations of Western navigators, nineteenth- and twentieth-century merchants and military forces of Europe established worldwide empires that dominated almost the entire Islamic world.

The development of Western seafaring began in the fifteenth century and grew out of the need for a better way to secure trade with Asia. Produce from Asia was in demand in Europe—silks and gems for the wealthy, spices such as nutmeg and cloves, and herbal medicines for the poor. Genoese merchants had earlier developed a thriving commercial business in these commodities by sailing up the Bosporus into the Black Sea, where they met caravans from East Asia, but the Turkish conquest of Constantinople had closed off that avenue, forcing Western merchants to use the southern route via Egypt. When Egyptian sultans increased their duties and tariffs, Italian traders from Genoa and Venice, and others as well, realized they needed a connection with Asia that would avoid these expenses. That meant a route around the lands of Islam, and ocean travel offered the only possibility. The discussion begins with the case of Christopher Columbus, even though his voyages were almost ancillary to those that resulted in the colonial empires.

CHRISTOPHER COLUMBUS

The year of Columbus's first transatlantic voyage, 1492, was, as earlier noted, the year King Ferdinand and Queen Isabella completed their conquest of the Moors, united the kingdoms of Aragon and Castile, and ordered the expulsion of Jews from their realm. On the 3rd of August, when Columbus's little fleet slipped its moorings at Palos, Spain, to float down the Rio Saltés on the morning ebb tide, his sailors probably saw a second fleet departing for the Netherlands bearing the final group of Jewish exiles to depart from Spain. The preceding day, August 2, was the last day unconverted Jews were permitted in that land. One of Columbus's crew was a converted Jew (who spoke Arabic), but Columbus planned to allow no Jews in the lands he would claim for his sovereigns. The future carried an irony: the lands he would "discover" would in time become the safest that Jews would know.

Islam was also on Columbus's mind. In a letter he penned to Ferdinand and Isabella on that first voyage, he told of his great joy in having seen "the Moorish king come out of the gates of [Alhambra] and kiss the royal hands of Your Highnesses," "enemies of the sect of Mahomet" as his monarchs were.[3]

---

[3] *The Journal of Christopher Columbus,* trans. Cecil Jane (New York: Bonanza Books, 1960), 3-4.

did Columbus not understand that the one God of Islam was the same one God of Christianity? Obviously!

124   *The Sea Explorers and Western Colonialism*

Jerusalem and the holy places of Palestine occupied his thoughts as well.[4] Indeed, from the beginning he seems to have thought of sailing around the world in order to strike Islam in the rear, thereby restoring Jerusalem to Christendom.[5] At bottom Columbus fancied himself another crusader, a man who thought to dislodge the infidel Muslims from the Holy City of Jerusalem. There was no Renaissance calmness here. The old rivalry was alive and well. The navigator-sailor from Genoa sought an end to the ungodly rule of Islam in the Holy Land.

After his third voyage to the West Indies, the Admiral of the Ocean Sea (as he had then been named) collected all the prophetic passages from the Bible he could find on the islands and lands of the sea as well as parallel passages from Christian writers and published them in a *Book of Prophecies* he said would prove that Spain would conquer Jerusalem. He also took note of a prophecy of the fiery twelfth-century Joachim of Fiore that "someone from Spain would restore the arch of Zion,"[6] and applied it to himself. Columbus hoped to use the wealth of the Indies to finance the next Crusade, thereby enabling his sovereigns to realize the ambitious title they had inherited, King and Queen of Jerusalem. His plan to find a sea route to Asia failed, of course, and his hopes of funding another Crusade and conquering the Holy Land went unfulfilled, but both were important elements in his explorations.

THE PORTUGUESE NAVIGATORS

The Portuguese succeeded where Columbus failed—they found the sea route to Asia. Their success can be traced back to Prince Henry the Navigator, son of the Portuguese King John I. Prince Henry instigated this search and supported it with financing, his personal prestige, and his good imagination, even though, in spite of his name, he did none of the sailing.

---

[4] He also hoped to find the location of the Garden of Eden. "I believe that if I were to sail beyond the Equator . . . [to] where the world reaches its highest point . . . that there the earthly Paradise is located, where no man may go, save by the grace of God" (quoted by Felipe Fernández-Armesto, *Columbus* [Oxford and New York: Oxford University Press, 1991], 131). A book by Pierre d'Ailly, a prominent theologian of the fourteenth-fifteenth century, provided Columbus with many of the ideas that lay behind his plans, including the suggestion that the Indies could be reached across the Atlantic. Columbus's copy with his notes survives. The apocryphal 1 Esdras says in its account of creation that one-seventh of the earth is covered by water, a proportion that gave Columbus a way to estimate the time a sailing vessel needed to cross it.

[5] "To it [crossing the Atlantic] could be added a remoter 'grand design' to take Islam in the rear and reconquer Jerusalem, such as Columbus first advocated before 1492, and returned to at intervals, developing it, as time went by, in increasingly eschatological terms, with increasingly millenarian constructions" (Fernández-Armesto, *Columbus*, 26).

[6] *The "Book of Prophecies" Edited by Christopher Columbus*, ed. Roberto Rosconi, trans. Blair Sullivan, Reportorium Columbianum (Berkeley, Los Angeles, and London: University of California Press, 1997), 31.

By the mid-fifteenth century, Portuguese sailors had newly designed ships called caravels, which carried rigging derived ironically enough from Arab dhows or *caravos*, small ships that plied the Arabian Sea. Their name is the source of the word "caravel." Columbus's Niña and Pinta were such ships. This triangular fore-and-aft rigging ("lateen" sails they are called) gave Portuguese ships more speed and maneuverability than the square rigging they had been using, including the ability to sail both south and north along the coast of Africa.

Supported by a papal bull, Prince Henry's stated purpose was to spread Christianity in Asia and to link up with fellow Christians who were believed to have been led by one Prester John, an imagined Christian prince said to rule a vast Christian kingdom in Asian lands. The thought of this Asian ruler and his great Christian realm had held the imagination and often the hopes of Latin Christians for centuries.

Henry's captains sailed south, exploring the western coast of Africa, but got only part way down it. King John II the Perfect continued Henry's exploration program, and in 1488 one of his captains, Bartolomeu Dias de Novais, sailed all the way to the southern tip of Africa. Tradition says that Dias named it the "Cape of Storms," but King John renamed it the "Cape of Good Hope," thinking of the gold that awaited him when his ships would sail around the cape to Asia.

The actual opening to Asia came in 1498 when Vasco da Gama, sailing on orders from the same King John, who was by then deceased, rounded the cape and sailed on to India. His pilot for navigating the Indian Ocean was a Muslim from Malindi in East Africa. When da Gama landed at Calicut, the major port of trade on the western coast of India (not to be confused with Calcutta on the eastern coast of India), he announced that he was looking for fellow Christians and for spices. The Portuguese found Christians there well enough, but unrelated to the imagined Prester John, stories of whom they now learned were fictions. These Indian Christians were members of the Church of St. Thomas, established in the first century, it was believed, by the apostle Thomas, one of Jesus' Twelve.

The Indian Ocean had been controlled for centuries by Arabs and then Turks as well, but now these Muslim sailors were forced to give way to Westerners, save in the Red Sea, where Turkish naval power retained control. Vasco da Gama confronted the Muslim presence on his second voyage, when he met and captured a ship bringing Muslim pilgrims from Mecca back to India. When the pilgrims refused to hand over their gold, he ordered both passengers and crew killed (some 380 men plus women and children) and the vessel burned to the water line. It was in this way that the relations of Christians with the Muslims of South Asia began. When Portuguese sailors destroyed an Arab-Egyptian fleet in 1509, European control of the Arabian Sea was complete. In 1510 the Portuguese seized Goa as an Indian base, and in 1511 they took Malacca, commanding the Malay Straits in southeast Asia. In 1515 Ormuz on the Persian

Gulf fell to their conquest. European military presence in south and southeast Asia had begun.

A SHIFT IN POWER

The sixteenth century saw the expansion of three Islamic empires; the Ottoman Turks moved into southwest Asia, southeast Europe all the way to Vienna, and across North Africa. The Safavids developed a powerful empire in Persia, and the Moguls in India enjoyed their greatest days under Babur and Akbar. Istanbul, Isfahan, and Delhi, the centers of these three great empires, were splendid cities with safe and quick communication, and they ruled their subjects with a relatively common system of law and religion. These empires represented an impressive peak of Muslim power and influence. But they were the last success before decline set in.

By the end of the seventeenth century, power began to shift to the Latin West. The Turkish navy that had dominated the Mediterranean had been destroyed earlier at the Battle of Lepanto in 1571.[7] By then the passage around the tip of Africa to the Far East was open, and Europeans controlled the sea lanes to Asia that had been dominated by Arabs. In 1683 Turkish troops withdrew from Vienna for the last time, now in clear defeat. The subsequent peace treaty of Carlowitz of 1699 marked the first instance in which Muslim rulers bowed to terms dictated by Westerners, a staggering loss for Islamic leaders, but a sign of the new energy and power of the West. Western Europe had begun its period of ascendancy, while the Islamic world pulled more and more into itself. For one thousand years, a full millennium, Europeans had lived with the threat of invasion by Muslim forces, but that era was now at an end.

An Islamic threat remained in one area only, the Mediterranean coast of North Africa. In the seventeenth and into the eighteenth centuries Algerian corsairs, or pirates, ventured into Mediterranean sea lanes attacking British, French, and even American shipping, reaching as far as Iceland, and in one case to England. In defense of American vessels, the American naval officer Stephen Decatur, Jr., captain of the *Enterprise*, engaged Islamic forces at Tripoli, Libya, in the years 1803 to 1805, and after 1815 as well. He accomplished his most famous exploit in 1804, when he sailed a captured Libyan ketch renamed the *Intrepid* into the harbor of Tripoli, where his sailors burned the United States frigate *Philadelphia*, which had fallen into Libyan hands. The familiar line "to the shores of Tripoli" in the *United States Marine Hymn* derives from the deployment of Marines from Decatur's ship to attack Libyans of North Africa. Only later would the European problem with North African pirates be resolved.

---

[7] Miguel Cervantes, the author of *Don Quixote,* lost a hand in the battle (Miguel de Cervantes Saavedra, *The Ingenious Gentleman Don Quixote de la Mancha,* vol. 2, trans. Samuel Putnam [New York: Viking Press, 1949], 505, 989, n. 4 of "Prologue").

WESTERN IMPERIALISM:
THE NINETEENTH AND TWENTIETH CENTURIES

The Latin West, long overshadowed by the Islamic world, now began to surpass its Islamic-based competition. The sea power of the Portuguese and Spanish, and soon of the Dutch and English, took Europeans directly to Asia. The
great Muslim cities of the East that once possessed a splendor absent from the
Christian West had long since been equaled by the magnificence of the Renaissance cities of Florence, Rome, and Venice. The West, with its powerful new
armaments, advanced sailing vessels, the new technology of movable type and
the printing press, and the subsequent explosion of knowledge and literature,
surged ahead as the Islamic world, seemingly mired in its old ways, moved
more and more onto the defensive. The nineteenth-century development of
Western industrialism sealed the matter. Western power was now superior.
Western rulers began to sense the advantages they enjoyed. Emboldened by
their underlying conviction of the religious and moral privileges of Christendom, they looked beyond Europe's borders for new lands to conquer and turned
their attention to Africa and Asia. The result was Western colonialism.

By the end of World War I, Asia and Africa were virtually covered by West-
ern soldiers, traders, merchants, missionaries, and teachers. In the Crusades
Europeans may have rushed to the Holy Land, but then they went to the Near
East only, and tentatively at that. In the nineteenth and twentieth centuries they
ran to virtually all of Asia and Africa, and did so with overwhelming force.
Immediately behind the adventurers, in some cases even before them, went
Christian missionaries with their gospel of salvation and with schools and hos-
pitals as well. Thus, empires were established: Spanish and French in the Amer-
icas and North Africa; Dutch in the East Indies (present-day Indonesia);
Portuguese in Brazil, western India, and China (Macao); and, greatest of all, the
British, on which it was said the sun never set. Ovey N. Mohammed has
observed that thereby "King George V, de facto, became the ruler of more Muslims than any caliph in history."[8]

In the minds of Westerners this expansion was fully justified. The gaping
maw of nineteenth-century industrialism needed mountains of raw materials,
and the benighted inhabitants of foreign lands needed the truths, methods, and
ideals of the West. The swap was seen by Westerners as good for both sides—
prosperity for the West and salvation for the East.

The exchange was not always appreciated in the East. One would later hear
Mahatma Gandhi say that he would rather be ruled badly by his own people
than well by outsiders. In that statement he credited the efficiency and power of
the British administration of India but was also offering a higher value, the right

---

[8] Ovey N. Mohammed, S.J., *Muslim–Christian Relations: Past, Present, Future* (Maryknoll,
N.Y.: Orbis Books, 1999), 40.

of self-determination as against outside interference. How dear that principle can be was well borne out, as the French and Americans came to realize, by the great sacrifices the Vietnamese would endure in order to expel first the one and then the other from their land. The West still struggles from the backlash of peoples who remember with no pleasure the days of Western rule in their country.

For Muslims, Western imperialism brought an especially painful problem. The lands of Islam, the *dar al-Islam* that was to be ruled only by Muslims, were now controlled by the infidel.

NAPOLEON AND THE FIRST SIGNS OF IMPERIALISM

Napoleon Bonaparte's invasion of Egypt in 1798 can serve to mark the beginning of Western imperialism over Islam. Equipped with the new armaments of the West, his forces entered Egypt with dominating military power. Napoleon's goal was to establish a base for invading Palestine and Syria, and finally, like Alexander two millennia earlier, for striking across southwestern Asia into India. The philosopher Gottfried Leibniz had once told King Louis XIV that the future for France lay with a canal across the Suez. "'It is in Egypt that the real blow [against England] is to be struck' wrote Leibniz. 'There you will find the true commercial route to India. . . . There you will secure the eternal domination of France in the Levant.'"[9] This advice lay behind Napoleon's campaign whereby he not only planned to establish the greatest Western-based empire since the Romans and create a better passage to Asia, but thought to create in Palestine a new homeland for the Jews, the first major European leader to so propose. Once all of that was complete he would return to Europe as master of the world.

The fate of Napoleon's enterprise was signaled with the destruction of the French fleet by Lord Nelson's British ships in the Battle of the Nile shortly after Napoleon landed in Egypt. Even so, Napoleon moved his troops north up the Mediterranean coast to face the Turks and Egyptian Mamelukes at Acre. "The fate of the East is in the fort of Acre," he said.[10] From there he issued his proclamation to the Jews, "the rightful heirs of Palestine." In what was little more than a dramatic gesture, he called upon them "to arise," and "claim the restoration of civic rights among the population of the universe which have shamefully been withheld from you for thousands of years."[11] But his attack on Acre ended in defeat at the hands of the British, who entered the Levant as part of their new policy of supporting the Ottoman empire in order to protect their trade route to India, a policy that allowed no room for France. This time, 1799, the British fought at Acre for the Turks and won: in 1291 they had fought against the Turks

---

[9] Barbara W. Tuchman, *Bible and Sword: England and Palestine from the Bronze Age to Balfour* (New York: Ballantine Books, 1984), 164.

[10] Ibid., 165.

[11] Ibid., 163.

and lost. Napoleon, having lost his fleet and much of his army, returned to France, his glorious plan a failure. Twenty years later at St. Helena, he said "Acre once taken . . . I would have reached Constantinople and the Indies. I would have changed the face of the world."[12] He had failed in his attempt at a world empire, but he had announced what would later become an important Western policy, namely, the establishment of a home for Jews in Palestine.

Had Napoleon succeeded in his plan to repeat the successes of Alexander, he would have controlled both of the traditional trade routes to the East, the overland route across Iraq and Iran, which was lost with the fall of Constantinople, and the sea route that used Egypt and the Sinai peninsula to reach the Arabian Sea. In the latter case, his plan called for a canal that would have enabled ships to sail directly to Asia without going around the great land mass of Africa. But all of this came to naught and he left the Middle East in the hands of the failing Ottoman empire. Thus the first major attempt to breach the Christian–Muslim divide came to an end soon after it started, but due more to British power than to the power of Islamic forces themselves, a harbinger of an unfavorable future for Turks and Arabs.

COLONIALISM AND ISLAM

Although European colonialism was not initially focused on Islamic areas— the purpose of the sea passage was to go around them—the Portuguese command of the Arabian Sea and the Indian Ocean, the Dutch conquest of the East Indies (presently Indonesia), and the British takeover of India with its substantial Muslim population all affected Muslims directly. But the great heartland of Islam, North Africa and the Middle East, lay largely untouched by European colonialism until well into the nineteenth century.

THE MEDITERRANEAN

Direct entry into the western areas of Islam began as a result of the Algerian piracy in the Mediterranean Sea that was noted above. To eliminate the base for these continued attacks, Charles X of France ordered the occupation of the cities of Oran and Bone in 1830. When Algerians mounted a revolt in 1834, France enlarged its control over Algeria and created the first lasting European colony in North Africa and, save for Sicily and southern Spain, the first European sovereignty over a traditionally Muslim area since the Crusades. In 1881 the French established their protectorate over Tunisia.

European power in North Africa moved eastward when the British took control of the Suez Canal in 1875 after the Egyptians defaulted on their loan payments to the French. In December 1882, Italy began its occupation of Eritrea and its colonization of Africa, which led to Italy's occupation of Libya in 1911.

---

[12] Ibid., 165.

Libya later came into British hands in 1943 through the British campaign in North Africa.

As an increasing number of Europeans settled in the Near East to conduct trade and diplomacy, the European powers asked the Porte, the "White House" of the Ottoman empire, for legal authority over their citizens. In time this control was granted, but the shift undermined the classical Islamic method of handling non-Muslims, the "protected minorities" within Islam. With this new arrangement the Western powers were asking Islam to exempt Europeans from Islamic law as it had applied to them. Many Muslims saw this demand correctly as an intrusion into Islamic society.

When World War I opened, the Ottoman empire still controlled the Middle East, at least nominally, but when the Ottomans lost the war (they sided with Germany), the Middle East came under the domination of Europeans. The Ottomans had been a declining force in the Near East for a century or more, their poor, even corrupt administration and management being the root cause. Several of the lands they held had already been given over to a virtual independent status—Egypt and much of the Levant were ruled in name only. With the downfall of the empire, these Ottoman areas came under mandates of the League of Nations and were divided between the French and the British. Thus France and Britain became key players in the history of Syria, Lebanon, Palestine, Iraq, and much of North Africa. The classical Islamic pattern of the *dar al-Islam* was violated. Three Islamic countries that avoided this control were Afghanistan, Turkey, and Saudi Arabia. Afghan resistance had been able to fend off British attacks earlier in the nineteenth century. Turkey, after staging a successful revolt against their new rulers, established a Western-style nation-state shortly after World War I. Saudi Arabia was able to negotiate its separateness with Britain.

Egypt and its Suez Canal were a special case. The canal was built under the auspices of France in order to shorten the sea connection with Asia for Europeans and, ostensibly, to provide income for Egypt. It was completed in 1869. Financing for the project was so convoluted and unfavorable for the Egyptians, apparently by European design, that an enforced bankruptcy brought the operation of the canal into the hands of the British in 1875. British military occupation of Egypt came after their victories in World War I. Never outright rulers of Egypt, as they were in India, the British nonetheless dominated much of Egyptian political life until they negotiated a gradual withdrawal in 1936. When Gamal Abd-al-Nasser, president of Egypt, nationalized the canal twenty years later, the British and the French, with the assistance of Israel, mounted a joint military action to retake it, but they withdrew their forces quickly in response to strong opposition by the United States and others. Since then the canal has been owned and operated by Egypt.

BRITISH OCCUPATION OF PALESTINE

Jewish Zionism and the background of British support for that movement will come under review later. The present discussion will be limited to the political and military side of Britain's involvement in the establishment of the state of Israel. Britain announced its support for Palestine as a "National Home for the Jews" in its famous 1917 Balfour Declaration. Save for Napoleon's grandstanding statement a century earlier, the Balfour Declaration was the first formal pledge to this goal by a national power. Prior to World War I, Britain, long interested in Palestine as a base for its strategic interests in Asia, had played a waiting game with the Ottomans, supporting "the sick man of Europe," as some called the Ottomans, until events brought the empire's fall toward the end of the war. Empowered by the mandates of the League of Nations that ensued, France moved into Lebanon and Syria, and England into Palestine.

Jerusalem had fallen to British forces on December 9, 1917, a month after the Balfour Declaration. When the city surrendered, General Edmund Allenby, the British commander, dismounted from his horse in respect for the Holy City and entered Jerusalem through the Jaffa Gate on foot. The date was December 11, 1917.

Ironies and contrasts abound in these events. The British general had succeeded where in 1192 the English king, Richard the Lionheart, had failed. King Richard had sought the land for Christians; General Allenby, under British policy, was taking it for Jews. The First Crusade began by massacring Jews in the German Rhineland; the British sought a homeland for Jews to escape such massacres. The crusaders' capture of Jerusalem could not have been more violent; Allenby's entrance was peaceful and respectful. Medieval fanatics of the First Crusade believed that killing Jews would hasten the Second Coming of Jesus; some Protestant supporters of the Jewish homeland believed then and believe now that the event would be hastened by settling Jews in Palestine. But the population of Palestine was Arab and largely Muslim, and the interests of Arabs and Muslims were ignored.

Westerners had ruled Jerusalem first in Roman rule from 63 B.C. to A.D. 324, then under the Christian empire to 638; under the crusaders from 1099 to 1187, and very briefly under an agreement the emperor Frederick II made, from 1229 to 1244. But now, the British, with a religion that came from the Jews, conquered it not for themselves but for the descendants of their spiritual ancestors. Britain ruled the city until the establishment of the state of Israel in 1948.

RESULTS OF WESTERN COLONIALISM

Even though Western colonialism was not as specifically anti-Islamic in its ideology as the medieval Crusades had been, almost all of the Muslim world was affected, from the Atlantic shores of North Africa on the west to the East Indies and the southern Philippines in the east. The lands of Islam either posed a threat to British and European trade or were important for their resources and raw materials. By the end of World War I, when the imperialist campaign of Europe reached its peak, these areas were largely under Western domination. One can understand how pious and thoughtful Muslims found this new and unexpected situation disturbing. The glory days of Islam had passed, and a time of subjugation had come, bringing a crisis for Muslims that was not just economic and political but religious and psychological as well. For the first time in their long history they were ruled by the infidel.

Two developments changed this situation: the withdrawal of the Western powers when they dismantled their European-based empires following World War II, and the discovery of oil in several Islamic countries. The first allowed the principles of the *dar al-Islam* to be reestablished in Muslim lands. The second brought wealth that supported the economic and military power of several Islamic counties. With these developments has come a resurgent Islam intent on both implementing Islamic principles in society and separating as far as possible from the West. But the West is still present in its technology and science, in its conflicts with nations such as Iraq, Iran, even Libya, with the terrorism of groups such as those of Osama bin Laden, and most of all in the modern nation-state of Israel. These topics will return at the end of the book.

12

Modern Views of Islam

From Rejection to Acceptance

It is sometimes assumed that when religious and theological misunder-standings are cleared up, Muslims and Christians will automatically enjoy more cordial relations. This needs to be balanced by the realization that when all is said and done . . . there is a good chance that a Muslim will still be genuinely repelled and even offended. . . . The same would have to be said, mutatis mutandis, of Christians. . . . [B]ut as in life generally, one does not need to denigrate those with whom one disagrees.
—Kate Zebiri[1]

As Western power increased from the seventeenth century on and Islamic power decreased, the Islamic threat also lessened and Western writers found it easier to think of Islam as a religious movement rather than a direct enemy. Western knowledge of Islam slowly began to increase, first with the study of Arabic, then with the publication of various Arab and Muslim documents, and then with the writings of people who met Muslims on the mission field. With this new knowledge, books on Islam multiplied and the views they carried diverged as well.

A foretaste of those developments was a book published in the 1670s by Henry Stubbe, *An Account of the Rise and Progress of Mahometanism: With the Life of Mahomet and a vindication of him and his religion from the calumnies of the Christians.* Stubbe denied that Islam had been spread simply by the sword, and he identified several unfavorable stories as "inventions," including the reports that Muhammad learned his teachings from Jews and Nestorian Christians, that his tomb hung suspended between two lodestones, and that he claimed his tame pigeon was the Holy Spirit. Stubbe interpreted Muhammad's Night Journey and Ascension to heaven as a vision, a reading known within

---

[1] Kate Zebiri, *Muslims and Christians Face to Face* (Oxford: Oneworld Publications, 1997), 234.

Islam. At the same time he continued to deny that Muhammad was a legitimate prophet, although he did praise Muhammad for his social and political accomplishments.

THE STUDY OF ARABIC

The study of the Arabic language was part of this new interest. A Chair of Arabic was established at the Collège de France in 1539 and at the University of Leiden in 1613. The accomplished Arabist Edward Pocock was appointed to the new Laudian Chair of Arabic Studies at Oxford in 1636. The earlier charge of the fourteenth-century Council of Vienne to establish schools for the study of Arabic, implemented briefly in the Renaissance, was coming to life once again. English-language versions of the Qur'an soon appeared, the first by Alexander Ross in 1649, and in 1734 a much more accurate and successful one by George Sale. The quality of Sale's work is attested to by the fact that Norman Daniel used Sale's version in his *Islam and the West: The Making of an Image.*[2]

In his "Prefatory Discourse" to the Qur'an Sale offered a much-improved description of Muhammad, saying that the Prophet had been improperly maligned: "Praises due to his virtue ought not to be denied."[3] He rejected the charge that Islam had been spread by the sword, but he did say that the religion was "no other than a human convention."[4] His portrait of Muhammad was so favorable that some readers even accused Sale of being a "closet Muslim."[5] Voltaire thought Sale had spent twenty-five years among Arabs, when in fact he never left England.[6] Norman Daniel says of Sale that he had "no axe to grind. He wants to elucidate the facts."[7]

EARLY WRITERS FROM THE ENLIGHTENMENT

Enlightenment thinkers brought an entirely new approach to religion and thus to both Christianity and Islam. They rejected the principle of divine revelation in favor of an appeal to reason, axioms of thought that were held to be

---

[2] Norman Daniel used it "as best expressing in English the meaning traditionally understood in Islam" (*Islam and the West: The Making of an Image* (Edinburgh: University Press, 1960), 14.

[3] Clinton Bennett, *In Search of Muhammad* (London and New York: Cassell, 1998), 98.

[4] Ibid., 99.

[5] Clinton Bennett, a confessing Christian, reports something similar from his own experience. "Some of my Muslim friends have said that they cannot understand why someone who knows so much about Islam can remain a non-Muslim" (*In Search of Muhammad,* 8).

[6] Ibid., 23.

[7] Ibid., 99, quoting Daniel's 1993 edition of *Islam and the West*. The 1960 edition simply says "Sale grinds no axes" (p. 300).

self-evident and universal. The question then became not which religion but whether any religion at all. The seventeenth-century philosopher John Locke spoke of "religion without mystery," that is, without divine revelation, and his view became the hallmark of the new interpretations of religion.

Count Henri de Boulainvilliers is a good illustration. In his hands Muhammad became an Enlightenment philosopher. In a biography published posthumously in 1731, he stripped Islam of its religious elements and portrayed Muhammad as a free thinker, the creator of a religion of reason. The count said that if one took away the miracles and mysteries, Muhammad's religion was true in its essentials. The Prophet's religion required no mortifications of the body, no severe disciplines, and offered no mysteries that could be troublesome to reason. While that much of the Frenchman's view was not far from the truth of Islam, the denial of the divine removed the heart of the Islamic faith. On the count's view, Muhammad became an Arab deist, not the fiery Meccan prophet with the powerful revelations of the Qur'an. This is quite a change from Peter the Venerable's view of Muhammad as a man inspired by Satan. No Muslim would have accepted Peter's ideas, but they would have understood him. The count's presentation would probably have been a mystery.

Edward Gibbon discussed Muhammad in his famous *History of the Decline and Fall of the Roman Empire* (1776-1788) and gave mixed reviews to both Muhammad and Islam. He described the Islamic movement rather fulsomely, "not as something separate and isolated, nor as a regrettable aberration from the onward march of the Church, but as a part of human history," to use the words of Bernard Lewis.[8] But the old biases and prejudgments remained. "From his earliest youth Mahomet was addicted to religious contemplation; . . . in the cave of Hera, three miles from Mecca, he consulted the spirit of fraud or enthusiasm, whose abode is not in the heavens, but in the mind of the prophet."[9] Gibbon's description of the Qur'an is as reprehensible as it is colorful: "the endless incoherent rhapsody of fable, and precept, and declamation, which seldom excites a sentiment or an idea, which sometime crawls in the dust and is sometimes lost in the clouds. . . ."[10] The Muslim confession of one God with Muhammad as his prophet was "compounded of an eternal truth and a necessary fiction."[11] But in praise of the Meccan Prophet he could say: "He breathed among the faithful a spirit of charity and friendship; recommended the practice of the social virtues; and checked, by his law and precepts, the thirst of revenge, and the oppression of widows and orphans."[12]

---

[8] Bernard Lewis, *Islam and the West* (New York and Oxford: Oxford University Press, 1993), 9.

[9] Ibid., 97.

[10] Ibid.

[11] Ibid.

[12] Edward Gibbon, *Great Books of the Western World*, ed. Mortimer J. Adler, vol. 38, *Gibbon II*, 2nd ed. (Chicago: University of Chicago Press, 1990), 253.

THEOLOGICAL VIEWS: POSITIVE ELEMENTS IN ISLAM

A Theologian: J. F. D. Maurice

As the nineteenth-century missionary movement progressed, British Christians had direct contact with Islam in both India and Africa. Some continued the tradition of rejecting the religion altogether, while others saw positive elements in it. Though not a missionary himself, the writer who can be called the theologian of the latter view was John Frederick Denison Maurice, whom one scholar has called "the most important [British] thinker in the middle of the nineteenth century."[13] In his book *The Religions of the World*, Maurice explained, rather like Nicholas of Cusa before him, that Christians should accept good wherever they find it, even in religions traditionally thought to be unworthy. Albert Hourani says, "For Maurice, the essence of religion was 'the faith in men's hearts.'"[14] Maurice suggested that because humans are made in the image of God, all have some innate sense of divinity, and thus some portion of divine revelation. Maurice not only rejected the view that Islam was an enemy of Christianity, but said that, because of its high sense of morality, its strong religious practices, and its clear monotheism, it was a preparation for Christian faith and a religion that fitted into the overall plan of God's providence.

A Missionary's View: Bishop Crowther

Bishop Samuel Adjai Crowther, a Yoruba clergyman and missionary to his own people in West Africa, did not study with Maurice, but his method of communicating Christianity would probably have pleased the King's College professor. Crowther learned early that arguing over beliefs "where one party cries 'Jesus is the Son of God' and the other 'No, he is not' was useless."[15] Seeking a common ground between Christianity and Islam, he focused on themes common to both religions, such as Jesus' role as prophet and his miraculous birth. Instead of arguing, he used Christian scripture with Muslims, reading stories from the Bible, and, if asked questions, he cited an appropriate biblical text. He said, "there was no argument, no dispute, no objection made, but the questions were answered direct from the Word of God."[16] His audience often noted that Crowther's scripture was in their language, Yoruba, not a foreign tongue. Andrew F. Walls says of him:

---

[13] Hubert Cunliffe-Jones, quoted by Clinton Bennett, *Victorian Images of Islam* (London: Grey Seal Books, 1992), 46.

[14] Albert Hourani, *Islam in European Thought* (Cambridge: Cambridge University Press, 1991), 20-21.

[15] Andrew F. Walls, *The Cross-Cultural Process in Christian History: Studies in the Transmission and Appropriation of Faith* (Maryknoll, N.Y.: Orbis Books, 2002), 144.

[16] Ibid., 145.

Crowther, the African leader of an African mission, had developed an African Christian approach to Islam in an African setting. It parted company from the assumptions about Islam that had been current in missionary writing in Crowther's formative years; there was no denunciation, no allegations of imposture or false prophecy.[17]

His approach was to present Christianity as the fulfillment of Islam, not as its opponent and contradiction.

REGINALD BOSWORTH SMITH

Reginald Bosworth Smith, a Harrow schoolmaster, added two things to Maurice's view, namely, results from the new field of comparative religions, and the idea of evolution. Believing that all religions are based on a commitment to the moral life, Smith credited Muhammad with raising the moral level of Arabs, and thus bequeathing to his followers a strong sense of ethical principles. Christianity was the pinnacle of religion's evolution and thus superior to all other religions, but it was an ally, not an enemy, of Islam, since both have sought the elevation of humanity. He believed that British policy should encourage Islam, not fight it, because it could serve to improve the life of Britain's subjects abroad. Smith was the first Christian writer to name Muhammad a prophet. Muhammad, he said, "claimed for himself that title . . . which . . . the truest Christianity will one day, I venture to believe, agree in yielding to him—that of a Prophet, a very Prophet of God."[18]

THEOLOGICAL VIEWS: THE NEGATIVE SIDE

SIR WILLIAM MUIR

The traditional negative views continued. Sir William Muir, perhaps the most notable missionary writer of the nineteenth century, learned of Islam from Muslims in India, where he served as a missionary. A first-rate scholar, well trained in Arabic and often praised for the accuracy and fairness of his scholarly work, Muir published a four-volume *Life of Mahomet* as well as an English-language account of the *Apology* of al-Kindy, partly a summary, partly a translation, with Arabic text. Muir received praise for the scholarship of his *Life of Mahomet*, but he rejected Islam as a religion. "Mohammedanism," he said, was "perhaps the only undisguised and formidable antagonist of Christianity."[19] He said two factors had prevented Christians from destroying Islam: one was the Christians' use

---

[17] Ibid., 146

[18] Quoted by Clinton Bennett, *Victorian Images of Islam* (London: Grey Seal Books, 1992), 86.

[19] In an 1845 article printed in the *Calcutta Review* (Norman Daniel, *Islam, Europe, and Empire* [Edinburgh: University Press, 1966], 32).

of images, and the other was the Muslims' bigotry, concubinage, and preference for a lower level of morality. Opponent of Islam as he was, his insistence on accurate descriptions of Islam is impressive, but Muslim readers might have seen little gain in an accuracy of facts in the light of his overall negative evaluation of their religion.

Muir is a clear example of colonial imperialism. As a missionary in India, he believed that the Christian West had a responsibility to bring enlightenment and health to demented Asians living in the darkness of their old traditions. His commitment to Christianity as absolute truth was part of this attitude, but part also was his embrace of the principle of the "white man's burden," the idea that the "civilized" Christian West had a responsibility to bring light to the heathen in their darkness.

HENDRIK KRAEMER

In 1938 the Protestant theologian Hendrik Kraemer published *The Christian Message in a Non-Christian World*, probably the most important book of the mid-twentieth century on the subject of Christianity and other religions. Like the famous Karl Barth, the twentieth-century Protestant theologian par excellence, Kraemer distinguished between "religion," those beliefs and practices created by humans, and "revelation," the truth that God gives to humans. Barth and Kraemer placed Christianity in the second category, all other religions in the first—they had only human beliefs and no divine presence. Kraemer's views defined the attitude of the majority of Christians toward other religions for decades.

ROMANTICISM: THE MIDDLE EAST AS EXOTIC

If thinkers in the Enlightenment turned Muhammad into a philosopher, and some theologians found authentic religion in Islam, the popular mind turned to romanticism. This began with the translation of *The Thousand-and-One Nights*. The book was first put into French in 1704 by Antoine Galland and then into English in 1885 by Richard Burton, the adventurer and writer famous for his visit to Mecca.[20] The book's portrayal of the mysterious customs and manners of the Orient with sensual harems, chivalrous behavior, and exciting travels piqued the interest of European readers and led many of them to the Middle East as tourists. One report says that for a time this book was second only to the Bible in sales in England. The problem was that the exoticism Europeans drew from the book was more the creation of the European mind than something characteristic of Islamic or Arab culture. Europeans again saw in Islamic and Arab life largely what European eyes could behold, not what that culture

---

[20] Non-Muslims are prohibited from the Holy City upon pain of death. A few have entered, however, Burton being one.

was in itself. "The great change . . . was to reduce polemic, and to replace it by exotic entertainment."[21]

Sir William Muir considered Washington Irving's *Life of Mahomet* a romantic novel. He said that Irving had "amid the charms of a romantic bias too often lost sight of truth."[22] Muir, the scholar who knew well the Muslim sources, including those available in English translation, complained that British writers did not avail themselves of these sources, several of whom Muslims respected, but resorted to their own imagination instead. Irving revived the old charge that Muhammad suffered from hallucinations and delusions.

In one well-known case, the romantic approach came out in art. The noted lithographer David Roberts created a series of 248 depictions of street scenes, buildings, and historical monuments, half in Egypt and half in the Holy Land, that are collectors' items. Muslim mosques, the tombs of the Mamelukes, an Egyptian coffee shop, as well as the Pyramids and the Sphinx, and the famous temples at Karnak and Thebes plus the Valley of the Kings are all portrayed here in a spirit that is respectful and a style that is romantic.[23] Pastel colors, dignified poses, quiet gatherings, and impressive architecture all give an impression of the dignity of classical Egypt and an Islam that is staid and serious, but very comfortable. Roberts portrays placid, subdued landscapes and simple shops with people going about their business without stress or conflict. Islam here is a religion practiced by peaceful people within large, spacious mosques of architectural grandeur where Muslims gather in quiet conversation. No hint of violence or dogmatism is to be found.

THE ACADEMIC STUDY OF ISLAM

While the contacts of missionaries with Muslims had brought a new openness of outlook to some missionary writers, nothing would equal the changes that the academic study of world religions would bring. This work began in the middle of the nineteenth century, intensified in the first half of the twentieth, and then mushroomed following World War II. With the dismantling of colonies by Europeans, the basis for Western superiority quietly eroded and scholars could approach Africa and Asia in a more evenhanded way. When they delved into the religions of these continents, they found an impressive religious life wedded to sophisticated philosophy and literature, and the practice of denigrating Asian religions began to wane.

New studies of Muhammad and Islam came from scholars who knew Arabic and other Mideastern languages and read the texts in those languages, something only a few of the earlier writers could do. Louis Massignon, the great

---

[21] Daniel, *Islam, Europe, and Empire*, 9.

[22] Quoted by Bennett, *Victorian Images*, 114.

[23] I report here only on the descriptions of Egypt, since they are all I have seen. These are available on line at www.museum-tours.com.

French scholar of Islam, is probably the most prominent of the group.[24] Baptized a Catholic in his teens, he lost his Catholic faith only to regain it while an Arab Muslim family in Iraq cared for him during his fight with malaria. Massignon had a strong doctrine of the Holy Spirit, and although he still affirmed the superiority of Christianity, he believed that God's Spirit was active within Islam. As one writer says, "He . . . had no doubts that Islam bound men and women to God."[25] Massignon was a powerful figure in encouraging the study of Islam and was a factor behind the Catholic Church's important statement on Islam at the Second Vatican Council.

Other scholars followed. Examples are Tor Andrae, a twentieth-century Scandinavian scholar, whose biography *Mohammed: The Man and His Faith* still draws positive comments; William Montgomery Watt, professor at the University of Edinburgh, whose numerous books on Muhammad and Islam are monuments of careful and respectful scholarship; and Karen Armstrong, whose recent *Muhammad: A Biography of the Prophet* has been cited in this work. These and many more represent attempts by Western scholars to get to the heart of the story of Muhammad. Their method is the so-called objective method of modern historical study, which does not argue for the truthfulness or falsehood of the religion under consideration, though some will challenge received traditions and opinions. The recent work of Patricia Crone and Michael Cook illustrates the latter.[26] They argue that the Qur'an, in part at least, is not from Muhammad but was composed after his death, and that the information about him in the *hadith* is less reliable than Muslims have claimed. Others have revived the old view that Muhammad drew on both Jewish and Christian materials in developing Islam.

ORIENTALISTS: IMPERIALISTS OF THE BOOK

The heavy work of research and translation was done by "Orientalists," Western scholars who became experts in Asian life and culture, particularly of the Middle East. The early Orientalists were linguists who read and translated Middle Eastern texts, usually Arabic-language materials, but soon their group broadened into historians who wrote on Middle Eastern history and culture. They followed the modern historical-critical method, which claims to be objective and nonjudgmental. But critics charge that their interpretations were biased in favor of the West and that these scholars not only shared the viewpoint of Western colonialism but often worked in support of the colonial powers as consultants and advisers. Philip Hitti, Lebanese by birth and cited several time in

---

[24] Hourani reports that a photograph of the Allied entry into Jerusalem on December 11, 1917, shows both Massignon and T. E. Lawrence among the officers entering the city (*Islam in European Thought*, 116).

[25] Hugh Goddard, *A History of Christian-Muslim Relations* (Edinburgh: Edinburgh University Press, 2000), 155, quoting B. Breiner.

[26] Patricia Crone and Michael Cook, *Hagarism: The Making of the Islamic World* (Cambridge: Cambridge University Press, 1977).

this study, and Massignon are examples of Orientalists with whom Edward Said, a Columbia University professor and the most prominent of these critics, finds fault. He argues that the Orientalists' factual, impersonal approach to other peoples and their beliefs is disrespectful and hypocritical, and that even its claim of objectivity masks an inherent posture of superiority.[27]

Said's criticisms have merit. For one thing, Western accounts of Islamic and Arab life sometimes have a sterile quality about them that can appear, rightly or wrongly, as condescension. The so-called objective approach often tends to reduce the religion and/or the culture under consideration to an "it," thereby ignoring the spirit and life that radiate within the reality. The late Professor Fazlur Rahman makes the point: "The Orientalists, although they have made a remarkable contribution and have been, by definition, pioneers of modern studies of Islam, have studied Islam merely as a historical datum, as a dead body, so to speak, to be analyzed."[28] To write accurately and sensitively about another religion is a demanding, often controversial task, and many object to the cool, relatively dispassionate approach that characterizes much of the modern study of religion and religious texts. Crossing the gulf between the West and Islam may be harder than Nicholas Cusanus and Theodore Bibliander had thought.

INTERRELIGIOUS DIALOGUE

As the evidence mounts of deep spirituality, high motivation for ethical living, and a clear awareness of the divine in other religions, many theologians have found it increasingly difficult to downplay and ignore these religions. The late Catholic theologian Karl Rahner, for example, affirmed that if God is present in other religions, people in those traditions may know God too. Thus he said there are a number of different ways to salvation, Christianity being only one. He called those believers "anonymous Christians."[29]

An especially important illustration of this shift in theological attitude among Christians is the Catholic Church's Declaration on the Relationship of the Church to Non-Christian Religions (entitled *Nostra aetate* [*In our time*]) promulgated by the Second Vatican Council in 1965. Following a similar announcement on Judaism, the document reads:

> Upon the Moslems, too, the Church looks with esteem. They adore one God, living and enduring, merciful and all-powerful, Maker of heaven and earth and Speaker to men. They strive to submit wholeheartedly even to His inscrutable decrees, just as did Abraham, with whom the Islamic faith

---

[27] Edward W. Said, *Orientalism: Western Conceptions of the Orient,* 2nd ed. (London: Penguin, 1995), e.g., 4-9.

[28] Fazlur Rahman, *Islam* (Garden City, N.Y.: Doubleday, Anchor Books, 1968), 312.

[29] See Karl Rahner, *Theological Investigations,* vol. 5, *Christianity and the Non-Christian Religions* (New York: Seabury, 1974), 115-34.

is pleased to associate itself. Though they do not acknowledge Jesus as God, they revere Him as a prophet. They also honor Mary, His virgin mother; at times they call on her, too, with devotion. In addition they await the day of judgment when God will give each man his due after raising him up. Consequently, they prize the moral life, and give worship to God especially through prayer, almsgiving, and fasting.

Although in the course of the centuries many quarrels and hostilities have arisen between Christians and Moslems, this most sacred Synod urges all to forget the past and to strive sincerely for mutual understanding. On behalf of all mankind, let them make common cause of safeguarding and fostering social justice, moral values, peace, and freedom.[30]

The council reaffirmed the traditional Christian commitment to the finality of the revelation in Jesus, but its statement recognized positive values in Islam (and other religions also), thereby opening a door to conversations with their representatives.

Both the Catholic Church and the National Council of Churches have since established formal offices for interchange with Muslim leaders.[31] Protestant denominations in the United States have also put forth statements on Islam. In 1985 the General Assembly of the Presbyterian Church (U.S.A.) encouraged its membership to understand Muslims and cooperate with them on issues of social justice, and the denomination established an Interfaith Office.[32] Universities have established study centers, among which are the Institute for Christian-Islamic Studies at Selly Oak Campus at the University of Birmingham, England, and the Center for the Study of World Religions at Harvard University. Numerous schools and professional academic associations have sponsored study seminars and discussion groups. And universities, religious and secular, in both the West and Islamic areas, have shared speakers and faculty. As a result the last few decades have seen the proposals of John of Segovia, Nicholas of Cusa, and Theodore Bibliander for face-to-face conversations come to fruition. These conversations are aimed at gaining information and understanding, but they also

---

[30] *The Documents of Vatican II* (New York: Guild Press, America Press, Association Press, 1966), 663.

[31] In the Catholic Church, the Pontifical Council for Inter-Religious Dialogue. In the National Council of Churches, the Commission on Interfaith Relations.

[32] Byron L. Haines distinguishes three approaches Protestant churches have made toward Islam: the conciliatory approach of the Presbyterians (U.S.A.), the evangelistic approach of the Southern Baptists, and the moderating approach of the Reformed Church of America, which is relatively open in part but still somewhat evangelistic ("Perspectives of American Churches on Islam and the Muslim Community in America: An Analysis of Some Official and Unofficial Statements," in *The Muslims of America*, ed. Yvonne Yazbeck Haddad [New York and Oxford: Oxford University Press, 1991], 39-52). In 1987 the Presbyterian Church (U.S.A.) published a study book on Islam: *Christians and Muslims Together: An Exploration by Presbyterians,* ed. Byron L. Haines and Frank L. Cooley (Philadelphia: Geneva Press, 1987).

intend to share the meaning and experience of religious faith, replacing the "it" of academic study with the living presence of the religion.

Developing such interchanges is not easy.[33] Not only is there a long background of animosity and hostility, but Christians and Muslims tend to understand the role of religion differently. For present-day Christians, religion tends to be private, separate from civic and governmental matters, and even the subjects and concerns of the secular world. Islam, on the other hand, combines the two areas; faith and society are intermixed. Seyyed Hossein Nasr, an Iranian Shi'ite Muslim with a Ph.D. in science and history from Harvard, comments on this by recalling Jesus' command to render to God what is God's and to Caesar what is Caesar's. He says that Islam has never had the problem of distinguishing God and Caesar. From the beginning Islam "tried to integrate the domain of Caesar itself, namely political, social and economic life, into an encompassing religious world view."[34] Further, he notes that in every dialogue between Islam and Western Christianity, "there is a third partner which is secularism in the modern secular West," and this makes "dialogue much more difficult."[35] In that point Nasr offers a particularly important insight, and his observations illustrate how something begun with good intentions can founder on unexpected problems.

The May 5, 2001, visit of Pope John Paul II to the famous Umayyad Mosque in Damascus is an example of such risks. Because the mosque stands on the site of the former Church of St. John the Baptist, it was an appropriate place for the pope to visit. In the early days of Islam, both Christians and Muslims used the church for their prayers. Muslims later bought the church and replaced it with a mosque. Since Christians and Muslims claim that the head of Jesus' forerunner rests in the mosque, the mosque is sacred to the two groups of believers. Pope John Paul II's visit was the first of a Roman Catholic pontiff to a Muslim mosque, and the Umayyad Mosque was certainly fitting. But some Muslims, aware of the traditional position of the Catholic Church on non-Christians, wondered if the pope did not also have a private hope for the eventual conversion of Muslims to Christianity. (There are Muslims who wish the same for Christians in respect to Islam, of course.) Thus, a visit that on the surface seemed generous, open, and friendly raised the suspicions of the visited. Such is the nature of dialogue across religious lines. History, tradition, and formal definitions have been so strict and exclusive that bridging those separations is not easy.[36]

---

[33] Kate Zebiri has an excellent chapter on the subject and history of interreligious dialogue: "Factors Influencing Muslim-Christian Relations," in *Muslims and Christians Face to Face*, 15-43.

[34] Quoted by Ataullah Siddiqui, *Christian-Muslim Dialogue in the Twentieth Century* (New York: St. Martin's Press, 1997), 154.

[35] Quoted by Siddiqui, *Christian-Muslim Dialogue,* 155.

[36] The preceding December the Catholic International Theological Commission issued an important statement entitled "Memory and Reconciliation: The Church and the Faults of the Past," which says, following an earlier papal statement, the church must repent of "the use of force in the service of truth," confesses that "the history of the relations between Jews and Christians is a tor-

Muslims have generally been less eager to begin interreligious discussions and have often felt themselves invited guests, suspecting that the motivation for these conversations comes from a continuing colonialism or orientalism or missionary interest. Evangelical Christians tend to advocate the latter as the only legitimate approach Christians can make to non-Christians. And the statement of Vatican II itself implies a continuing commitment to missions, as a later papal proclamation explained.[37] Some Muslims have favored conversations with Christians, however, in the interest of clarifying what Islam really is. The World Muslim Congress (*Mu'atamar al-'Alam al-Islami*), The Muslim World League (*Rabitat al-'Alam al-Islami*) as well as other Islamic international organizations have supported and engaged in dialogue with Christian representatives.[38]

IS THE QUR'AN THE WORD OF GOD?

No more direct approach to Islam has appeared than that proposed by Wilfred Cantwell Smith in his 1963 Taylor Lectures at Yale Divinity School, "Is the Qur'an the Word of God?" Smith began by noting that no Christian scholar had asked this question before. Christians have seen the Qur'an as the word of Muhammad (if not the word of Satan), but not the Word of God as Muslims see it. If the Qur'an is approached as a book that actually leads people to God, it becomes not just a document from a different religion but a book to be respected for its authentic religious power, and even a book that can speak to Christians, or Jews, or others.[39]

---

mented one," and asks whether "today's conscience [can] be assigned 'guilt' for . . . the Crusades or the Inquisition." In neither that text nor the published statements of the Pope in Damascus are there any statements regarding Muslims, however. The text is found under www.vatican.va/ roman_curia/congregations/cfaith/documents.

[37] *Dominus Iesus*, promulgated August 6, 2000, by the Congregation for the Doctrine of the Faith, which offers clarification of the Vatican II statement, has been seen by some as pulling back from the earlier position. But the new statement probably only refines the earlier one, emphasizing the more traditional elements of evangelism and the necessity for the Catholic Church and its sacraments in the divine economy. *Dominus Iesus* says, "Inter-religious dialogue, therefore, as part of [the Church's] evangelizing mission, is just one of the actions of the Church in her mission ad gentes [to the nations]." The statement denies the view that "one religion is as good as another," but sees the prayers and rituals of other religions as a preparation for the gospel.

"Certainly, the various religious traditions contain and offer religious elements which come from God, and which are part of what 'the Spirit brings about in human hearts and in the history of peoples, in cultures, and religions' [Quoting John Paul II, "Encyclical Letter," *Redemptoris missio*, 29]." But these elements need the completing work of the Catholic sacraments. *Dominus Iesus*, published by the Congregation for the Doctrine of the Faith at www.zenit.org/english/archive/documents/Dominus-Iesus.html.

[38] Siddiqui, *Christian-Muslim Dialogue*, 175-84. The congress has been especially interested in religious minorities, since almost one-third of Muslims live as a minority. This in turn has made the representatives mindful of the situation of religious minorities within Islamic lands.

[39] A valuable and informative illustration of the latter is a recent book by one of the advisory

Laying aside the question of whether the text is true or false in a formal sense, Smith affirms that both the Qur'an and the Bible can produce the same result, namely, bringing the reader or hearer into contact with the Mystery of God. He observes further that both Orientalists and orthodox Christian religionists have made the error of reducing Islam to its doctrines and ideas while ignoring the quality of personal faith that is the living reality in the religion— the Orientalists in the interest of an objective, impersonal study of Islam, the latter in the interests of orthodox doctrine.

Clinton Bennett proposes a similar approach when he recalls the ninth-century Nestorian Catholicos ("Patriarch") Mar Timothy, who said that Muhammad "had walked in the path of the prophets." Bennett observes that, had Greek Orthodox theologians in those first centuries followed Timothy's view of Muhammad, "the result [among both Greeks and Latins] might have been different."[40] Like Catholicos Timothy and Reginald Bosworth Smith, Wilfred Smith saw Muhammad as a prophet.

The idea of interreligious dialogue is not simple. The hostility that developed over the centuries is not dead, and the Muslim fear of Western colonialism and the Christian tradition of triumphalism are not easily overcome. When one adds political questions to the mix—Western support for the state of Israel, the case of the recent Gulf War and the continuing embargo and air strikes against Iraq, the American military presence in Saudi Arabia, not to mention the background of the medieval Crusades and nineteenth-century colonialism, and what Muslims see as a decline in morals and spirituality in the West—one can understand that many Muslims may not respond favorably to such discussion. And many, perhaps most, Christians are not eager to enter into such conversations.

FROM THE MUSLIM SIDE

Muslims have their own opinions about Christianity and the West. Obviously traditional Islam considers Christianity to be in error. Muslims have generally considered the Christian attribution of divinity to Jesus to border on, or perhaps even to be, blasphemy, because it violates the Muslim (read "divine") command against associating anything or anyone with God. Christian scriptures, and Jewish as well, are held to be corrupt, and the Christian and Jewish refusal to recognize Muhammad as a true prophet of God is a denial of divine truth.[41] In these respects the traditional evaluation of Christianity continues as the majority opinion.

---

readers of this book, Professor John Kaltner: *Ishmael Instructs Isaac: An Introduction to the Qur'an for Bible Readers* (Collegeville, Minn.: Liturgical Press, 1999). Kaltner's book compares several stories common to the Bible and the Qur'an with a view to considering how the Qur'an can illuminate biblical passages.

[40] Bennett, *In Search of Muhammad*, 79.

[41] Zebiri reports on a number of Muslim popular-level books on Christianity intended for

But Kate Zebiri describes a number of Muslim thinkers who are relatively open to Christianity. One, Hasan Askari, like Wilfred Cantwell Smith, looks at the world religions as variations on the human response to God and thus fits Christianity, Hinduism, Buddhism, and others into a rationale that includes Islam as legitimate ways of serving and worshiping God.[42] Other Muslims recognize that many of the traditional Islamic criticisms of Christianity are unjustified, and thus find it easier to enter into dialogue than their predecessors may have been.[43]

Beyond the disagreement with Judaism and Christianity over doctrine lie substantive criticisms of Western society. Many Muslims see in the West an indiscriminate and loose sexuality, a commitment to hedonism, a weakened family structure, and violence and drug addiction. Many Muslims claim that the cause of loose morals and weakened social structures is the abandonment of religion as the foundation of society. They argue that the separation of church and state and the loss of an overall religious commitment by Western societies has brought a secularization of society that has undermined social values and morals, problems that Western societies struggle with and that Muslims want to avoid.

Finally, the history of the Crusades and colonialism and the attitude of superiority that went with them is not forgotten. Some Muslims see little difference between those attitudes and two aspects of the contemporary West, Christian missions and support for the state of Israel. Of the two, the question of Israel is the more serious, and the resolution of that situation would lessen tensions dramatically.

Muslim readers and finds that their criticisms of Christianity go beyond these traditional matters and move into misunderstanding and misrepresentation, rather like the medieval Christian material on Islam (*Muslims and Christians Face to Face*, especially chapter 2, "Muslim Popular Literature on Christianity," 44-93).

[42] Ibid., 164.

[43] Zebiri's chapter is entitled "The Study of Christianity by Muslim Intellectuals" (ibid., 137-82). The views of Muslim writers she reports on under the heading "Irenical Views of Christianity" contrast sharply with the views she describes in "Muslim Popular Literature on Christianity" (ibid., 162-70 and 44-93 respectively).

13

Zionism and the Establishment of the State of Israel

The Hebrew [settlements in Israel] and the state of Israel were shaped and structured by a continuous struggle against the Arab-speaking population of Palestine and the neighboring Arab countries supporting it. This process also shaped the character and consciousness of the Arabs, who now began to regard and define themselves not only as Arabs but also as Palestinians, although a separate Palestinian national consciousness had arisen among them even before the intensification of this struggle.

—Boas Evron[1]

The major contemporary instance of Western involvement in an Islamic area is the creation of the state of Israel, founded by the European Jewish movement called Zionism. The plan for such a state was advanced early in the twentieth century and even before by Britain, whose support was crucial for the establishment of the new country. While Westerners may not think of this development as in any way parallel to the Crusades of the Middle Ages or even to modern colonialism, many Arabs and other Muslims think of it in just those terms.

The conflict between Israel and the Palestinians is a struggle between two national movements, the Jewish-Zionist movement to establish the nation of Israel, and the Arab-Palestinian desire for an independent Palestinian state. Both interests date back to the early years of the twentieth century, but only the Jewish-Zionist cause is familiar in the West.

When the European powers relinquished their colonial possessions following World War II, the British and French withdrew from the Middle East, the British from Palestine and the French from Syria and Lebanon. The British left

---

[1] Boas Evron, *Jewish State or Israeli Nation?* (Bloomington and Indianapolis: Indiana University Press, 1995), 134.

Palestine as the conflict the Israelis call their War of Liberation, which established Israel as a nation, was just breaking out. Syria, Lebanon, and Jordan, areas that had been under French control, emerged into their nationhood about the same time, but without the violence that took place in Palestine. Those were Arab countries populated largely by Arabs; Israel was a Jewish country founded in an Arab land.

Most of the Jews who established Israel came from Europe to establish their new country in an area that had been Arab for centuries with no invitation from the Arab inhabitants, the Palestinians, to do so. The success of the Jewish-Zionist movement owed much to the support it received from Britain earlier in the century, though the 1948 military campaign was fought wholly by Jewish fighters using resources they had largely gathered themselves. In order to survive, Israel has needed the support of Western nations, principally the United States, for whom Israel is something of a client state, an outpost of the West in the locale where much of the world's reserves of petroleum is found.

Jews, of course, are descendants of the Israelites, many of whom were driven from their ancient homeland in a series of invasions stretching from the Assyrians in the seventh century B.C. and the Babylonians in the sixth century B.C. down to their final expulsion from Jerusalem and environs by the Roman emperor Hadrian in A.D. 131. Romans named the area *Palestina*, in order, as Mordecai Chertoff says, "to erase even the memory of Jewish sovereignty."[2] The Latin word *Palestina* (in English "Palestine") is a derivative of "Philistine," the name of Israel's ancient enemies who lived along the Mediterranean coast. One quickly recognizes the irony in using a word derived from Israel's past enemies for the people with whom they are now in conflict.

For the better part of two millennia most Jewish people lived in the Diaspora; that is, they were "dispersed" from their homeland, and relatively few lived in Palestine. Save for a brief participation in the Persian war against Byzantium in the seventh century and modest support for the Arab takeover a few years later, the handful of Jews who did live in Palestine dwelt there peacefully throughout this period. The canard one sometimes hears that the present conflict between Jews and Arabs in Palestine is just a continuation of a centuries-old conflict needs to be laid to rest. The truth is just the opposite: the conflict is recent.

The full story of the new nation of Israel is complex, but the outline is relatively clear and the principal actors are easy to identify: European Jews who adopted the Zionist cause of settling in Palestine; Britain, with its strategic and imperial interests in the Middle East; the Turks, with their crumbling Ottoman empire; and Arabs, both Arabs of the neighboring states and Palestinian Arabs. Following World War II the United States can be added to this list and on some occasions the former Soviet Union.

---

[2] Mordecai S. Chertoff, ed., *Zionism: A Basic Reader* (New York: Herzl Press, 1975), 83.

THE BEGINNINGS OF ZIONISM

The Jewish movement to create a national homeland began in Europe at the end of the nineteenth century and took the name Zionism, "Zion" being a biblical word for the sacred hill in Jerusalem on which the ancient Jewish temple stood, and by extension a name for the Holy City. After their defeat by the Babylonians in the sixth century B.C., Jews lived in an ever-widening Diaspora. With the spread of Islam, Jews in the Near East, like Christians, came under Islamic rule. Baghdad, for example, the great Islamic capital, possessed a large number of Jews for centuries. Since Jews, like Christians, were relegated to a secondary status within Islam, their life was not ideal, but it was generally peaceful and productive, and, as we noted above, talented Jews often served in the courts of Islamic rulers.

The situation for Jews in Christian Europe was not as satisfactory. The massacres of the First Crusade were soon followed by official Christian decrees intended to suppress Jews. In 1215 the Fourth Lateran Council ordered distinctive dress for Jews and prohibited their entering the professions. Then followed the expulsion of Jews from various European countries, the 1555 papal bull *Cum numis,* which created Jewish ghettos, and the 1558 collection of papal and conciliar decrees for controlling Jews. In spite of these difficulties, Jews managed to survive, moving from place to place, finally settling largely in eastern Europe. In the early to mid nineteenth century, events seemed finally to be turning in their favor in France and Germany, and Jews began to think of the possibility of becoming accepted in European society. Following the lead of the noted eighteenth-century philosopher Moses Mendelssohn many Jews entered the public arena of culture, the arts, and literature. In 1791 Jews gained French citizenship and did the same in England in 1858. Their campaign for "emancipation," that is, full citizenship, continued apace, and the future looked bright.

Then things turned against them. In the 1880s Eugen Karl Dühring, a German philosopher and political economist, published a series of attacks on Jews calling for Europeans to cancel Jewish civil rights and force Jews back into their ghettos. Inspired by the anti-Semitism of Richard Wagner, Dühring declared: "The 'Jewish question' . . . should be 'solved' by 'killing and extirpation.'"[3] His criticism of Christianity as a Semitic religion was almost as severe, but it carried no call for violence. Then, during Holy Week 1881, the week that celebrates the crucifixion of Jesus, for which Jews had traditionally been blamed, a horrendous pogrom fell upon the Jews of Russia (*pogrom,* a Russian word meaning "riot," or "storm"). "Within three days all of Western Russia from the Black Sea to the Baltic was smoking with the ruins of Jewish homes."[4] One hundred sixty villages had been savaged, "a degree of brutality

---

[3] Paul Johnson, *A History of the Jews* (New York: Harper & Row, 1987), 394.

[4] Barbara W. Tuchman, *Bible and Sword: England and Palestine from the Bronze Age to Balfour* (New York: Ballantine Books, 1984), 231, citing Lucien Wolf.

unknown since the Middle Ages."[5] In May of the following year in Russia the Temporary Laws were announced, restricting where Jews could live and setting quotas for entrance into the universities. A tightening of the laws in 1890 prohibited Jews from owning land and banned them altogether from the universities or professions or government service. These "temporary" laws lasted until 1914. Hitler would later add concentration camps and gas chambers, the most horrible part of the European persecution of Jews, but, save for those instruments of murder, much of the rest was in place in Russia by the 1880s. Modern anti-Semitism as official governmental policy had begun.

Then in France in 1894 came the trial of Captain Alfred Dreyfus, a Jewish army officer accused of treason. The trial sparked an outburst of anti-Jewish sentiment with mobs crying "Death to the Jews,"[6] bitter emotions for which the Jews of France, indeed of the rest of Europe, were unprepared. European Jews had trusted the Enlightenment ideas of human rights and equality, and many Reform Jews had responded to the call to leave their ghetto-like life of seclusion and modernize their religion and customs. Now the policy of assimilation was challenged, even rebuked, and Jews were thrown into shock.

The reasons for this anti-Semitism are manifold, and the prejudice goes back many centuries, but the core of it was that Jews were something of a separate nation living within nations of non-Jews. Not only were they of a different religion and different ethnic group, but they carried a different culture and language. While not a political "nation," as a group they possessed many qualities that mark nations. Zionism would be based on that principle, namely, that Jews in fact comprise a "nation."

Although many European Jews were too deeply hurt by these threats and brutalities to respond immediately, some realized that something had to be done. Foremost among them was a widely respected Viennese journalist, Theodor Herzl. Ever since reading Karl Dühring's book, Herzl had brooded over the Jewish situation and had pondered the possibility of a Jewish state. Herzl covered the Dreyfus trial as a reporter and heard the shouts of the mobs. The call to send Jews back to the ghetto, the violence in Russia and similar attacks on emancipated Jews of Austria-Hungary and Germany, plus the Dreyfus affair in France, "the seat of reason,"[7] brought him to propose the formation of a Jewish state, and so, in 1896 he published his epoch-making little book, *Der Judenstaat* (*The Jews' State*).[8]

Herzl was not the first to speak of "Zionism." That distinction belongs to another Viennese journalist, Nathan Birnbaum, who established a Jewish nationalist fraternity in 1882 and in 1885 founded a journal, *Self-Emancipation*,

---

[5] Ibid., 232.

[6] Ibid., 284. "*A mort les Juifs!*"

[7] Ibid.

[8] The German title has usually been rendered "the Jewish State," but Henk Overberg argues for "the Jews' State," a more literal rendering (Theodor Herzl, *The Jews' State: A Critical English Translation*, trans. Henk Overberg [Northvale, NJ; Jerusalem: Jason Aronson Inc., 1997], 3-4).

in which the term Zionism was first used. But Herzl made Zionism a household word and sparked the movement. From then until his untimely death some eight years later, Herzl gave himself unstintingly to this new cause, a virtual Moses pressing for a new exodus.

The hope of Jews for a return to their ancient land had been kept alive during the centuries while Jews struggled for survival within Christendom. Family and synagogue celebrations often ended with the motto "Next year in Jerusalem." The developments in the late nineteenth century raised difficulties for Jews to an alarming level once again. Herzl then put the question bluntly: "Are we to 'get out' and where to? Or may we yet remain? and how long?"[9]

Herzl opposed the plan then popular that Jews should simply move to Palestine and settle there, arguing that immigration into Palestine could be stopped at any time by whatever authority controlled the area and that nothing short of possessing their land as a Jewish nation-state could secure the future of the Jewish people. Thus his little book begins: "The concept with which I am dealing in this pamphlet is very old. It is the establishment of the Jews' State."[10] He described growing anti-Semitism as the propelling force behind his proposal and proceeded to lay out a plan for financing and implementing the establishment of a nation-state for Jews. Herzl even thought that anti-Semitic sentiments would aid Jews in this goal, supposing that Europeans would be glad to see Jews leave, but in this he was mistaken. In his insistence on land, sovereignty, and statehood he did not budge.

Herzl's pamphlet and public appearances immediately stirred the consciences of European Jews thereby enabling him to call them to a European congress. When his followers met in Basel in 1897 as the first Zionist Congress, they stated plainly: "The aim of Zionism is to create for the Jewish people a home in Palestine secured by public law."[11]

The Zionist movement had problems in securing finances and political support for the plan, and some Jews even rejected the idea of a nation-state. Orthodox rabbinic leadership tended to oppose the political movement, arguing that the restoration of Jewish people to the Holy Land was in the hands of God and his Messiah, and that the use of political methods compromised faith and even bordered on idolatry. Assimilationists, who favored accommodating to Western culture, felt the movement would aggravate the Jewish situation by calling attention to the differences between Jews and Gentiles. Others thought that energies expended in a political cause would lessen resources needed for other

---

[9] Tuchman, *Bible and Sword*, 281.

[10] Overberg, in Herzl, *Jews' State*, 123. Overberg argues for "establishment" over the usual "restoration," following a literal translation of Herzl's German word, *Herstellung* (pp. 215-18).

[11] Tuchman, *Bible and Sword*, 289. Abraham Shulman reports that from 1919 to 1923 over thirty-five thousand Jews emigrated to Palestine, almost all from Russia and eastern Europe (*Coming Home to Zion: A Pictorial History of Pre-Israel Palestine* [Garden City, N.Y.: Doubleday, 1979], 59). The first thirteen arrived on August 11, 1882, having traveled from Kharkov, Russia, joining a colleague already there, making fourteen (ibid., 8, 63).

activities, and some feared the activity could result in increased oppression against Jews.

Herzl was surprised at the opposition he received, particularly from emancipated Jews who feared that his plan to remove Jews from Europe would contradict their goal of acceptance and assimilation into the larger Western community. It is clear now, in the light of the German Holocaust, that their hopes for acceptance, at least in Germany, were in error. In spite of numerous objections to the plan, by the time of Herzl's death the idea of a Jewish homeland had been firmly fixed in the minds of many European Jews. The question then became when and how this goal would be accomplished.

BRITISH SUPPORT FOR ZIONISM

While Jews in Europe began to work toward Herzl's goal, the country that took up the cause was England, whose policies of empire had already called for a foothold in the Middle East. Barbara Tuchman, whose excellent survey of Britain's involvement with both the Jews and Palestine is a source for much of what follows, says:

> The origins of Britain's role in the restoration of Israel . . . are to be found in two motives, religious and political. One was a debt of conscience owed to the people of the Bible, the other was the strategy of empire which required possession of their land. . . .
>
> Long before Britain was an empire . . . the Bible . . . came to be adopted, in Thomas Huxley's phrase, as "the national epic of Britain." Thereafter England had, so to speak, one foot in Palestine. The other foot was brought in by the requirements of empire. . . .[12]

Dr. William Thomson, archbishop of York, addressing the Palestine Exploration Fund in 1875, even said, "Our reason for turning to Palestine is that Palestine is our country," meaning that it had given him the "laws by which I try to live" and the "best knowledge I possess," the Bible.[13]

As early as the Puritan Revolution the idea of Jewish resettlement in Palestine drew the attention of various influential Englishmen. Had not the prophets foretold that the Messiah would return after the Jewish people were converted and had resettled the Holy Land? Was it not also necessary that the people of Israel first be "scattered" throughout the world, even into England? Some stressed the second point, arguing that England should open itself to Jews, the only "isles" that lacked a Jewish population. Jews had been ordered out in 1291.

---

[12] Tuchman, *Bible and Sword*, xiii, xiv.
[13] Ibid., 1.

In 1649 Joanna and Ebenezer Cartwright presented a formal petition to the Puritan leader Lord Fairfax and the Council of War requesting that Jews be allowed to return to England.[14] The Cartwrights were thinking not so much of Jews as of their own Christian-based view of history whereby the conversion and resettlement of the Jews would usher in the great events of the end of the age. Nine years later a plan was proposed for Jews to enter England but approval came after so much haranguing and debate that most Jews felt they had received a cool invitation at best.

In the Puritan period interest in Jews, in the Hebrew language, and in the Old Testament mushroomed. Awareness of Arabs also grew with the establishment of the first chair of Arabic at Oxford University, occupied by Edward Pocock, the Arabist, who served as chaplain for the Levant Company in Aleppo, Syria, from 1630 to 1635.

No British leader argued for the restoration of Jews in Palestine more vigorously than Anthony Ashley Cooper, the seventh earl of Shaftesbury. Lord Shaftesbury was the great advocate of social reform in nineteenth-century Britain and, according to Barbara Tuchman, "the most influential non-political figure, excepting Darwin, of the Victorian age."[15] Inspired by the prophecies he read in the King James Bible, Lord Shaftesbury claimed that the British had a special responsibility to care for Jews and see them converted to the Christian faith and settled once again in their biblical homeland. Only with the conversion of the Jews and their move to the Holy Land would the time be right for the Last Days and the return of the Messiah. Engraved on Lord Shaftesbury's ring were the words "Oh pray for the peace of Jerusalem."[16] That peace would involve both the return of the Jews to the Holy Land and their conversion to the Christian faith.

Lord Shaftesbury's ideas on biblical prophecy were formed by the teachings of a sometime Anglican priest, later a member of the Plymouth Brethren Church, John Nelson Darby, who authored an interpretation of biblical prophecy called after him "Darbyism," or more commonly "premillennialism," which accords great importance to the return of the Jews to Palestine as a precursor of the Second Coming of Jesus. Both Lord Shaftesbury and Lord Arthur Balfour of the Balfour Declaration were reared in churches that shared this teaching.[17]

---

[14] Ibid., 121-23, 136. Tuchman observes that the first call for a restoration of Jews to the Holy Land was in 1621 by Sir Henry Finch: *The World's Great Restauration or Calling of the Jews and with Them of All Nations and Kingdoms of the Earth to the Faith of Christ*. He "predicted the restoration in the near future of temporal dominion to the Jews and the establishment by them of a world-wide empire" (Tuchman, *Bible and Sword,* 131).

[15] Tuchman, *Bible and Sword,* 176.

[16] Ibid., 178, quoting Edwin Hodder, Shaftesbury's biographer. Tuchman says that Shaftesbury "regarded the Jews as somehow passive agents of the Christian millennium" (p. 199).

[17] Donald Wagner's excellent article "Evangelicals and Israel: Theological Roots of a Political Alliance," discusses this fully (*The Christian Century,* November 4, 1998, pp. 1020-26). His article describes the connections of Protestant evangelicals with Zionism.

Although Shaftesbury was an advocate for the Jews, his interest was wholly within the framework of Christian doctrine, whereby he saw Jews as potential Christians. He did not envision a self-governing Jewish state in Palestine, but he did believe that settling Jews in the Holy Land would bring the principles and practices of European civilization to Palestine and that strong Jewish support for this program, including the financial backing of wealthy Jews, would be forthcoming. Shaftesbury believed, as did the Jewish leader Sir Moses Montefiore and the British traveler and writer Eliot Warburton, that if Jews could settle in the Holy Land they would undo the barrenness and decay that had set in over the centuries and the land would once again bloom and become prosperous, a theme often trumpeted by supporters of Jewish return to the Holy Land. So when Theodore Herzl announced his campaign for a Jewish homeland in Palestine, the proposal came as something already familiar in Britain.

BRITISH POWER INTERESTS AND ISRAEL

British commercial interests in the Levant began as early as the sixteenth century, when pilgrim journeys of Catholics to the Holy Land were replaced by the journeys of Protestant merchant adventurers. Commerce, not salvation, became "the new lure of the East."[18] These merchants were the first to put England into contact with the Ottoman empire, and they laid the foundation of Britain's later massive involvement in the Middle East. They traded for raw cotton, later a major factor in British mills and industry, for spices, gems, and even flowers (irises, lilies, crocuses, hyacinths, daffodils, and laurel), but not coffee—the coffee bean they spurned. To manage this trade the British formed trading companies, first the Levant Company for the Middle East (1581), and then the East India Company, founded by merchants from the Levant Company (1601). The second company was formed in order to break the Dutch and Portuguese monopoly on Asian trade, a monopoly that had brought a twofold increase in the price of the trade goods. The East India Company became a powerful factor in India and eastern Asia, an economic engine that was "destined to transform England into an empire."[19]

When the British took possession of the Suez Canal in 1875, the land of Palestine assumed major military significance: it was the eastern flank of the British position in Egypt. By then a booming trade with India was under way, the British Empire was beginning to take shape, and control of the southeast Mediterranean was crucial to those interests. The prospect of a European-type Jewish state in the Middle East was attractive, a client state able to help Britain defend its interests, particularly the land and sea connections with Asia. Some even dreamed that the establishment of such a country would stabilize the area, since it would replace the corrupt, graft-ridden Ottoman empire in Palestine to which all objected, both Arabs and Europeans. Thus Joseph Chamberlain, the

---

[18] Tuchman, *Bible and Sword*, 104.
[19] Ibid., 111.

colonial minister, made an agreement with Theodor Herzl that Britain would support Jewish colonization of the Sinai if Jews could get Egyptian approval. Britain thereby became the first nation to negotiate officially with Jews as a political entity and offer them the actual occupation of territory.

THE BALFOUR DECLARATION

The famous Balfour Declaration, named for Lord Balfour, prime minister at the time, was issued on November 2, 1917. General Allenby's forces were already in the Holy Land in a campaign against the Ottoman empire, which had allied with Germany, and they took Jerusalem five weeks later. The declaration proposed that the new Israel should occupy all the land from southern Palestine north through Syria, and from the Mediterranean on the west to the borders of present-day Iraq on the east. The French and Italians soon endorsed the plan, and in 1922 the League of Nations incorporated the declaration into its mandate for Britain to govern Palestine. This declaration would guide British policy until the late 1930s and early 1940s, when their need to prevent the Arabs from supporting Hitler caused them to retreat from it. Even so, the Balfour Declaration laid the basis for actions that would finally result in the nation of Israel.

The British envisioned a new era for Palestine, when Jewish settlers would put into practice modern scientific agricultural methods to make the desert blossom, thereby returning the land to the productivity it had enjoyed in ancient times, before, as the British believed, Arabs and Turks let it fall into ruin. Because the mandate of the League of Nations gave international approval to the British conquest of Palestine, it was presumed to support the Balfour Declaration. Palestine was open to Jews once again.

PALESTINIAN ARABS

While Jews, supported by the British, were forming a movement to create a Jewish state in Palestine, Arabs thought in terms of an Arab state. When Arabs of Palestine came out from under the less than charitable rule of the Ottoman Turks only to find themselves subject to the British, they began to look toward independence. They may have lacked the ideology and organization of the Zionist movement, but the more they saw of Zionism and the Jewish plans for Palestine, the more they realized that they needed their own state, free of British imperialistic rule, and without the Jewish nation they thought Zionism had in mind. Although the Arabs of Palestine had an embryonic consciousness of being a "nation" early in the twentieth century, it was finally the conflict with Zionism that brought this concept clearly to the fore. According to Boas Evron, "The Palestinian nation [as Palestinians think of it today] is a new entity, largely shaped by the conflict with Zionism."[20]

---

[20] Evron, *Jewish State or Israeli Nation?* 134.

Thus, by the 1940s two nationalistic movements were under way in Palestine: Zionism, with its plans for a Jewish "homeland," and Palestinian Arab nationalism, with its hope of expelling British imperialism and preventing the formation of a Jewish nation. The collision of these two nationalistic movements forms the heart of the conflict that has raged off and on for over fifty years in Palestine.

Zionist plans for creating a Jewish homeland, or even a Jewish state, had a great deal of idealism behind them, but their lack of constructive arrangements for the Arabs of Palestine proved disastrous. Nor did the British have a plan for handling the impact Jewish settlers would have upon the Arab population. In fact, many held the romantic view that because the Arabs were cousins to the Jews—both being descendants of Abraham—they were a positive and promising feature of the land.

Supporters of Zionism, like many others, thought of Palestine as a relatively unpopulated region that Arabs and Turks had turned into little more than a desert. Mark Twain's description of Palestine in *Innocents Abroad* would have suited them well: "Palestine sits in sackcloth and ashes," its valleys " unsightly deserts," a land of "far-reaching desolation." Jerusalem, he said, was "a pauper village," Capernaum "a shapeless ruin," the borders of the Sea of Galilee "a silent wilderness," and Magdala "the home of beggared Arabs."[21] Twain's description may be exaggerated, but it points up the fact that had Palestine been more organized politically and developed economically, it would have been difficult if not impossible for the Zionist experiment to succeed.

Rather than attempting to negotiate with the Arabs, Zionists concentrated their energies on Britain and the help the British could provide. There was realism in this approach. The Arabs would hardly have been amenable to a plan that took their land and made them little more than second-class citizens, and the Zionists knew that they needed a powerful ally external to Palestine who could provide leverage over the Arabs. Nonetheless, the attitude of trading the Palestinians away to gain land for Jews, ignoring the Arabs and the possible national aspirations they might have, was certain to bring trouble. This callous attitude for the swap they had in mind is well reflected in a slogan that became common in the Diaspora: "A country [Palestine] without people for a people [Jews] without a country."[22] Boas Evron observes that the old-time Jewish residents of Palestine would never have said this; they knew from firsthand experience that the Palestinians were a nation, and that they could not be ignored.[23]

---

[21] Quoted by Chertoff, *Zionism*, 22-23. Jews and others often charged Arabs with having deforested the land. Benjamin Kedar says that the seventh-century *Revelation* falsely attributed to Methodius predicted that "all the trees of the woodland will be cut down, the shape of the mountains undone, towns deserted, regions made roadless, humanity diminished" (*Crusade and Mission: European Approaches toward the Muslims* [Princeton: Princeton University Press, 1984], 29). In referring to this work earlier I noted that it presented in predictive form things that had already taken place.

[22] Donald Wagner credits Lord Shaftesbury with the creation of this slogan: "A land of no people for a people with no land" ("Evangelicals and Israel," 1021).

[23] Evron, *Jewish State or Israeli Nation?* 139. Evron quotes the 1923 statement of Ze'ev

The text of the Balfour Declaration purported to recognize the rights of the Arab people. According to the declaration, "[N]othing shall be done which may prejudice the civil, and religious rights of existing non-Jewish communities in Palestine."[24] But a later private, unpublished memorandum of Foreign Minister Balfour contradicted that policy: "Whatever deference should be paid to the views of those who live there, the Powers in their selection of a mandatory do not propose, as I understand the matter, to consult them."[25] Arabs had not been consulted in the formation of the declaration, and they were not to be consulted in its implementation.

Nor did the Jewish leaders themselves attempt to negotiate with the Palestinians. In fact they self-consciously planned an expulsion of Arabs from Palestine or, as they termed it, a "transfer" of Palestinians to other Arab lands. Israel Zangwill, an Anglo-Jewish writer, expressed the widely held Jewish view that Arabs had done little with the land and thus did not deserve it as their home.

> We cannot allow the Arabs to block so valuable a piece of reconstruction.
> . . . And therefore we must gently persuade them to "trek." After all, they
> have all Arabia with its million square miles. . . . There is no particular rea-
> son for the Arabs to cling to these few kilometres. "To fold their tents" and
> "silently steal away" is their proverbial habit; let them exemplify it now.
>
>   Many are semi-nomad, they have given nothing to Palestine and are not
> entitled to the rules of democracy.[26]

Thus Jewish leaders worked on plans to move Arabs out of Palestine. Their ideas included buying land from Palestinian landowners (but not selling it back), persuading Palestinians to leave, and if necessary even forcing them from their land. All of these methods were finally used. Nur Masalha, who has written on the Jewish policy of transfer, offers this interpretation: "At the root of this notion—that the Palestinians did not have to be dealt with directly—was the denial of a distinct Palestinian identity or any semblance of Palestinian nationalism."[27] This view considered the Arabs of Palestine to be simply Arabs, members of the large, widespread Arab populations, not "Palestinians," citizens who belonged to the specific land of Palestine. This would mean that Palestine

---

Jabotinsky: "[The land of] Israel is only 170th part of the immense area occupied by the Arabs. . . . The requisitioning of a tract of land from a people of vast holdings to make a home for a wandering people—this is an act of justice. And if the owner refuses (which is quite natural) he must be forced into it" (ibid., 150, quoting Jabotinsky's "The Morality of the Iron Wall"; the iron wall was to be the Jews' invincible military force).

[24] Elmer Berger, "The Real Issues in the Arab–Israeli–Zionist Conflict," in *Zionism, the Dream and the Reality: A Jewish Critique*, ed. Gary V. Smith (New York: Barnes & Noble, 1974), 236.

[25] Berger, "Real Issues," 234. The statement was made two years after the Balfour Declaration, but was not made public until some thirty years later.

[26] Nur Masalha, *Expulsion of the Palestinians: The Concept of "Transfer" in Zionist Political Thought, 1882-1948* (Washington: Institute for Palestine Studies, 1992), 14. Masalha's book describes the thoughts and plans of Jewish leaders in great detail.

[27] Ibid., 17.

as an entity had no legal legitimacy. Jewish leaders usually spoke in more muted tones, but the theme was the same: Jews deserved to be in the land, and the Palestinians did not. Jews would occupy the land, and the Palestinians would leave, one way or another. Most of them did.

To plant a people in a land they had not occupied for centuries for the purpose of forming a nation-state without clear prior approval of the occupants was certain to bring problems. Dr. Nahum Goldmann, long-time president of the World Zionist Organization and a person closely involved in creating the state of Israel, has described the error well:

> However legitimate its claims, the Zionist movement should never have lost sight of the fact that it represented an exception to the universally valid rule that a territory belongs to the majority of the population that lives there. In other words, from the ideological and ethical point of view, as well as from the point of view of practical politics, Zionism should have tried from the first to reach an understanding with the Arab world.[28]

Apologists for the Israeli cause cite a notable exception to this lack of consultation, namely, negotiations with the Emir Faisal ibn Husayn, perhaps the chief Arab leader at the time of the Balfour Declaration. Chaim Weizmann, Zionist leader and the first president of Israel, testified before the United Nations Special Committee on Palestine, October 18, 1947, that in 1918, on a mission to Palestine, he met with the Emir Faisal and reached an agreement with him. Weizmann said, "[T]he Emir Feisal [*sic*], later king of Iraq, made a treaty with me declaring that if the rest of Arab Asia were free, the Arabs would concede the Jewish right freely to settle and develop in Palestine which would exist side by side with the Arab state."[29] The agreement was part of a larger plan of the British to install the sharif of Mecca, Husayn ibn Ali, as the head of an Arab kingdom that would encompass Syria, Transjordan, and Palestine, within which the Jews would occupy a province. Faisal, Husayn's son, was at the time of the agreement commander of the Arab forces under General Allenby and a close associate of the famous T. E. Lawrence. Felix Frankfurter, one of the most prominent of the American Jewish leaders, received a letter from the Emir in March 1919, affirming the cooperation of the Arabs and the Zionists, stating that "there is room in Syria [the term in this usage included Palestine] for both [Jews and Arabs]. Indeed I think that neither can be a real success without the other." "We are working together for a reformed and revived Near East, and our two movements complete one another," he said.[30]

Weizmann argued in 1947 that the terms of the agreement had been met, the Arabs of Asia were independent, and the treaty should be honored. While the

---

[28] From Goldmann's *Autobiography* (quoted in Berger, "Real Issues," 235).

[29] Weizmann's testimony before the U.N. Special Committee on Palestine, October 18, 1947 ("Feisal-Frankfurter Correspondence," in *Zionism: A Basic Reader*, ed. Chertoff, 11).

[30] Ibid., 12.

reports of these agreements are probably reliable and the agreements perhaps credible enough in themselves, they certainly were neither openly publicized nor widely approved. Arabs have generally ignored the agreement, claiming that Faisal had no authority to make it. Nor can the document be used to argue for a Jewish state, since it speaks of an "Arab state" within which Jews would settle and live.

EARLY SETTLERS

Long before the political entity "Israel" was formed in 1948, Jewish immigrants had begun settling in the land, joining a small number of Orthodox Jews who already lived in Palestine. There were five major immigrations. The first was a group of fourteen Jews in 1882. Further immigrations for farming came in 1904-1914. A third began in 1919 after the outbreak of the Russian Revolution. The fourth was that of Polish Jews who had been "ruined by economic calamities deliberately produced by an anti-Semitic government." The fifth was the influx of Jews from the Holocaust following World War II. But Jews were not the only immigrants—between the two World Wars some one hundred thousand Arabs immigrated into Palestine, attracted, Israeli apologists claim, by the economic development Jewish settlers had brought to the land. Jewish population increased faster, however, due largely to their own immigration. Jewish inhabitants in Palestine increased from 8 percent in 1918 to 31 percent in 1948, from 83,790 in 1922 to 700,000 in 1948. Britain sought to limit this immigration for a time, but their constraints were only partially effective.

Jewish leaders expected that economic improvement would help resolve the problem of Jewish–Arab relations, but they were wrong, and the resulting tensions sometimes turned into armed conflict. The most serious of these was the Great Arab Rebellion of 1936-1939, which cost a sizable number of Jewish lives and was put down only with difficulty by British forces. Arabs were profiting from their better standard of living, but they feared the ultimate goal of the Jewish leadership, namely, a Jewish nation in their Arab land. Jews did not recognize that the Arabs' first interest was their own nationhood, not just an improved economic situation. Longtime Jewish residents knew better; they were aware of Palestinian desires, but the Zionist leadership did not listen to them.

THE FAILURE OF ATTEMPTS TO EXTRICATE JEWS

By the late 1930s the Western democracies had become aware of the plight of Jews in Germany and worked to extricate them from the peril that awaited them, a plan with which German authorities agreed, at least for a time. The problem was finding a place for Jews to locate. Proposals included Angola, British Guiana, Mindanao, Ethiopia, and the Dominican Republic, but for various reasons, all were rejected.

The Jewish situation worsened when Britain issued its White Paper of May 1939, announcing a limit on further Jewish immigration into Palestine and in five years an end to all Jewish immigration. The announcement also restricted the right of Jews to purchase Arab land. These were policies proposed as early as 1930, but now they were official.

Meanwhile, Western leaders had found themselves unable to rescue the Jews of Europe. Henry Feingold says that because of these two developments, namely, the failure to save Jews from Europe and the restrictions imposed on Jews in Palestine, "the Zionist view of a beleaguered world Jewry surrounded by a murderous world community became a fixation which is still in evidence."[31]

Because the Zionist movement was so small, its leaders needed an outside power for leverage against the Arabs. When Britain gave up this role, the Zionists found their answer in the United States, from wealthy Jews who contributed financial support and from political leadership in the government. "Zionism never veered from the basic tenet that it needed an alliance with a big power with vested interests in the region to back it against the resistance of the local population."[32]

The 1939 British policy against immigration into Palestine bore tragic results. That same year the British refused permission for three freighters overloaded with escaping Jewish refugees to disembark their passengers in Palestine. A similar event took place at Istanbul in 1942, where the *Struma*, carrying refugees from the Holocaust, broke down outside Istanbul and was towed into the harbor. When British authorities denied a Turkish request for the refugees to enter Palestine, Turkish authorities allowed a pregnant woman and two families to disembark and then had the vessel towed back to sea where it drifted until it was torpedoed and sunk by a Russian submarine. All but one of the 769 Jewish refugees perished.[33] Later the same year Jewish passengers of another ship, the *Patria,* were prohibited from entering Palestine, and the ship was scuttled at her moorings in Haifa killing some 252 Jews and British personnel. A later investigation charged that the explosion was probably caused by a Jewish sympathizer seeking to cast blame on Britain.

In spite of these constraints Jewish presence in Palestine increased during the period of World War II by some 25 percent. Their military strength grew through the development of a military arsenal and the recruitment of members of the Jewish Brigade that fought in Europe in the waning years of the war plus the immigration of refugees from Russia who had fought in the Red Army.

---

[31] Henry L. Feingold, *The Politics of Rescue: The Roosevelt Administration and the Holocaust, 1938-1945* (New Brunswick, N.J.: Rutgers University Press, 1970), 33.

[32] Evron, *Jewish State*, 133.

[33] On September 3, 2000, some sixty relatives of the perished refugees went by boat to the location where divers believe the ship sank, and in a ceremony of remembrance and grief offered prayers for the dead. The single survivor, David Stoliar, nineteen at the time, now of Bend, Oregon, did not attend but sent a letter of support (*Macon* [Georgia] *Telegraph and News*, September 4, 2000, 12A).

THE CREATION OF THE STATE OF ISRAEL

Following World War II, tensions and violence in Palestine increased. Britain had its hands full in trying to administer the area in the face of the increasing hostilities. In 1946 Jewish agents bombed the King David Hotel in Jerusalem, which contained British government and military offices, and in 1948 a Jewish force massacred some 254 men, women, and children in the Arab Village of Deir Yasin near Jerusalem. In reprisal Arabs ambushed a medical convoy a few days later, killing 79 doctors, nurses, and students. A British force some two hundred yards away did not intervene.

On November 29, 1947, a United Nations commission recommended that Palestine be partitioned into Jewish and Arab sectors and that Jerusalem be declared an international city. The proposal was unacceptable to the Arabs, who voted against it (one of the few cases where Arabs had a voice in decisions affecting them). Jewish leadership had objections, but they saw merit in the plan because it both recognized the principle of a Jewish state and defined its territory. Under this plan some 55 percent of Palestine would be allotted to Jews, who held only 8 percent of the area. In words that were as wrong as they were hopeful, President Harry Truman said the partition plan "could open the way for peaceful collaboration between the Arabs and the Jews."[34] The results have been anything but peaceful.

Because the United Nations plan had not been approved by both Arabs and Jews, Britain refused to participate, and the British high commissioner for Palestine departed on May 14, 1948, removing a British presence in the area. On that same day the General Zionist Council at Tel Aviv issued its Declaration of Establishment, which announced the formation of the Jewish state of Israel. The declaration stated that "the State of Israel will be open for Jewish immigration and for the Ingathering of the Exile." This policy was formalized in the 1950 Law of Return, which in effect "confers on every diaspora Jew the immediate right to become an Israeli citizen."[35] The proposal Herzl made in his book *The Jews' State* had been realized.

De facto recognition of Israel came from the United States immediately and de jure recognition by the Soviet Union on May 17. Arab forces from the five surrounding Arab countries had already invaded on May 15, and the first Arab–Israeli war was under way. The war ended in 1949 with a Jewish victory and the new nation of Israel in possession of some 77 percent of Palestine, considerably more than the 55 percent proposed by the United Nations in 1947. Forty years earlier Jews owned only 8 percent.

---

[34] Alfred M. Lilienthal, "Israel Is Created," in *Zionism: The Dream and the Reality*, ed. Smith, 129. "It was anti-Semitism and political and economic insecurity, not the attraction of a community, that led to the great waves of immigration to Palestine" (Georges Friedmann, "Jews and the State of Israel," in *Zionism: The Dream and the Reality,* ed. Smith, 36).

[35] Dilip Hiro, *Sharing the Promised Land: A Tale of Israelis and Palestinians* (New York: Olive Branch Press, 1999), xix-xx.

Three more wars ensued: an Israeli invasion of the Sinai following Egypt's nationalization of the Suez Canal in 1956, the Six-Day War of 1967, and the Yom Kippur War of 1973, all of which were won by the Israelis. Israelis fought the first of these wars primarily with their own resources, but in the later ones they were aided by Western supplies and equipment, mostly from the United States. Indeed, foreign aid from the United States continues to be the lifeline for the Israelis as well as a basis for the Arab charge that Israel is another case of Western imperialism.

Behind the conflicts between Jews and Arabs lies a single question: the right of Jews to create a nation-state in an area formerly held by Arabs. The conflict over Israel is sometimes read as a religious war between Muslims and Jews, or as an ethnic struggle between ethnic Jews and ethnic Arabs. While those factors are certainly present and exacerbate the problems, neither is the original cause. "The conflict [between Israel and the Arabs] . . . in origin and in essence was a clash between two movements for national liberation: the Jewish one and the Palestinian one. . . . The dilemma, in a nutshell, was that the Jewish aspiration to sovereignty in Palestine could not be reconciled with the Palestinian people's natural right to sovereignty over the same country."[36]

In order to deflect criticisms, defenders of the Israeli nation point to several positive factors in the establishment of Israel. The terms of the agreement between Weizmann and the Emir Faisal were met. All of the Arabs outside Israel are independent, a status gained through the Allies' victory over the Ottoman empire in World War I and their subsequent liberation of the Arab nations after World War II. In addition, Israelis point out that jobs created through the phenomenal growth of Israel's economy have benefitted Arabs as well as Jews and have prompted the immigration of Arabs into Israel. Arguing from these points and more, the apologists claim that the state of Israel has not only not harmed the region and its Arab population, but has improved both. Furthermore, they argue that Jews of the world needed a place of their own to exist as a nation that can protect them as other peoples are protected and supported by their nations. Since the land was originally Israelite, at least as far back as the thirteenth century B.C., they say that the Jewish claim on Palestine is just.

Arab defenders say that Arabs as a group had no say in the creation of Israel and that the Israeli nation was forced upon them by the power of arms. Moreover, when Arab armies entered Palestine in the seventh century of the current era, the land had not been ruled over or even lived in by Jews in any significant number for centuries. The fact that Arabs have lived and ruled there over a thousand years supersedes any claim Jews may have from the ancient past. Furthermore, while any Jew anywhere in the world is automatically a citizen of Israel, few Arabs are granted that privilege. Israeli citizenship for Arabs has

---

[36] Avi Shlaim, *The Iron Wall: Israel and the Arab World* (New York, London: W. W. Norton & Co., 2000), 598.

been controlled in order to make it legally possible to expel Arabs as resident aliens in case of dire emergency. And for years Arabs were denied representation in the Knesset, the Israeli legislature, due to the ban on Arab political parties, requiring Arabs to stand for election in Jewish parties, meaning they could hardly represent their own constituency. In the territories Israel captured in the 1967 War, Israeli citizens and Arabs live side by side, but the latter are "deprived of all political rights,"[37] since they live under Israeli military occupation. International law requires that such military occupation be temporary, but thus far the Israelis have refused to withdraw and return the land to the Palestinians.

Restrictions on the right to land ownership and land use are another problem.

Jewish settlement land, bought by the Jewish National Fund largely with money acquired from American, English, and European Jews, constitutes about ninety percent of Israeli farmland. This Jewish National Fund land may not be sold nor leased to Arabs. (On some of the land Arabs may not even work.) Leasing this land to Arabs became illegal with the passage in the Knesset of the Agricultural Settlement Law on 1 August 1967.[38]

Then there is the problem of the displaced Arabs. "The Zionist dream of de-Arabizing the country and realizing a clear Jewish majority finally came about during the 1948 war, when 750,000 Palestinians, or more than 80 percent of the Arab inhabitants of what became Israel, took up the road of exile."[39] Descriptions of the causes of the exodus vary, but one historian has suggested that one-third fled out of fear, one-third were forcibly evacuated by the Israelis, and one-third were encouraged to flee.[40] West Jerusalem, captured in the 1948 war, became almost wholly Jewish, enabling David Ben-Gurion, then prime minister of Israel, to announce: "Since Jerusalem was destroyed by the Romans [in A.D. 131], it has not been so Jewish as it is now."[41] Many of the former landowners were compensated for their land, but often the actual occupants were tenant farmers, sometimes families who had lived there for more than one generation, who were simply displaced with no compensation. In some cases entire villages were destroyed, the inhabitants turned into refugees, and the site then occupied by Jewish settlers. Many of the Palestinian refugees managed to emigrate to other countries, but most were left to fend for themselves, mainly in camps in Jordan which has had to struggle with feeding, clothing, and administering this massive influx. These Arab refugees became the base for the Palestinian Liberation Organization headed by Yasser Arafat.

---

[37] Evron, *Jewish State or Israeli Nation*, 203.

[38] Norton Mezvinsky, "The Zionist Character of the State of Israel," in *Zionism, the Dream and the Reality*, ed. Smith, 251.

[39] Masalha, *Expulsion of the Palestinians*, 175.

[40] Meir Pa'il, cited by Masalha (*Expulsion of the Palestinians,* 179).

[41] Ibid., 180-81.

THE TWO INTIFADAS

On September 28, 2000, Ariel Sharon, at the time leader of the right-wing Israeli Likud political party and former prime minister, visited the Temple Mount (the *Haram al-Sharif* or Noble Sanctuary to Muslims) in the Old City of Jerusalem accompanied by an entourage of security officers and fellow political leaders. It was the day before Rosh Hashanah, the Jewish New Year. While the visit itself was peaceful at the time, it proved to be provocative, and the next day violence broke out on the part of Arabs that has led to a continuing conflict resulting in several hundred Arab deaths and a smaller but still large number of Jewish deaths. Dubbed the al-Aqsa Intifada, or "uprising" (the name "al-Aqsa" is sometimes used for the Temple Mount as well as for the mosque that carries that name), this was the second such prolonged series of riots and attacks upon Israelis. The first Intifada lasted the better part of five years, from 1988 to 1992.

The quantity of violence in these uprisings effectively demonstrates the pent-up frustrations and bitterness of many Palestinians and is alarming not just for the injuries and deaths that have resulted, but because these are relatively spontaneous protests from the population itself and are not necessarily the result of a call for demonstrations from their official leaders, even though the Palestinian terrorist organizations seem to support them.

EXTREMISTS AND THE USE OF VIOLENCE

At least two Islamic terrorist organizations operate within Israel, Hizbullah and Hamas. Hizbullah ("the Party of God") was founded after the Israeli invasion of Lebanon in 1982, which drove the Palestinian Liberation Organization out of Lebanon. Hizbullah, a Shi'ite-oriented group based in Lebanon, is the origin of many suicide-bombers, including the 1983 attack on the U.S. Marine barracks in Beirut. The reader may recall that Shi'ite Islam emphasizes the principle that suffering in a righteous cause is efficacious. Reports suggest that the principal support for Hizbullah comes from Iran, a strong center of Shi'ite Islam. The membership of both groups is small, a mere fraction of the total population of Palestine, but their dedication, their methods, and their resources are so large that their power far outweighs their numbers.

Westerners speak of "suicide-bombers," but Hizbullah calls these people "martyrs," just as Christian writers speak of the eighth-century "martyrs" of Cordoba. The cases are not exact parallels, of course. The Muslim dies in effect by his own hand, while the Christians died at the hands of Islamic authorities. But the actions are similar, since in both cases the agents intend their death to create a result that reaches beyond their death. The Cordoba martyrs sought to hasten the Second Coming of Jesus; the Muslim suicide-bombers seek the destruction of Israel.

The second organization, Hamas—the name is an Arabic acronym for the Islamic Resistance Movement in Palestine—was founded in 1988 during the first Intifada. The movement is dedicated to the eradication of Israel in the belief that Palestine is a *waqf*, a technical Islamic term that identifies a grant made in perpetuity, in this case the land of Palestine, which Hamas holds to be a permanent part of the *dar al-Islam* that Muslims are obligated to defend. Hamas leaders view Western support of Israel as intended to remove Palestine from Islamic control, yet another development in the long history of Crusades, Western imperialism, and even Christian missionary activity and scholarly Orientalism, all of which they understand to have sought to weaken or even destroy Islam. Thus they are dedicated to their form of *jihad* as a means to defeat Israel completely, and even eliminate its existence. On the positive side, they provide significant social services in the Gaza Strip.

Hamas officials say their support comes from various organizations within several Middle Eastern countries. Analysts claim that both groups have been supported by Iran, perhaps Syria as well, and that they serve as agents in the fight of those countries against Israel, with the goal of eventually eliminating Israel as an independent nation.

THE NATURE OF THE CONFLICT

The city of Jerusalem is one of the most serious points of dispute. Sacred to Jews as the site of their ancient temple, and to Muslims as the place from which Muhammad was taken to heaven, and sacred as well to Christians as the place of Jesus' crucifixion and resurrection, the city is laden with conflicting claims and sentiments. Michael C. Hudson observes that were there no state of Israel, "Jerusalem would not only have remained under Arab control, but it might also have been the capital of an independent Palestinian state with an Arab majority and a Jewish minority."[42] But instead of experiencing a normal liberation from colonialism, the area was planted with a new state, one that was brought from outside the land and imposed on the earlier inhabitants.

An equally severe problem is the Palestinian demand for the return of displaced Palestinians to their former homes in land that Israel controls. If the problem of the Temple Mount/Noble Sanctuary faces difficulties of tradition and religion, the call for the right of return includes logistical problems, not the least of which would be matching people and property after half a century of separation. The goal of repatriation has had United Nations backing in the past. Following the 1967 War the United Nations in its Resolution Number 242 proposed that Israel hand back to the Arabs the territories seized in that war and recognize the right of return for refugees. The principle behind this approach was clear: Israel would get peace with its neighbors in exchange for returning to Arabs the land taken in the Six-Day War. Egypt and Jordan agreed to the plan; Syria did not. Israel publically accepted the Resolution in 1970, and in the 1978 Camp David Accords Prime Minister Menachem Begin agreed to the Resolution "in all its parts,"[43] but the occupied territories of the West Bank and Gaza have not yet been returned to the Arabs. Rather than returning the land,

---

[42] Michael C. Hudson, "The Transformation of Jerusalem, 1917-1987 AD," in *Jerusalem in History*, ed. K. J. Asali (New York: Olive Branch Press, 2000), 250.

[43] Shlaim, *The Iron Wall*, 260, 375.

Israelis have continued to settle in the West Bank in violation of that resolution, international law, and the more recent Oslo Accords. This continued pattern of military occupation of the areas taken in the 1967 War with the concomitant disenfranchisement of Arabs living there has only served to exacerbate the original problems. The metaphor of "powder keg" may be an understatement for the seriousness of this situation.

SUMMARY

The nation of Israel appears to be a permanent fixture in the midst of Arab states. While smaller than the Arab countries surrounding it, Israel has been no David among Goliaths since its military power has been superior. Now, however, Israel and its neighbors stand much nearer to parity in military strength. Israel's security is ensured by the support it enjoys from the United States and other Western countries, an assistance that may provide for Israel's survival but has done nothing to endear the West, especially the United States, to Arabs, or to the Islamic world in general.

The establishment of the modern state of Israel is another case of Western engagement with Islamic peoples, an encounter hauntingly similar to the medieval Crusades with their passion for land and their disrespect for the settled population.[44] In this case the conflict is not between Christians and Muslims per se. Instead, the principals are better described as Western powers, Jews, and Arabs. In fact many of the Arabs who have opposed Israel are themselves Christians. Even so, an old pattern has returned, namely, an attempt by powers within what once was Christendom to impose a non-Arab, non-Muslim state upon Arabs, most of them Muslims, and to continue that support by the force of arms. Nothing rankles Muslims, both Arab Muslims in the Middle East and Muslims of other lands, more than the events within Palestine of the last fifty-plus years. That grievance is a direct source of the continuing Arab and Islamic terrorism toward Westerners and Israelis. The terrorism may not be justified, but its precipitating cause is easy to identify and will not be removed until a peaceful settlement between Israelis and Arabs is achieved. Even then much of the hostility may remain.[45]

---

[44] One can also observe the invasion of the Canaan by the Hebrews of the exodus reported in the Old Testament. Many modern scholars will say that those events were in fact far less dramatic than scripture reports, but even so the story remains.

[45] For the reader who wishes current information on the Palestine–Israel situation, the Internet provides a rich variety of sources. Palestinian views can be found in the sites for the Palestinian Authority and the Islamic Association for Palestine. The Middle East Media Research Institute (MEMRA), a private, nonpartisan organization, gives translations of both Palestinian and Israeli documents, articles, and speeches—an excellent resource for information. Information on Israel can be found at the Israeli Embassy site, www.israelemb.org.

14

An Overview of Islam and the West Today

What had previously seemed to be an increasingly marginalized force in Muslim public life reemerged in the seventies—often dramatically—as a vibrant sociopolitical reality. Islam's resurgence in Muslim politics reflected a growing religious revivalism in both personal and public life that would sweep across much of the Muslim world and have a substantial impact on the West in world politics.

—John L. Esposito[1]

We are witnessing the "end of the progressive era" dominated by Western ideologies and are moving into an era in which multiple and diverse civilizations will interact, compete, coexist, and accommodate each other.

—Samuel P. Huntington[2]

We [i.e., God] have made you peoples and tribes so that you can get to know each other.

—Qur'an 49:13[3]

The Western world's view of its relationship to Islam was turned upside down on September 11, 2001, with the attacks in New York City and Washington, D.C. American financial markets were sent reeling, travel was curtailed, security measures were strengthened, and thousands of families found themselves in sorrow and grief. The nation was thrown into shock by a small group of terrorists who conducted an attack with methods no more sophisticated than

---

[1] John L. Esposito, *The Islamic Threat: Myth or Reality?*, 3rd ed. (New York and Oxford: Oxford University Press, 1999), 9-10.

[2] Samuel P. Huntington, *The Clash of Civilizations and the Remaking of World Order* (New York: Simon & Schuster, 1996), 95, citing Eisuke Sakakibara, "The End of Progressivism: A Search for New Goals," *Foreign Affairs* 74 no. 5 (Sept./Oct. 1995): 8-14.

[3] The citation as abbreviated by Hugh Goddard, *Christians & Muslims: From Double Standards to Mutual Understanding* (Richmond, England: Curzon, 1995), 11. The full text as Arberry renders it is: "We have created you male and female and appointed you races and tribes, that you may know one another."

boarding scheduled airline flights with legitimate tickets, carrying "weapons" that apparently fitted within the guidelines of security measures then in effect. The subsequent highjackings allowed them to achieve their diabolical goals.

While terrorism is the most dramatic and visible pattern of activity from Islamic areas, it is only one of several competing currents of social, political, and religious life. The most significant trend is the revival of Islam as a religious and political force across the entire Muslim world. Contrary to this so-called Islamization[4] is the intrusion of the West with its technology and science, but much more troublesome for traditional Muslims are its sexual laxness, materialism, and secularism. A third current running among the people of Islam is a desire for participatory government, itself opposed by yet another pattern, namely, authoritarian rule. These four patterns—Islamization, Westernization, democracy, and authoritarianism—plus terrorism, mark the outline of the struggle that Islamic societies have as they shed the colonialism they left fifty years ago and move into the world of modern nation states. Muslims are not having an easy time with this transition, and the uncertainties that these changes bring lie behind the turmoil evident within Islam.

A RESURGENT ISLAM

The most prominent of these movements is the resurgence of Islam. Fifty years ago few observers of Islam would have predicted the revival of conviction and commitment that has come to pass among Muslims. When Muslims were liberated from European colonial powers in the mid-twentieth century, their societies were hobbled by poverty, limited resources, and undereducated populations. Almost as troubling, they faced the powerful Western world with its intimidating science, technology, and wealth. Muslims found themselves living and competing within a twentieth-century world for which they were unprepared. To a considerable extent those factors are all still present, but within that setting Muslims have rediscovered Islam, turned to its traditions and teachings with pride, and have been working to adapt it to their new situation.

THE PRINCIPLE OF ISLAMIZATION

We can illustrate the idea of Islamization by the work of two twentieth-century Islamic theorists, Hasan al-Banna (1906-1949) and Mawlana Mawdudi (1903-1979), the former from Egypt, the latter from India, who proposed Islam

---

[4] The term "Islamization" and its cognate, "Islamist," are controversial in that they tend to distinguish one group of Muslims from another. I use the terms here to identify those people and movements that forcefully assert the power and relevance of Islam for today's world. Some of these are strict and dogmatic ("fundamentalist"), some even violent, but many simply seek to construct an authentic Islamic society that is able to compete and live well in the modern world.

as a third way for social life alongside capitalism and Marxism. They rejected capitalism and Western democracy, claiming that the West's separation of church and state had created a secular society devoid of religious and moral guidelines. Marxism was easy to dismiss—its atheism made it unacceptable. The proper alternative, they said, is Islam, because it is a total system combining law and religion, the social and the spiritual-moral. While some Muslim leaders were blaming the West for Islam's difficulties, al-Banna and Mawdudi argued that the fundamental problem in Islam was that Muslims had not been faithful to their own tradition. Hence they called for Islam's renewal.

Other voices have joined in this call, and as a result much of the Islamic world has renewed its commitment to the values and way of Islam. Muslim leaders have faced numerous problems in following this path, namely, whether to establish a moderate or strict form of Islam, and whether to implement it through public participation or authoritarian control. Egypt and the kingdoms of Morocco and Jordan have opted for moderate Islam, while Libya and Saudi Arabia have been more strict. The latter have also followed the strong-leader approach, while others—Morocco, Jordan, and even Iran—have included a democratic component in their political process.

EXAMPLES OF THE RESURGENCE OF ISLAM

An early evidence of Islam's resurgence was Colonel Muammar al-Qaddafi's 1969 coup that overthrew King Idris I of Libya. Qaddafi announced that Libya was to be an Islamic state governed by Islamic law, *shari'a*. Qaddafi's rule of Libya has been largely authoritarian, strictly so in the beginning, less so more recently, but his authoritarian approach set a model for others to follow.

Qaddafi's coup, significant as it was, did not register with either Westerners or Muslims as strongly as did Iran's overthrow in 1979 of the Shah Muhammad Reza Pahlavi. The Iranian revolution, nourished in its beginning by the resentment of the Iranian people against the Shah for his oppressive regime, was taken over and completed by the Ayatollah Khomeini and his Islamic associates, who reinstalled Islam as the ruling force in Iran. Khomeini's group banished the Shah, took over the American Embassy, held its members hostage for 444 days, and imprisoned or executed any who opposed them. The revolution brought a return to the strict laws of Islamic *shari'a*. Women put on head scarves, long sleeves, and long dresses; Western-style banking was replaced by institutions operated on Islamic principles; Western amusements were banned; and the pattern of classical Islam was renewed. The overall pattern was authoritarian, but the new nation was given the name the Islamic Republic of Iran, because its organization included some semi-democratic elements, namely, the popular election of a parliament and president. Final authority was kept in the hands of the *ulama*, the clerics who interpret Islamic law, a novel form of the separation of powers.

Nations with substantial Muslim populations

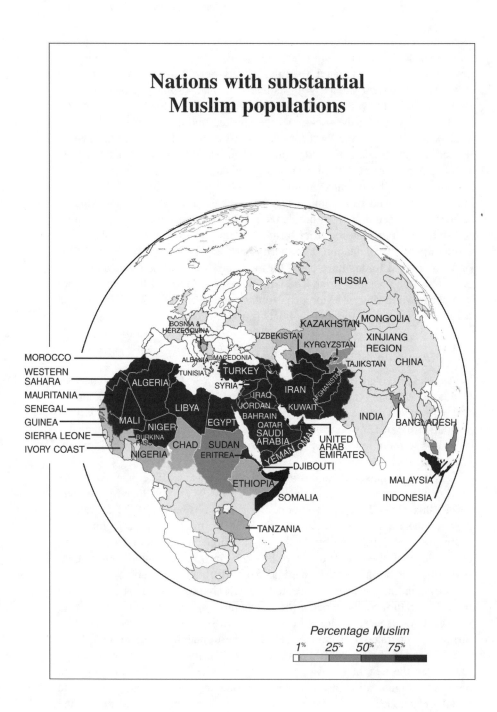

Predominance of Sunni and Shi'ite Islam in predominantly Muslim nations

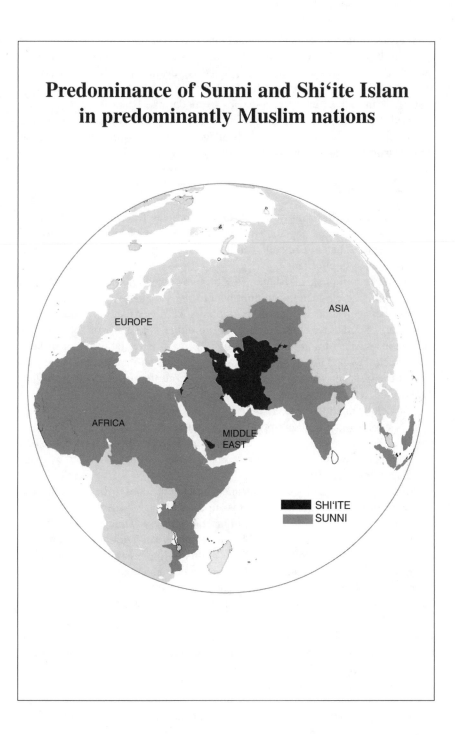

Many Muslims took renewed confidence and pride in Islam from these events in Iran. The West with its history of Crusades and colonialism had been ousted, and Islam was again in control of its own destiny. Muslim writers, political leaders, and anyone else who lived in public view behaved differently thereafter. Initiatives in other countries to modernize Islam were delayed or reversed, and soon it became fashionable to tout the glories of Islam against the alleged faults of the West, namely, its alleged godlessness, materialism, loose family structures, and open sensuality.

ADOPTION OF SHARI'A

The movement to Islamization meant a shift away from the secular side of Westernization to the acceptance of Islamic law as the social norm. Saudi Arabia, for instance, had already adopted the Qur'an as its constitution and named *shari'a* as its system of law.

But the requirement of Islamic law brought objections from non-Muslim populations. In the Sudan the commitment to *shari'a* aggravated long-standing disputes between south and north, prompting a civil war that has lasted almost fifty years. Southerners, most of whom are either Christians or followers of indigenous African traditions, have fought to resist the establishment of laws over which they had no say. Rivalries among leaders north and south have prolonged the war, and the discovery of oil in 1999 further inflamed the conflict. The United Nations estimates that the Sudanese civil war has resulted in two million deaths in addition to creating thousands of refugees.

In Nigeria several northern provinces want to reestablish the Islamic society they had before colonialism, but the southern areas, with a higher Christian population, are resisting. A result has been occasional violence, abetted by long-standing ethnic rivalries.

Algeria is an especially tragic instance of the conflict over reclaiming Islam, a dispute in this case among Muslims. In a 1990 election for municipal and regional officials, a radical Islamist organization, the Islamic Salvation Front, or FIS, won a stunning victory. The more moderately oriented government withheld funds in order to limit the FIS's ability to implement its victory. When the FIS won in both municipal and parliamentary elections a year and a half later, military leaders engineered a coup and took charge, cracking down severely on FIS leadership. A virtual civil war has followed since with atrocities on both sides and no resolution of the conflict. An irony in the dispute is that the fundamentalists represent the more democratic side since they won at the ballot box. The fundamentalists have more recently turned to violence and terrorism, a protest in this case against rulers who are themselves Muslims.

The most extreme case of resurgent Islam is the Taliban of Afghanistan. They banned television, music, and movies, instituted public executions and amputations, refused to let women work outside the home, and prohibited young women from attending schools. Strict regulations have been placed on non-Muslims, who have been ordered to wear distinctive clothing or special badges to distinguish them from Muslims. Their association with Osama bin Laden and his group's terrorist activities has now turned the Afghan form of Islamization into a war with the West, specifically the United States.

MODERATE ISLAM

Other Islamic countries such as the Kingdom of Morocco, by constitution an Islamic country, have followed a more moderate route. Even Colonel Qaddafi backed off from the rigid enforcement of *shari'a* in Libya when he wrote *The Green Book,* which announced socialism as the pattern for Libyan reform. The document placed him in the position of both political ruler and arbiter of religious law, the latter a place traditionally held only by the jurists and scholars of Islam. He has encouraged women to enter society and to become educated. The late King Hussein of Jordan established a constitutional monarchy with a parliament, rather like the Kingdom of Morocco. The late President Anwar Sadat of Egypt, a strong Muslim himself, attempted to steer his country on a moderate course in international affairs, ultimately giving his life when assassinated by a group of Islamic extremists. Malaysia, a Muslim country by constitution even though only 45 percent Muslim, has not required *shari'a*, but it does give priority to Muslims in education and government support.

Even Iran shows signs that its extremism may be abating. The moderate-oriented president, Mohammad Khatami, has recently won reelection by an overwhelming majority, larger than in his first election. His power is limited by the religious leadership, but the election shows a movement away from strict Islam on the part of the Iranian populace.

In all of these cases, however, both moderate and extreme, the life of Islam has been renewed. Muslims have become increasingly proud of their tradition, have committed themselves to regaining Islam's importance within the larger world, and are possessed of a certitude of Islam's value and truth. Westerners may be undergoing a crisis in religious faith—at least many observers claim they are—but most Muslims are not. Their confidence is strong. The problem lies in how to actualize that confidence in political and social programs that are faithful to Islam but avoid those Western social values that conflict with Islam.

PARTICIPATORY GOVERNMENT VERSUS AUTHORITARIAN CONTROL

Part of the Westernization package includes the option of adopting the political institutions of democracy and brings with it the question of the relation between Islam and the state and the status of other religions in relation to Islam and the state. John Esposito, a keen observer of contemporary Islam, says that the movements for democracy in Islamic states are just as powerful as the desire to keep Islam as the overarching value system.[5] On the surface, democracy might not seem to be a likely form of government for Muslims, but many Muslims believe the two are compatible. Islam has traditional principles that can work well with participatory political life, notably consultation (*shura*) and consensus (*ijma*), two traditions that over the centuries have provided Muslims with a cooperative method for resolving disputes in society and law.

The forms of democracy that Muslims develop will not be the same as those familiar in the West. The Islamic world possesses a different doctrine of human rights from the West. In Islamic doctrine rights are given by God, that is, granted through the Qur'an and traditional Islamic law. The supreme authority is God, and humans are his agents, even his viceregents, but they cannot be sovereign. The Western democratic concept of the sovereignty of the people is not an option for traditional Muslims, so how far Islamic societies can go in adopting some form of the Western idea of human rights is a question. In two areas, however, the pressure is already building, namely, the rights of women and the right of freedom of religion.

The two Islamic scholars cited above, al-Banna and Mawdudi, said they felt that the lowered level of morality in American society is due to its separation of church and state, a principle that underlies religious freedom. Islamic extremists come down hard on the West at that point, arguing that the West's attempt to export its values to the rest of the world threatens Islam and its commitment to a religiously oriented society. Some even claim that the West wants to destroy Islam, a view that few if any Westerners would admit to having. The argument that the West is out to eliminate Islam is a powerful propaganda force among the terrorists and the extremists who support them.

We saw earlier that classical Islamic law allowed Christians and Jews the right to practice their religion but placed restraints on them, including a prohibition against criticizing Muhammad and the Qur'an and against publicizing their own faith. Nor were Muslims free to convert from Islam to another faith. Enforcement of these rules varies from place to place today, strict in the Sudan and Afghanistan, liberal in Jordan and Egypt, but the principles remain and do not comport well with modernity.

Reports of Christians being compelled to become Muslims, though extremely rare, are even more troublesome. By Islamic tradition, indeed, by Qur'anic mandate,[6] Muslims are not to require religion. Such a requirement violates a fundamental principle of Islam. From Pope John Paul II to the Dalai Lama, religious leaders around the world have urged religionists to practice tolerance toward other religions, and democracy will require it. Islamic leaders may have to deal with that question more clearly to become fully respected members of the world community.

---

[5] John L. Esposito and John O. Voll, *Islam and Democracy* (New York and Oxford: Oxford University Press, 1966), 6.

[6] "No compulsion is there in religion" (Qur'an 2:258).

AUTHORITARIAN GOVERNMENTS

Under the surface lies yet another problem, namely, the unrest many Islamic peoples have concerning authoritarian governments. Some of these governments are semi-secular (Egypt, for instance) while others are strongly Islamic (Saudi Arabia). In both cases, whether secular or more Islamic, popular resistance to them has paraded itself under the rubric of Islamic ideals. Islamic radicals in Egypt assassinated Anwar Sadat on the grounds that he had compromised Islam. Saudi Arabia is a conservative Islamic state that cooperates with the United States, but many observers as well as many devout Muslims and even Osama bin Laden consider it corrupt because of its rulers' loose and self-serving use of their wealth, and even say they are not good Muslims. As a result Saudi Arabia possesses a social unrest parallel to Iran in the days of the Shah. Because America often allies with these authoritarian rulers, many Muslims believe that America does not act on its rhetoric of supporting the people—and to that degree is not a good example of democracy.

The adoption of democratic ways by Muslims will be difficult. Democracy is based on the principle that the people possess the power to elect representatives to govern them, but people who feel powerless, manipulated, and exploited by their rulers will be a source of restlessness, even rebellion. This is the case with Osama bin Laden, who is clearly a master at encouraging violence from people who do not feel empowered in their own political situation. In the West, bin Laden is seen to be focused on America, but his larger purpose includes unseating Islamic rulers, many of whom he considers un-Islamic.

PROBLEMS BETWEEN THE WEST AND THE ISLAMIC WORLD

THE NATION OF ISRAEL

Until the recent spread of terrorism, the conflict between the West and Muslims centered on the nation-state of Israel and its dispute with the Palestinians. Israel's decisive defeat of Egypt, Jordan, and Syria in the 1967 Six-Day War, an event Muslims call "the Disaster," raised the already intense conflict to a new level. In that war Jordan lost territory across the Jordan River called the West Bank, including East Jerusalem; Egypt lost the Gaza Strip along the Mediterranean and the Sinai; and Syria lost the Golan Heights in northern Israel. The Israelis later returned the Sinai to Egypt, but the other areas are still occupied and governed by Israel's military rule even though more than thirty years have passed since the conquest. But American support for Israel and the Israeli attempt to create a Western-style democracy have aligned Israel with Western politics, not Islamic or Arab.

It is difficult to imagine that this situation can continue much longer. The international community cannot allow a people to live permanently under military occupation, nor can the Israelis maintain their control forever. A solution must be found, even though at present the parties seem unable or unwilling to find it. One can hardly exaggerate the positive results for Western–Islamic relations that would follow if that conflict were concluded. However, any peace accord that officials sign that does not have the support of the respective populations will be of no value. Meanwhile, the violence continues, and the populations on both sides suffer. Economic development is on hold, unemployment abounds, and families continue to lose loved ones.

The United States has often been quick to condemn the invasion or conquest of one nation by another, and the United States backed the United Nations' condemnation of Israeli actions against the Palestinians. But America has also given Israel financing that has supported the takeover, and it supplies the arms Israelis use to control the Palestinians. Palestinians who observe these things claim that the behavior of the United States reveals America's true interests, and thus they accuse the Americans of double-dealing.

Beyond the fundamental question of the existence of the state of Israel in a formerly Arab and largely Islamic area lie three especially thorny matters: first, the Palestinian claim for restitution of property that was lost when Israel was established, second, control of and access to the Temple Mount, as Jews call it, or the Noble Sanctuary (Haram al-Sharif), as Muslims name it, and, third, the desire of Palestinians for their own state. The United Nations has endorsed the Palestinian claim for restitution to former landowners, and Israeli and Palestinian officials have negotiated on the matter from time to time, but no agreement has been reached. Allowing people to return to specific properties they owned forty or more years ago seems impossible, but economic restitution may be conceivable.

The Temple Mount is not only the site of the ancient Jewish Temple, but contains the al-Aqsa Mosque and the famous Dome of the Rock, both especially sacred to Muslims. After capturing the area in the 1967 War, Israel ceded control to Muslims by virtue of the holy mosques there, but that meant that Jews could not go onto the Mount to pray. Arranging satisfactory access for both groups proved a major sticking point in the Camp David discussions in 1978. Ariel Sharon's visit there in September 2000 accompanied by an armed escort, resulted in the Second Intifada noted above. Proposals range from total Israeli control of the site, to total Palestinian control, to some form of international management for the city of Jerusalem. At present none of these seems acceptable.

The question of a Palestinian state is probably the least intractable of these three problems. Both the international community and Israeli leaders have from time to time given their approval to the principle. But implementation is another matter. The state certainly will not emerge until the violence is controlled, and then will have Israeli support only to the extent that the Israelis are certain that the safety of their nation is guaranteed.

While the specific conflict is over land, behind the quarrel lie religious claims, Jewish, Christian, and Muslim. Most of the Arabs who lost land in the establishment of Israel were Muslims, but some were Christians (some 6 percent of the Palestinians at large are Christian; the number is smaller in Palestinian areas and larger in Israel proper). While both Christians and Jews consider Palestine to be their Holy Land, the area is sacred to Muslims as well, partly because of the story of Muhammad's ascent to heaven from Jerusalem, but also because for centuries it has been part of the *dar al-Islam*, the geographical area in which sacred Islam dwells. For non-Muslims to take over land sacred to Islam is a violation of fundamental Islamic belief and tradition and one of the classical justifications for Islamic *jihad*. Sorting out these problems will obviously be extremely difficult, but a solution must be found for peace to be possible.

TERRORISM

Part of the legacy of the Palestinian–Israeli conflict is the development of international terrorism by Islamic extremists. Already a problem before September 11, the violence of that event has galvanized the United States, the Western nations, and other lands as well into forming a concerted campaign against terrorism, now clearly seen as a worldwide threat.[7] President Anwar Sadat was assassinated by a radical Islamist group, and the late King Hussein of Jordan survived more than one assassination attempt by extremists. Reports have it that King Hussein's son and successor, King Abdullah, and President Hosni Mubarak of Egypt have both escaped assassination attempts by members of bin Laden's organization. We have earlier seen two such groups active in Israel, Hamas and Hizbullah, but the prominent one now is al-Qaeda ("the base"), the organization believed to be led by Osama bin Laden.

As a radical Islamist, bin Laden fights what he sees as an American attack upon Islam. This attack on Islam, as bin Laden sees it, consists of America's support for Israel, its cultural invasion by the film, television, and music industries, its attacks and embargo on Iraq, and its military presence in Saudi Arabia. Beyond that he claims that the projection of American power into Islamic lands through its technology, financial power, and culture also constitutes an attack on Islam. He and his supporters have raised the Islamic response to Western modernization to a new and unprecedented level, fearing that traditional Islamic societies will change if they embrace this new worldwide movement, and in that fear he is probably correct.[8]

In light of the history of the Western involvement with Islam, one must admit there is reason for Muslims to be angry with the West. Westerners have not behaved over the centuries with exemplary righteousness and selflessness.

---

[7] An earlier case of Western defense against terrorist activities originating among Muslims was the campaign of British and American navies in the late 1700s and early 1800s to rid the seas of pirates based in Algeria. Stephen Decatur's role in that effort was described above on p. 126.

[8] And yet bin Laden's movement makes use of international networks connected with modern technology, as if to suggest the problem is not modernization and globalization but who controls these processes.

Western governments and businesses can be greedy and thoughtless, and the baser sides of Western society would be a threat to classical Islam. One can also debate American policy in respect to Israel, Iraq, and Saudi Arabia, and some American leaders do. But it is also true that American political and military intervention saved many Bosnian and Albanian Muslims from the genocide that Serbian Christians were threatening them with in the 1990s.

The process of Westernization is another question. Whether called that, or modernization, or globalization, the momentum of these developments will continue. Individual societies will find their own ways to adapt to this process, and not everyone will accept it all. One can hope that, as parts of the West are adopted, a sense of morality and spirituality will accompany them.

Meanwhile, many Islamic countries have cells of terrorists within their borders, supported in some cases by the government itself. Libya was behind the massacre of eleven Israeli athletes at the 1972 Munich Olympic Games, and the bombing of a discotheque in Germany in April 1986 that injured some eighty American servicemen, as well as the bombing of Pan Am Flight 103 over Lockerbie, Scotland. Authorities also claim that Syria, Lebanon, and Iran support terrorist organizations such as Hamas and Hizbullah.

Terrorism is doomed to fail in the long run, however. When civilians, including children, are killed by deliberate military actions, sympathies go to the victims, not the perpetrators, and terrorism then becomes counterproductive. It has not prompted Israel to change its commitments; if anything Israel's resolve has been strengthened. The September 11 attacks have caused the United States to announce a war on international terrorism, a war American leaders say they will prosecute with all of the resources in their possession. Westerners have been repulsed and embittered by these attacks, and a new spirit of patriotism has emerged among Americans. Many Muslim leaders have called these attacks a violation of true Islam. Unfortunately, because of these events, many are again claiming that Islam is a religion of violence. The ancient charge against Islam is in danger of returning.

THE WEST

The West has changed as well. It is no longer a Christian society with a legally established Christianity to which citizens are expected to conform. Religion is now a private matter, and secularism has replaced it as the norm for public policy. No basis exists for religious Crusades as in the Middle Ages or even for a new colonialism as in the nineteenth century. The West should therefore be more capable of a greater tolerance toward other religious orientations and other types of societies.

Muslim observers criticize the West for its secularization, but Muslims who live in the West enjoy the freedom that secularization brings. Their right to practice Islam in the West is absolute, a privilege they did not enjoy in the glory days of Christendom, and a freedom their guests from the West do not always have in Islamic countries today.

Western technological skills flow virtually unhindered to Islamic lands. Students, professors, scientists, technicians, not to mention representatives of corporations that profit from the new technologies, move back and forth constantly. Significant amounts of trade passed between the West and the Islamic world in the Middle Ages, but the quantity of that intercourse could not begin to equal the communication taking place today.

At the same time, the industrial world focuses on the Mideast for its great reserves of oil, and while most Muslims live outside that area, that part of Islamic geography is of crucial importance for industry, and therefore a potential source of conflict.

OTHER PROBLEM AREAS

Not every disagreement with Islamic powers relates directly to Islam. Indonesia's annexation of East Timor in 1975 is an example. Located on the southeastern edge of the Indonesian archipelago, East Timor had been a Portuguese colony with a significant Catholic population, but when the Portuguese withdrew, Indonesian troops invaded and annexed the area. Indonesia is a Muslim country, but the invasion's purpose seems to have been political and economic, not religious. The United States and its allies acted with dispatch and power when Iraq invaded Kuwait in 1990 but did nothing years earlier for East Timor. The media have reported that President Gerald Ford and Secretary of State Henry Kissinger, who were present in Indonesia only hours before the action, tacitly agreed to the Indonesian plan to take East Timor by force. But the East Timorese resisted, leading to a bloody conflict that sometimes pitted Muslims against Christians.

In 1999 under auspices of the United Nations and with the approval of the Indonesian central government, the East Timorese held a referendum in which some 98 percent of the voters chose independence. The Indonesian military, whose leaders opposed releasing the province, intervened causing hundreds of deaths and thousands of refugees. At times the conflict has been religious, with both sides, Christian and Muslim, guilty of hostilities, but a resolution has now been achieved that grants the East Timorese political autonomy.

The Gulf War against Iraq has been the most dramatic case of Western–Islamic conflict, but the problem was Iraq's invasion of Kuwait, an oil-rich country, not Islam. The conflict continues through U.S. control of much of Iraqi airspace and trade embargoes imposed by the United Nations. The cost of the embargo has been high for Iraq, and the lack of adequate medicine has resulted in an alarming increase in the deaths of children, though some Westerners claim Saddam could afford medicine if he spent less on arms.

The West's intervention in the Balkans was the reverse, an attempt to aid Muslims. United Nations troops, including both air and ground forces from the United States, acted to rescue Muslims suffering from the "ethnic cleansing" campaign of Serbian Christians against Bosnian and Albanian Muslims. A fully settled situation is yet to be created in the area, but the case is a notable one for the support the West gave in defense of Islamic people.

Finally there is war in Afghanistan against al-Qaeda and the Taliban. Afghanistan is a poor country, ravaged by its war against the Soviet Union as well as internal conflicts among various ethnic groups. It is difficult to foresee the results of the current hostilities, but the hope is for a peaceful Afghanistan fairly governed with adequate food and support for its citizens.

ISLAM IN THE WEST

The greatest change in the West's relations with Islam has come in increased numbers of Muslims in Europe and America. Although Muslims have been on the American continent since early slavery,[9] only in recent decades has their number become appreciable, approaching perhaps six million in the United States alone. Islam may soon be the second largest religion in the United States, with Judaism third. Most of these Muslims are immigrants or children of immigrants, but an estimated twenty thousand are converts.

The formation of the Nation of Islam in the early 1930s was the first publicly noted Islamic development in the United States, a movement of African Americans that was often characterized by the demonization of whites. Elijah Muhammad, the reorganizer of the movement, said that the white race had come from the Devil. Because racism has never been a mark of Islam, Elijah Muhammad's extreme views were an embarrassment to traditional Muslims, as was the claim that he was a prophet (against the Islamic belief that Muhammad was the final prophet), and orthodox Muslims declined to recognize the organization. Malcolm X, the best-known member of the Nation, left the Nation and, after a life-changing experience on pilgrimage in Mecca in 1964, renounced his earlier racism. The following February he was assassinated.[10] Elijah's son and successor, Wallace, who later took the name Warith Deen Muhammad, gradually brought the Nation into line with standard Sunni Islam, so close in fact that he was given authority to certify the credentials of American Muslims going on pilgrimage to Mecca. He renamed his movement the American Muslim Society.

Louis Farrakhan, who separated himself from W. D. Muhammad's more moderate group, revived the name Nation of Islam in 1978 and with it a substantial amount of the earlier anti-white racism. Recently Farrakhan has renounced the earlier extremism of his movement, doing so after his own pilgrimage to Mecca, like that of Malcolm X.

---

[9] Two recent books discuss this story: Allan D. Austin, *African Muslims in Antebellum America: Transatlantic Stories and Spiritual Struggles* (New York: Routledge, 1997); and Sylviane A. Diouf, *Servants of Allah: African Muslims Enslaved in the Americas* (New York: New York University Press, 1998).

[10] Malcolm's associates claimed that the murder was ordered by leaders of the Nation of Islam, but that was never proved. Elijah Muhammad denied any connection.

Warith Deen Muhammad's American Muslim Society, Louis Farrakhan's Nation of Islam, plus the great influx of Muslims into the United States have catapulted Islam into a major presence in American cities, a situation unimaginable fifty years ago.[11] The presence of Muslims in the West is a challenge for both Muslims and non-Muslims. The former, particularly the immigrants, live as Muslims in a society that is not Muslim and gives them no special privileges. Women's conservative dress and the Muslim need for times and places for prayer create problems, not to mention simply living outside the *dar al-Islam* with the support it provides. Westerners must adjust too, since they now meet customs that are foreign but must be welcomed.

Conservative Christians may continue to evangelize Muslims, but Muslims often find their approach demeaning, since they are viewed as prospective converts, not as people of faith in their own right. The results of such efforts have usually been sparse. For Christians not inclined to evangelism, the presence of Muslims brings a new possibility: the opportunity to learn firsthand about another religious tradition.

CONCLUSION: THE PLACE OF RELIGION

While the problems described above are in considerable part political and social, a fundamental element is religion. One can ask where the specifically religious component fits in. There are at least five possibilities. First, there is the religious fanaticism that underlies international terrorism. It is said that young Muslims who offer their lives as suicide bombers do so in the belief that their sacrifice for the Islamic cause will purchase them immediate entrance into Paradise. But more than that would seem to be at work. Dr. Robert Jay Lifton, a psychiatrist who has studied several terrorist movements, believes an ideology that typically drives such movements is an "apocalyptic" orientation that thinks the radical change they believe society to need can be produced only through a purgation involving violence and killing.[12] If one thinks of the martyrs of Cordoba or the vicious attacks upon Jews at the beginning of the First Crusade, one sees that principle at work. In the first case the tool was a form of suicide, in the second, murder, but in both cases the Christians saw violence as a means to a larger, more nearly global end. Present-day Islamic terrorists claim a divine sanction for their efforts as well, namely, the belief that only violence can displace the evils of the West that have infiltrated Islam. We may call that religious fanaticism, but fanatical or not, those emotions and beliefs are powerful, dangerous, and the actions they produce are difficult to defend against.

---

[11] Richard Brent Turner, *Islam in the African-American Experience* (Bloomington and Indianapolis: Indiana University Press, 1997) is an excellent survey of the history.

[12] Robert Jay Lifton, *Destroying the World to Save It: Aum Shinrykyo, Apocalyptic Violence, and the New Global Terrorism* (New York: Henry Holt, 2000).

Second, the attachment that Muslims and Jews, as well as Christians, have to Jerusalem and Palestine drives much of the passion in that conflict. In part this is a claim for land—land that Jews say was promised to them by God. That is a religious conviction. Arabs counter by saying that they, as descendants of Abraham, have a divine right to the same land. Further, they say that since they were the last to possess it, and since they had held it for over a thousand years, they should not have been removed from it. Only a compromise that would divide the land and provide adequate living space for all can settle that argument. The problem of access to the holy places on the Temple Mount, the Haram al-Sharif, is even more volatile.

Third, and on the Christian side, the strongest support for the nation of Israel comes from certain fundamentalist Christians who believe that the resettlement of Israel by Jews is the fulfillment of biblical prophecy, part of the providential plan that will lead to Jesus' Second Coming and the apocalyptic End of the Age. While the number of Christians who hold these specific views is small, their support for Israel is virtually absolute, and they contribute not only moral and political support but financial support as well. Unfortunately such views add to the problem, since, to whatever degree Muslims feel that the intent of Western Christians is to destroy Islam, either through missions or their support of Israel or a hoped-for apocalyptic cataclysm, to that extent the response of many Muslims will be hostile.

Fourth, an increase in the knowledge that Christians and Muslims have of each other's faith can help considerably. This book has attempted to demonstrate that the West has inherited a tradition of bias and disrespect toward Islam and Muslims, a tradition that must be called into question. Muslims have a similar tradition on their side. Our forebears may have erred on the side of misinformation and prejudice, and we could be guilty of the same. To be sure, much that we hear, especially of the violence of Islamic extremists, helps to reinforce a negative view of Islam as a religion. Even so, it behooves us to become better informed about Islam, its teachings, its ideals and practices, and the hopes and aspirations of contemporary Muslims, as well as what they think of us. This can come through study or interreligious dialogue, or both.

Finally, the Second Vatican Council called for Christians and Muslims to unite in a "common cause of safeguarding and fostering social justice, moral values, peace, and freedom."[13] Perhaps the time will come when members of these great traditions, Judaism included, will put their differences behind them, emphasize what they have in common, and join hands in efforts to help the people of the world improve their lives. All three religions emphasize peace and justice, and all three hold to the virtue of helping the needy. Should such a partnership come to pass, the descendants of its creators would, in the words of the Old Testament, rise up and call them blessed.

---

[13] Declaration on the Relationship of the Church to Non-Christian Religions 3 (*The Documents of Vatican II* (New York: Guild Press, America Press, Association Press, 1966), 663.

Suggestions for Further Reading

Numerous English-language biographies of Muhammad exist. Perhaps the easiest to obtain would be Karen Armstrong's *Muhammad: A Biography of the Prophet*. The standard but older *Muhammad: The Man and His Faith*, by Tor Andrae, is useful as well. Clinton Bennett's *In Search of Muhammad*, while not a formal biography, discusses the general problem of writing a biography of the Prophet and surveys the various attempts that have been made. Bennett's book also surveys a variety of issues in the study of Islam and is notable for the author's sensitivity to the religious aspects of Islam.

As the reader learned from discussions above, reading the Qur'an in English usually fails to provide an authentic taste of Islam, but the exercise can be valuable nonetheless. I happen to like A. J. Arberry's *The Koran Interpreted*. His rendering of the Arabic text has received good marks from reviewers, and his English reads well. *The Holy Qur'ān* by A. Yusuf Ali is often recommended by Muslims and carries both extensive annotations and the original Arabic. Arberry and Ali are both Muslims. A recent book by Michael Sells entitled *Approaching the Qur'ān: The Early Revelations,* the first of a planned two-volume work, provides a new and elegant "translation" of Qur'anic texts together with introductions and explanations. A CD of chants of the texts accompanies the volume. John Kaltner's *Ishmael Instructs Isaac: An Introduction to the Qur'an for Bible Readers* compares stories from the Qur'an with their parallels in the Bible in order to shed light on the biblical stories and in doing so provides valuable insights into both the Bible and the Muslim holy book. A second volume to follow will study the stories of Joshua.

General surveys of Islam are numerous. One of the best is by John L. Esposito, *Islam, the Straight Path*. Authored by a respected Islamics scholar, the book covers all major aspects of Islam. *The House of Islam* by Kenneth Cragg has been a standard introduction, as has the older and ill-named *Mohammedanism: An Historical Survey,* by Sir Hamilton A. R. Gibb. Karen Armstrong's best-selling *Islam: A Short History* is a recent account of the history. The important story of Muslims in the United States is well told in Jane I. Smith's *Islam in America*.

For a brief discussion of the Christian–Muslim encounter in the Middle Ages, nothing equals R. W. Southern's *Western Views of Islam in the Middle Ages*. These three lectures at Harvard University, while over forty years old, are still a wonderful source of information and judgment and are presented in elegant and clear prose. Norman Daniel's monumental *Islam and the West: The Making of an Image*, often cited above, is the premier study of Western views of Islam in the Middle Ages. *A History of Christian–Muslim Relations,* by Hugh Goddard, covers much of the ground of the present work in a more scholarly form and adds the Islamic side to give a balanced treatment of the history.

The history of the Crusades is well told in the recent *God Wills It! An Illustrated History of the Crusades,* by W. B. Bartlett. *The Cross and the Crescent: A History of the Crusades,* by Malcolm Billings, is also good for the general reader. Steven Runciman, *A History of the Crusades*, an older work in three volumes, remains a standby and is readable in spite of its length. Amin Maalouf, in *The Crusades through Arab Eyes,* has given us reports of Arab chroniclers of the Crusades that we did not have easily available in English before. Carole Hillenband's excellent *The Crusades: Islamic Perspectives* narrates in greater detail the history as told by Arabs and adds informative sections on culture and the way of war. The book is lavishly illustrated.

Interest in communication between Christians and Muslims has produced a number of helpful books. The slim volume by Charles Kimball, *Striving Together: A Way Forward in Christian–Muslim Relations*, is an excellent introduction to the subject and carries general information on Islam as well. His term "striving" comes from the first meaning of the Arabic word *jihad,* namely, "striving (or struggling) in the way of God," the spiritual and moral efforts required in faith. Hugh Goddard's *Christians and Muslims: From Double Standards to Mutual Understanding* and the Jesuit scholar Ovey N. Mohammed's *Muslim–Christian Relations: Past, Present, and Future* are more detailed studies. Kate Zebiri's *Muslims and Christians Face to Face* treats the subject and history of Christian–Muslim dialogue, as well as the views of contemporary writers on the two religions.

The present conflict between elements of the Islamic world and Western powers is discussed by Samuel P. Huntington, *The Clash of Civilizations and the Remaking of World Order,* and Anthony J. Pennis, *The Rise of the Islamic Empire and the Threat to the West.* Both Huntington and Pennis write in a relatively alarmist mode, warning of increased conflict between the two civilizations. John Esposito, *The Islamic Threat: Myth or Reality;* Bruce B. Lawrence, *Shattering the Myth: Islam beyond Violence;* and Shireen T. Hunter, *The Future of Islam and the West: Clash of Civilizations or Peaceful Coexistence?* foresee a less conflicted future.

The development of the modern state of Israel has produced mountains of books. Perhaps there is nothing better for an introduction than Thomas L. Friedman, *From Beirut to Jerusalem*, his personal account of experiences in the two cities. Friedman, Jewish himself, is a Pulitzer-prize-winning reporter with the *New York Times* and writes as both reporter and balanced interpreter. Barbara Tuchman's *Bible and Sword: England and Palestine from the Bronze Age to Balfour* recounts the history of Britain's relations with the Jewish people and tells in detail the story of the founding of the modern state of Israel.

Index

Abbasid dynasty, 22, 33, 37
'Abd al-Muttalib, 'Abdallah ibn, 4
'Abd al-Muttalib ibn Hashim, 4
'Abd al-Rahman, 35
Abdullah (king of Jordan), 177
Abraham, 7, 11
Abrahamic religions, 1, 25, 37, 46
Abu Bakr, 7: as successor of Muhammad, 26-27, 32
abū-Qurrah. *See* Theodore of Carra
Abu Talib, 4, 7, 42
Adhémar of Le Puy (bishop): as papal legate of First Crusade, 72, 73
Aeneas Silvius Piccolomini. *See* Pius II (pope)
Afghanistan: Taliban in, 172, 180
Ahmed, Leila: on women in Islam, 22-23
Aisha (wife of Muhammad), 16, 22, 57
al-Adawiyya, Rabi'a, 22
al-Aqsa, 16; mosque, 40n. 5, 176
al-Aqsa Intifada, 164
al-Banna, Hasan, 168-69, 174
Albert the Great, 97
al-Damiri, 17
Alexius Comnenus I of Constantinople (emperor): and First Crusade, 63-64
Alfonso VI of León, 62
Algeria: conflict over Islamization in, 172-73
Ali (cousin of Muhammad), 7, 32-33
al-Idrisi, abu-Abdullah Muhammad ibn-Muhammad, 99
al-Kamil (sultan): and al-Mu'azzam, 101-2; and St. Francis of Assisi, 88; truce with Frederick II, 102
al-Kindy: *Apology* or *Risalah* of, 81, 83, 113, 137; influence of, on Nicholas of Cusa, 109

al-Lāh ("the God"). *See* Allah
Allah: meaning of name, 7
Allenby, Edmund, 158; and capture of Jerusalem, 76, 131, 155
almsgiving: as one of Five Pillars, 23, 24; *see also* tithe
al-Mu'azzam Isa (sultan of Damascus), 101
al-Qaddafi, Muammar: and overthrow of King Idris I of Libya, 169; *The Green Book* of, 173; and moderate Islam, 173; *see also* Libya; terrorism; terrorists
al-Qaeda ("the base"), 177, 180; *see also* bin Laden, Osama; terrorism; terrorists
Alvar, Paul, 104: and Cordoba martyrs, 48-49
American Muslim Society, 180-81
Amina bint Wahb, 4
Andrae, Tor, 140
Antichrist: Muhammad as forerunner of, 91
anti-Judaism, 71: of John Chrysostom, 25; and Justinian Code, 51; of Pope Paul IV, 120; in Spain, 51; *see also* anti-Semitism; Jews; Judaism
anti-Semitism: of Eugen Karl Dühring, 149; reasons for, 150; of Richard Wagner, 149; *see also* anti-Judaism; Jews; Judaism
apocalypticism: and Cordoba martyrs, 48-49; and First Crusade, 131; and fundamentalist Christians, 182; and Jewish settlement of Palestine, 131, 153; and Jews in England, 153; and Marquardus de Susannis, 120-21; and terrorism, 181; and Turkish invasion in sixteenth century, 116, 119

Other Titles in the Faith Meets Faith Series